I0413633

We Will Lead Africa

Editors:

Yabome Gilpin-Jackson
Sarah Owusu
Judith Okonkwo

All rights reserved.

No part of this material may be translated, reproduced, stored or transmitted in any manner whatsoever without the written permission of the publisher except in the case of brief quotations in critical articles and reviews.

Copyright © 2017 Gilpin-Jackson, Owusu & Okonkwo

contact: submissions@wewillleadafrica.com

All rights reserved.

ISBN: 1545028427
ISBN-13: 978-1545028421

DEDICATION

Dedicated to the everyday African leader.

Thank you to each of the contributors who make up this collective story of leadership across Africa:

Adewale Ajadi
Chuma Asuzu
Bolanle Austen-Peters
Ajarat Bada
Toks Bakare
Liza Bel
Lue-Rachelle Brim-Atkins
Veronica Fynn Bruey
Chinezi Chijoke
Mina Girgis
Pablo Imani
Elizabeth Mujawamaliya Johnson
Ricardo Pinto Jorge
Mimi Kalinda
Adeline Sede Kamga
Robert Kalyesubula
Franck Kié
Chris Mulenga
Mwalimu Musheshe
Sal Muthayan
Daphne Nederhorst
Cecil Nutakor
Chinyere Nwabugwu
Ndidi Nwuneli
Simon Okelo
Nereya Otieno
Yeniva Sisay-Sogbeh
Julian Spezzati
Modupe Taylor-Pearce
Fatou Wurie

CONTENTS

Why?

Poem142:
Julianne Okot Bitek's "The Mundane, Sublime & Fantastical"

We've fallen into story

& inside story this is all there is

This is all there is this is all there is

This is all

We fall

We fall

We fall

Into lightness

Into being

Brightness into flight

This is all there is this

Is all there is this is

All there is this becoming

What they wanted us to be

Coming into becoming

Into being

Who are we who are we who are

We again?

Used with permission. All rights reserved by Julianne Okot Bitek
https://julianeokotbitek.com/

Preface

Who will lead Africa?

Forward, onward, fully into the land of its potential.

Into the realisation of the dream of prosperity held by so many for so long for the countries in this place we call home.

Again, we ask, *Who Will Lead Africa?*

~~~

In February 2016, we put out this African town crier's call, asking for responses from people who identify as African – people for whom Africa runs in their veins, their consciousness, and their very being. We asked for you, in all your colours, shades, and hues, whose heart beats with the drumbeat of Africa. You, who finds home first in her red dust soil, intermingling sounds of earth, animals, and peoples, all communicating, all at once. You, in who joy and passion bursts when you arrive at the airport of an African country and are greeted with a familiar yet always awe-inspiring scene of contradictions and cohabitations in swirls of bright colours: the Calvin Klein dresses and Dashiki tunics; a bucket on one's head and a briefcase in another's hand; iPhones, androids and tablets glittering in the sun while fax machines and typewriters reside on desks; children in back wraps, and suitcases in hands; local languages and imported languages; traditional greetings and hugs; a street preacher and hijabs; hip hop and soukous music; people walking into Mercedes-Benz' while a beggar child calls, and hawkers panhandle and push their wares.

Above all, we asked for everyday Africans, anywhere in the world, who embrace these contradictions and cohabitations and are choosing to lead change on the continent. We asked you to self-identify as African – by lineage, heritage, immigration/citizenship. We asked that if you are non-African, you interview and report on the work or impact of Africans. The vision was for a volume to include stories of capacity building, innovation, and development work from all over the geographic continent in all its complexity - North, West, Central, East, and Southern Africa.

This volume includes the response to that African Town Crier's call: thirty submissions or interview-based stories. Exemplars of everyday African leaders. Today's leaders, defying the narrative of impossible and working for the prosperity of Africa. These are but a sample of the movements we believe are already happening. People of African descent all over the world are packing up and returning to use their skills somewhere on the continent. Young Africans on the continent are innovating their own solutions. Many are giving up foreign aid and the handout mentality it created and are using their own readily available resources to move forward.

This is a story of leadership. Leadership in and for Africa now. It is a volume that speaks to action and practice. Work already underway by everyday leaders who are being the difference.

This volume is significant and important because, as one of the editors has shown elsewhere,[1] the current writings, literature, and narratives of leadership in Africa are overwhelmingly steeped in the political story of our historical marginalisation: slavery, colonial and post-colonial contexts, and the systemic economic pillage of wealth by dominant Africans colluding with outsiders. Just Google *leadership in Africa* or *leadership in African context* and see what shows up! These are real historical facts and contexts that help us understand how we've arrived at the challenges different African countries face today. And it is true that these dominant and systemic inequalities and wrongs continue even now. As we say in Sierra Leone, West Africa: *you nor go know ousyae you dae go if you nor sabi ousyae you comot* (you cannot know where you are going if you do not understand where you come from). These dominant narratives from our histories have and continue to serve the purpose of illuminating oppressions we have suffered.

However, as Brookfield (2000, p.145) notes, "critical reflection's focus on illuminating power relationships and hegemonic assumptions can be the death of the transformative impulse, inducing an energy-sapping, radical pessimism concerning the possibility of structural change."[2] We believe that in the life cycle

---

[1] Gilpin-Jackson, Y. (2016). African Leadership: Now and for the Future, in Quist-Adade and Royal (Eds.), *Re-engaging the African Diasporas: Pan-Africanism in the Age of Globalization.* Cambridge Scholars

[2] Brookfield, S. (2000). Transformative learning as ideology critique. In J. Mezirow

of social change and transformation, the initial points of pain and passion that fuel the need to name and uncover oppressive structures are necessary, but become counterproductive at a tipping point where transformation and positive change are possible. We believe we have reached that point for our African countries and continent. It is time to integrate our history into a more wholesome narrative, told by Africans, of the countries and the Africa for which we are working. It is time to share our individual and collective stories of change and transformation already happening to fill up the sea of change. Seeing the ocean expand before our eyes as we read stories of leadership actions in many countries across the continent will expand our horizons of possibilities. It will spark partnerships and collaboration. It will accelerate visions of the Africa we want such as the 50-year Africa Union Agenda 2063 for Unity, Prosperity and Peace.[3]

It is exciting to see the growing number of books, writings and theorising about the transformation, change and renaissance of Africa and the possibility of a new leadership on the continent. Examples include: Gail Cameron's *Authentic African Leadership: Authentic African Leaders Defined and the Techniques That Made Them Great*; Dr. Delanyo Adadevoh's *Leading Transformation in Africa*; Alan Rake's *African Leaders: Guiding the New Millennium*; Dr. George Ayittey's *Africa Unchained: The Blueprint for Africa's Future*; Global Shaper Community of the World Economic Forum's *The Africa 80: Transformation through Collaboration*; Dayo Olopade's *The Bright Continent: Breaking Rules and Making Change in Modern Africa*; Aubrey Hruby and Jake Bright's *The Next Africa: An Emerging Continent Becomes a Global Powerhouse*; and B. G. Jallow and F. Ngunjiri's *Palgrave Studies series in Africa Leadership*.

We Will Lead Africa contributes an open call to practitioners to join the conversation, and allow practice to further inform our theorising and conclusions of where we are now and what more is needed to attain the Africa we want. It is a shift from viewing leadership in Africa from the sociopolitical lens or theoretical lens, to a focus on leadership at every level. It neither denies the

---

(Ed.), Learning as transformation: Critical perspectives on a theory in progress. San Francisco: Jossey-Bass.

[3] African Union (2016). Retrieved, January 11, 2016, from:
http://agenda2063.au.int/en/home

overemphasised challenges of the continent, nor privileges the Africa-rising narrative. This volume simply draws on the power of personal narratives to highlight all the complexities of the challenges and inspirations of leading in Africa. It is about the power of storytelling to inspire even more change and shape the futures we want.

The collective of these inspiring leaders revealed some summative highlights of note:

1. Our final submissions yielded a near-balance of 14 submissions from men and 16 submissions from women.
    - We call this a near balance, because in a historical and contemporary context where women have been marginalised from leadership,[4] it is heartening to get this glimpse of women's active involvement.
2. We received eight submissions from people of Nigerian descent
    - We were not surprised that approximately a quarter of our submissions came from contributors from Africa's most populous nation.[5] We included all eight that met our criteria for this volume.
3. Submitters represented all regions of the continent, many of whose work cuts across multiple countries on the continent – North, West, Central, East and South. The intersectional and diverse nature of our continent is evident in this small slice of 30 submissions.
4. The stories in this volume cover a range of industries and topics for Africa's advancement. Many of the stories cut across multiple areas. However, for simplicity, they can be thought of in the following grouping:
    - **Eight on Literacy and Education** – meeting the massive education needs on the continent for literacy and primary education for rural and

---

[4] Bradshaw, Castellino & Diop (2013). Women's role in economic development: Overcoming the constraints – Background paper for the High-Level Panel of Eminent Persons on the Post-2015 Development Agenda. Sustainable Development Solutions Network.

[5] African Countries by population (2017). Retrieved March 25, 2017, from http://www.worldometers.info/population/countries-in-africa-by-population/

underprivileged/underserved groups all the way through higher education – Chinezi Chijioke, Elizabeth Johnson, Frankie Kie, Mwalimu Musheshe, Cecil Nutakor, Chinyere Nwabugwu, Yeniva Sisay-Sogbeh and Modupe Taylor-Pearce.

- **Eight on Social Entrepreneurship, Change and Policy** – including the stories from Adewale Ajadi, Ajarat Bada, Veronica Flynn Bruey, Chris Mulenga, Sal Muthayan, Daphne Nederhorst, Ndidi Nwuneli, Fatou Wurie.

- **Five on Arts and Culture** – Africans everywhere using expressions of Arts and Culture, from music to theatre to food to art and artefacts to inspire change, creativity and leadership in others, while providing development, employment and entrepreneurship opportunities. These submissions are from Bolanle Austen-Peters, Liza Bel (on behalf of four Africans), Mina Girgis, Ricardo Pinto Jorge and Simon Okelo.

- **Four on Healthcare and Wellness** – addressing healthcare needs and practices for those on the margins – girls, rural populations, autistic children, and youth seeking novel opportunities. These submissions are from Toks Bakare, LueRachelle Brim-Atkins, Pablo Imani, Robert Kalyesubula.

- **Four on Media and Communications** – with a clear call to own and tell African stores less told, by Mimi Kalinda, Nereya Otieno, Adeline Sede Kamga and Julian Spezzati.

- **One on Science, Technology, Engineering and Math** (STEM) innovations by Chuma Asuzu. It is worth noting that we were unable to get a similar submission about an all-girls code club[6] and to acknowledge the focus and role of STEM in Africa's sustainable development agendas.[7]

---

[6] Code Club Senegal: Where Women are Leading (2016). Retrieved March 24, 2017 from: https://www.theguardian.com/world/2016/jul/26/code-club-senegal-where-women-lead-the-way

[7] What STEM can do for Africa (2015). Retrieved March 24, 2017 from: https://www.weforum.org/agenda/2015/01/what-stem-can-do-for-africa/

We received so much more interest than what is included here! One observation of note is that our target of practitioners meant that we were seeking doers, who often do not stop long enough to write and document the work they are doing. Many expressed intentions to write but ultimately did not find the time or space to do so or to be interviewed by one of us. We wonder whether our African bent to oral history is part of this pattern. Given this pattern, we feel compelled more than ever that we Africans must document our stories, lest they continue to be told for us by others. As the well-known African saying goes: *Until the lion tells his side of the story, the tale of the hunt will always glorify the hunter.*

We also saw in this collective, evidence of the principle-based themes that inspires our thinking and philosophies of African leadership. While theories of leadership have been distilled to those most relevant for the African continent,[8] we have found from our praxis that effective leadership for change is principle-based and predicated on ideas of distributed and accountable leadership, dialogue, collective/collaborative action, narratives for the vulnerable, underprivileged and underserved, bridging all divides and courage and unity[9]. Hence our focus on:

We: Collaborative and accountable leaders, taking unified action.

Will: The leadership WILL, grit and courage to do something, anything, now and for the future, demonstrated through action-oriented and aspirational leadership.

Lead: Everyday leaders, motivated by service, in every sector, including emerging leaders from marginalised groups. All the authors who submitted stories shared a deep authenticity and integrity in their leadership. They focused on a values-driven path, even if it is challenging.

Africa: A focus on a prosperous continent, where divides are bridged and leaders work across boundaries and borders to achieve

---

[8] Van Zyl, Ebben (2016). Leadership in the African Context, 2nd Edition. Cape Town, SA.

[9] Gilpin-Jackson, Y. (2016). African Leadership: Now and for the Future, in Quist-Adade and Royal (Eds.), *Re-engaging the African Diasporas: Pan-Africanism in the Age of Globalization.* Cambridge Scholars

a broader success.

This volume is an ode to individual excellence and collective impact; it is an intellectual and affective rendition of leadership in and for Africa. You have arrived at the end of the opening, *the strophe of this ode* – which has been our poetic entry and this preface - signalling our need for stories, and new forms of story. The middle part - *the antistrophe* - are the stories themselves. They are presented alphabetically by last name within their groupings, delimiting hierarchy and denoting our collective, horizontal view. We invite you to read each story in this lyrical way, working with the flow and movement of each individual essay on leadership and action, while hearing the drumbeat of the collective. *The closing part – the epode of this ode – belongs to you and to us. Our epilogue question to you is: What leadership will this inspire in you? How will you lead and continue to lead - unapologetically from wherever you are – for the prosperity of Africa?*

And for those of you thinking it: yes, these rumblings feel like drops in the vast ocean of our needs right now. But that is exactly why you must join the action, join the movement, and change the narrative of the impossible. You are not alone. Remember that saying? Little drops of water, make a mighty ocean. We all need to do our part in service of a prosperous Africa, now and into the future. Let's find our leadership and strength in working together.

In Service and Leadership*,

Yabome, Sarah and Judith

Global Africans, Dreamers and Storytellers, committed to imagining and leading the futures we want. Contact us at submissions@wewillleadafrica.com or yabome@sldconsulting.org

*A note that our salutation reflects our logo and the inspiration from which we bring this work to life. Our logo is a horizontal variation of the Ghanaian symbol, NEA OPE SE OBEDI HENE. An Adrinka symbol of Kingship enacted in service and leadership - "He who wants to be king in the future must first learn to serve."[10]

---

[10] West African Wisdom: Adinkra Symbol and Meaning. Retrieved March 24, 2017 from http://www.adinkra.org/htmls/adinkra/neaope.htm

I. Literacy & Education

Chinezi Chijioke
Nova Pioneer Academies

The university town in the south east of Nigeria where I grew up, Nsukka, had a remarkable institution called the Children's Centre. It was started as a library in the storeroom of the university gymnasium by a group of women faculty. Through their inspiration, passion and perspiration it grew into a self-standing centre that offered – and I believe may still offer – a wide array of programmes for children; anchored by the library and all its reading programmes, it offered cooking classes, crafts clubs, excursions to gather clay at a nearby river banks, environmental hikes, volunteering at an orphanage, prison visits, Christmas caroling, and more. It made such a difference. I recall the Children's Centre was more powerful for my development – and the development of my passions – than the relatively good university primary school that many of us attended. The remarkable paths that the lives of so many of the children who my club-mates and library-mates at the Children's Centre is a testament to its formative power – and more generally, to the transformational power one great institution can have on the lives of young people.

It is no coincidence then, that shortly after I moved from Nigeria to the United States, I started dreaming of starting great youth-focused institutions back home. I first remember dreaming about starting schools at home on the Africa continent when I was 13. It was about two years after I had moved to the US from Nigeria and I can vividly remember being on a playground in Swarthmore, Pennsylvania daydreaming about starting a great school or university back home in Nigeria. Thinking about the remarkable talent and resourcefulness of the peers with whom I had grown up in Nuskka, I got was so excited about the possibility of a great school or university. It would be like fuel the flame of our talent and our drive. That was the dream that a general sense of purpose sharpened for me; a vision I could see, and it's never faded for me. I consider it a real blessing that I found that clarity of purpose and

2

energy to make it happen relatively early in life.

Over the years, that vision evolved. It started as a single great school or university (I couldn't decide which). I sketched campus plans, thought about what we could teach and the high standards we would set. I became a teacher after college to learn about learning, and I started forming clearer notions of the experiences and lessons I held to be most important for young people to gain at school. I was also a coach, and that led me for a time to the notion of sports academies - several of them across West Africa and possibly beyond; and in business school as I built a business plan for them, it was a step closer to action. Eight years after that, with the experience gained from working with McKinsey & Company's education practice with schools across the world, it crystallised into what is now Nova Pioneer Academies.

Nova Pioneer Academies are accessible 21st- century schools to develop young Africans as innovators and leaders. Our schools offer rigorous enquiry-based learning and conscious character development for students from ages 3 to 18. We have an amazing team of what is today 250 great educators and enterprise-builders, led by a team of kindred co-founders. Our goal over the next decade is to transform the lives and career paths of more than 50,000 youths across 100 schools, spanning all three regions of sub-Saharan Africa. Think of the transformative power of a single great institution of youth development, such as the Children's Centre in Nsukka. Now imagine a hundred or more excellent institutions of youth development all over the continent. I'm so excited about what we can accomplish through Nova Pioneer!

We are off to strong start. We opened our first school in South Africa in January of 2015, and as of January 2017, operate six schools in total, four in South Africa and two in Kenya. In 2016, our primary school students' growth in reading and mathematics significantly exceeded international growth norms, and in reading they doubled the international benchmark growth rate. If sustained, that's like gaining two years of reading competency per year in our school. Our secondary students are also making us proud; we recently had a group of 14 of our grade tens who are the first team in South Africa to register for a drone building challenge. Their work was featured on local cable TV and it's so cool to see our students pick up the initiative to take on such a project. Another example is a Kenyan student of ours who is in the finals for a global innovation forum. He is competing with University students and doing very well in entrepreneurship and innovation challenges.

Our mission at Nova Pioneer is to develop a generation of young people with the leadership and innovation skills to shape Africa. We live in a continent that will be home to nearly half of the world's youth under the age of 18 in 30 to 40 years --- but which certainly does not have half the world's jobs or educational opportunities. In fact, when it comes to educational opportunities, Africa offers our youth the lowest quality of education anywhere in the measured world. *That 40-50% of the world's young people who call Africa home are either going to be capable of shaping their world towards inspired and creative visions, or they're going to be frustrated and capable of burning it down. That is the challenge in front of us....and it's not just an African imperative, it's a world imperative. With such as large portion of the world's young people, the education and development of Africa's youth has to be a priority for the world for the next fifty years, or longer.*

Education also has to be on the agenda because it's a root-cause factor in every other lamentation or aspiration we hold for ourselves and our societies; pick any aspect of our lives or society: poverty and inequality, tolerance and pluralism, food security, healthcare, infrastructure, or good governance - literally anything. Whether you are lamenting its problems or setting an aspiration for its potential, if you ask "why?" (lament) or say "how might we?" (aspiration) five times, you get to root-cause issues of education: skills and character.

I got great advice from a mentor early in my career. I shared with him my dreams of starting schools of some form at home in Nigeria, and he said to me "if those are your dreams, why don't you learn something about teaching and learning." That's when I became a teacher and a coach. The wonderful students and athletes that I had the privilege of teaching and coaching helped me figure out what matters most to me about education; it is the opportunity to discover that you are fundamentally capable. That you can take on the challenge to pursue something you find meaningful (and difficult), that you can take the leap of faith to work hard at it, that you can get better at it through concerted effort, and from that experience discover that you are capable of far more than you ever imagined. The limits you have assumed for yourself are just imagined limits and don't serve you well. What serves you is the abiding confidence from the discovery that you are fundamentally capable. It does far less good for someone to tell you that you are capable than to discover it yourself, and great schools are a place where you do that.

We have a ton of work ahead of us to achieve our vision. Indeed, we've just barely got going. However, I feel great gratitude to be able to work with our team on a mission that we all find so meaningful. I am also grateful for the continual growth this endeavour requires of me and offers to me. Who I needed to be to work with a group of five to ten people three years ago, in planning our first school, is different from who I need to be for a team of 250 people across two countries and six schools who are working to build rooted culture and professional practices. It is different from who I will need to be four years from now as we operate 25 schools with over a thousand colleagues in south, east and west Africa. Trying to keep pace with the growth rate of our organisation, and of what leading it requires from me, is a constant stretch experience. It's both invigorating and challenging - and I'm thankful for both!

Most of all, I have a deep sense of gratitude for how the world has conspired to help make this path possible.

I'd like to end with a story about that. On the day before we opened the doors to students at of our first Nova Pioneer Academy, I remembered an experience that I hadn't thought about in almost 25 years; I remembered Sandy Sparrow. Mrs. Sparrow was my middle school principal at Swarthmore when I moved there from Nigeria and I would guess she is now in her early eighties. I was feeling a bit out of place in suburban Pennsylvania and out of what I now presume must have been a sympathetic desire to help me feel more at home, she asked me about Nigeria. She made a passing comment in that conversation that she would love to see Nigeria someday. I was 12 and I took her more seriously than I imagine she hoped I would, and asked my father whether I could invite my principal to visit us in Nsukka. He said yes.

She kept her word and she visited. It's funny to think about, but back then it felt very normal to me. I now realise how significant a step she was taking to follow through on her word for a new student in her school. It was quite an adventure and on that trip, I can remember her saying to me: "Dream big! Don't worry about the 'how' right now, but dream big." For many years, I hadn't thought about that, but on that first day of opening Pioneer Academy, the memory of her encouraging me to dream when I was twelve came back to me. Indeed, it was on an evening just one year later that I found myself hanging out in the playground of Swarthmore-Rutledge K-8 school discovering my own North Star.

Chinezi Chijioke is a Founder & CEO of Nova Pioneer Acadamies, a network of high quality and accessible 21st century schools across South Africa and Kenya. Chinezi was previously the Head of McKinsey & Company's African Education Practice, during which period he also worked with school systems across Asia, Europe, the Middle East, and the Americas. Chinezi started his career as a secondary school mathematics teacher, where he was nominated by his students to Who's Who Among American Teachers. He currently serves on the Global Advisory Council of Teach for All. A Nigerian, Chinezi lives in South Africa. Chinezi has a Bachelor of Arts in Psychology from Harvard University, a Master of Arts in Education, and an MBA from Stanford University in Palo Alto, California.

Elizabeth Mujawamaliya Johnson
Grace Rwanda Society

I have faced death numerous times and escaped during the 1994 Rwandan Genocide against the Tutsi. Once, I was with six to ten thousand people in one church; they came and killed and killed and killed. I was among maybe 30 to 40 people who survived that day. Many who died were better than I, more educated, wealthier - but I believe God wanted me alive today for a reason. That's why I don't take life for granted. I take life very, very seriously, and I've been working around-the-clock since then to live a life that is going to make an impact, not only on me, but also for the people around me. That's why I can say, "if it wasn't for the genocide, I don't think I would have co-founded Grace Rwanda Society." The Elizabeth who emerged from those 100 days in Rwanda was totally different than the Elizabeth before that. I realised that life sometimes can be very short. So, I started to say, "Yes, I survived; let me use my life to help others." I emerged with the determination that I survived something terrible, but my life didn't end. Actually it gave me more courage to say, "You know what? Work hard because you still have a long way to go – you survived for something greater than just surviving." I still had a future and hope and I wanted to make a difference not only to those who had suffered with me, but to those who had harmed me and my people, to those who can't even understand what happened, like the audiences in North America I often speak to, and for future generations.

After the 1994 Rwandan Genocide against the Tutsi, I immigrated to Canada in 1999 in a quest for more opportunities and more open doors to do better for my daughter and I, and maybe even to go and give back to Rwanda. I appreciate what we have in Canada and how much we can make a difference in the lives of so many people if we decide to do practical things with the knowledge and opportunities we have. So, ten years afterwards, in 2009, a friend, who is also a genocide survivor, and I founded a charitable organisation, Grace Rwanda Society. Grace Rwanda's goal is to bring literacy to Rwanda's youth and children in order to help them succeed in rebuilding their country. It is a grassroots diaspora organisation focused on education and literacy, starting in the areas and villages where we were born. Our first project was in the Eastern province of Rwanda. We helped the very school that I had attended as a little girl to make advances in literacy programmes, because we observed the link between basic levels of literacy - the ability to read and write – and students' orientation to general advancement and higher education. We decided that even if we helped a few children from our neighbourhoods, we will have done something towards rebuilding the lives of post-genocide Rwanda. We went from this modest goal all the way to signing an agreement with the Ministry of Youth for the literacy programmes we've been working on since 2013.

To-date we have helped install mini-libraries in six schools. We are already serving 15,000 children though these school libraries. Through the ministry contract we are building District Youth Centre Libraries. These libraries are being launched at each youth centre and we are planning to build 22. So far, we have completed six and have another 16 to go. Through each of these libraries, used only 100 out of the 365 days in a year, we modestly estimate we are serving 50 youth per day. We can say we are creating 5,000 literacy days annually per library or 110,000 for the 22.

We are a very small charity but we are committed to doing this work. We continue to advance our literacy initiatives through funding and support gained through our charitable organisation from private donors. Recently we've received about 35,000 books from Canada, such as dictionaries, reference books, and general fiction and non-fiction books. We have also acquired books published within Rwanda portraying local cultural contextual stories and content to support local authors and publication. One thing we are trying to encourage the people to do is to read in their own language, because most people in the rural villages and communities speak neither French nor English but only their indigenous language of Kinyarwanda. We are also trying to promote a culture of reading and writing through our work as aligned with what the Rwandan government is promoting nationally.

We started all this work while based in Canada but in 2016, my husband retired and we decided it was time to come to Rwanda and accomplish the work on the ground. We are paying attention now to how we can expand our work, based on the needs of locals, and on questions of personal ownership, sustainability, and generating local content. For example, we have done work with rehabilitated street boys, preparing them with literacy as well as other skills that will empower them long-term, like welding and sewing to name a few. We are also moving into community development in order to ensure local ownership and sustainability. I grew up poor, and am concerned with the economic livelihood and well-being of the people around us; therefore, doing what I am doing is about making sure others do not live and go through what I did myself. It is about thinking about what legacy I can leave, especially in post-genocide Rwanda. I am always asking, "what can I contribute?" I know I survived because God has a purpose for me and that purpose is to make a difference and a contribution to honour those who didn't survive, and even for those who survived.

The biggest challenge we've had since we started the organisation is all of the Nos we get to our funding request proposals. We receive no, after no, after no, for over 30 proposals. I think there is still some stigma out there in North America that when an African is taking an initiative to do work like this, they assume we may not fulfil their commitment, nor be trustworthy. I may be wrong, but I think that our work is not funded because there's a belief that we are not able. Therefore, we face the challenge of not having the funding to do what we need to do.

How am I overcoming this? We have a goal, we have a vision and whether we receive the funding or not, we will continue taking small steps as much as we can to work towards our goal. We will continue to make an impact at the local level, whether we have the support or not. This was one of the reasons we decided to pack up our lives in Canada and come into the field in the hope that our presence on the ground will help us grow with the international aid improving the outcomes we were achieving with what little we have.

Interestingly, people keep asking me, "Elizabeth why did you go back to Rwanda?" People believe that life in North America is better; however, I believe that if I come and make a contribution, and build capacity intellectually and financially, each of us can help one or two or three people. People may then point to that success, see something better is being done, and say, "look what people have done to make Rwanda a better country, to promote literacy for children, for future generations and the future of the world." This continues to be the motivation I had when we started. Yes, I believe a great wrong was done in 1994, but we can learn from the wrong and make our country a better country. People can also learn from us.

We are seeing the difference our work is making and relocating to Rwanda has definitely helped us expand our outreach. We are still receiving minimal monetary donations and shipments of books from Canada, as there are individuals who still believe in us and fund us on a small scale. I am also a Rotarian and continue to raise awareness and support through service clubs like Rotary International.

Usage of the libraries is growing. We are seeing children in elementary schools all the way to university students borrowing the books, reading, and using the library resources to do homework. Not only are we seeing impact with students but we are also expanding into the community. When you give a child a book, they share with the community and family members as well and so further spread impact. We are also reaching adults. We are seeing civil servants and educators coming into these centres. People are realising that they don't have to own the books to use them.

The usage and ownership of the ideas of literacy and education we're working for are starting to take hold in the communities that have libraries. We are not managing the centres personally; the local people manage them and that's the ownership we continue to strive for. We are seeing leadership grow as people come "out of their boxes" so to speak, and get involved with dignity. People are planning better for their future as well.

This experience has taught me that we can accomplish a lot with just a little, that we can keep moving forward in small steps, even without major access to resources – for example, large funding. I see us expanding and bearing more fruit in the future, because we now have more volunteers, more partnership opportunities, and strong motivation.

So, my message is, "don't be shy or afraid to follow your vision." Set your goals, go step by step, and don't lose your focus. If you lose your focus you end up not accomplishing much. For example, other possibilities have emerged, like working with the marginalised women and street youth. We are staying focused first to expand the literacy work and then, turn our focus to so many other things.

In order to get to sustainability, one has to focus on following one's vision and overcoming the challenges as they occur. Don't stand on the side lines, get involved and engaged in the battle, then you will advance one step at a time.

I have also learnt not to be intimidated by limited resources. *If you have a dream of impacting people, don't wait - just do it. For those in the diaspora, I say, 'don't get comfortable. If you have an idea to do something for your home country with your skills, with your finances, please do it.'* When you take a step, you will start making a difference; it may also encourage others and if we pool resources together, we will make international development better. I think when those of us from the African continent bring back the knowledge we have gained abroad and pool it with our background and local context, we do better with development work and can make a bigger difference.

To people who have gone through traumatic events, wars, poverty and other adversities I say, don't give up. You can do good and even use what you went through to have a positive impact on other people. After the genocide, I went back to school right away. I didn't speak English. I was using English in Rwanda, but it was my third or fourth language because I also speak French. I pushed through to get both a BA and an MA in Canada. I have allowed myself to heal, forgive and feel deeper compassion for others in spite of what happened to me. For example, after all is said and done, I decided that I can take something from my experience and go back blessing those people who actually harmed me and those I love. For example, we were helping and working with volunteers for the school we were building in Rwanda, some of whom probably killed my own people in that area; it can be tough because it's hard to accept what happened sometimes but I have that voice within me that says you can forgive and move on. Don't give up. You can do better. So, I think I gained a more loving and caring heart because I have seen the worst of humanity. I believe in and want to be part of being and doing our best. By that I mean, if we can do greater things for others and live with compassion, I think the world will be a better world.

Elizabeth Mujawamaliya Johnson was born in Rwanda and lived through the Rwandan genocide in 1994. While in Rwanda, she worked for the Ministry of Agriculture, Care Australia and World Vision. Elizabeth holds a MA in Leadership and a BBA in HRM. Her work includes developing public support for Grace Rwanda projects and speaking to groups across Canada to raise awareness about the genocide and its impacts. As a Rotarian, Elizabeth has a drive to serve above self and has a drive for international development. More information about Grace Rwanda can be found at www.gracerwanda.org.

Franck Kié
Promoting Education for Africa Rising

My name is Franck Kié and I am a 25-year old Ivorian, living and working as a Financial Analyst Consultant at Deloitte in Côte d'Ivoire. It's been two years since I came back home to start working after I did my studies and earned a BA(Hons) in International Business with a major in Finance at the European Business School London and an MA in International Security at the University of Warwick.

After my Master's degree, I did a 5-month internship at the leading provider of payment solutions in the Middle East in Dubai, before coming back to Abidjan. Up to this point, I believe you might think that the story I'm trying to tell you here is one of a young African who pursued his studies abroad and came back to Africa as a "repat" to work and develop his country. It could very well be that way, but my story is a little bit more complex than that. In fact, prior to going to the United Kingdom, I was born and raised in Côte d'Ivoire, but an unexpected event changed the lives of many of us who were living in that country.

In 2002, a failed coup that turned into a rebellion divided the country in two parts, with the north held by the rebels, and the south, where I was living with my family, controlled by the government. In 2004, an attempt by the government to regain control of the north accidentally killed 9 French military men and France's response was the destruction of the Ivorian army air fleet. This action caused a massive unrest from the Ivorian population which attacked every French symbol they could find in order to retaliate; restaurants, homes and schools were all destroyed. I was going to a French school that was burnt down, and my family and I had to fly to Morocco so I could continue to finish my high school there.

Unfortunately, everybody did not get the chance to travel to another country in order to pursue their studies. I was already aware of how fortunate I was to be raised with some privilege, but at that specific time, it was even clearer how lucky I was to have this

14

opportunity while others didn't. Over the years, the situation kept getting worse in the country, and as I was going home every now and then for holidays, I could see how the educational system was getting very badly affected.

With most of the budget of the State being used for the management of the crisis and students being manipulated by politicians, results of national exams such as the baccalaureate (high school diploma) would hit the lowest levels year after year. As I've always wanted to contribute to the development of my country, and have always been against inequality, I knew it was time to give back. I wanted to do something so that other children in Côte d'Ivoire could benefit from better access to education, even if they were underprivileged.

One of the values I believe in the most is meritocracy, and for the best to be rewarded for their hard work. We should all be equal so the rewards can be fairly distributed. In real life, it is obviously not possible to do so, but it's a dream we can all work on to make it come true. If we start by focusing on lending a helping hand to those who need it the most, we create more chances to reach equality.

Actions speaking louder than words; my father and I co-founded the Future Africa Foundation three years ago. Not too far from where we live, in the northern outskirts of Abidjan, there is a village called Akouedo, known for being the biggest waste depot of the country. On a Sunday afternoon, we decided to go there after a long discussion about how we could do something in order to help our community, and what we found was devastating. Children, living, playing, working, and even eating in this filthy place. They were being sent by their parents to collect plastic that they would resell later on. Witnessing that terrible situation made the idea of creating the Foundation obvious.

Creating the Foundation from a legal point of view was not the hardest part; it was really out on the field that we faced many challenges.

Our primary goal was to get these underprivileged children out of the waste depot and give them better access to education, but as it was their parents who sent them there to work, we realised that it would be a very complicated task. We first had to convince the parents that it would be more beneficial for them and their children in the long run if they sent them to school rather than sending them to work. It wasn't an easy task as most of the parents are themselves illiterate and didn't understand the benefits their children could get from getting an education. It was a very painful situation as it was obvious to me how they would be better off in the long run by doing so. As there is also a law forbidding children under 16 to work in Côte d'Ivoire, we also sometimes had to remind them of it to make them realise how bad it can be to send your child to work.

Since the closest school to the waste depot was in a very poor shape, our second biggest challenge was to do something about it so children and their parents would be more motivated to attend school rather than going to work in the waste depot. We therefore had to convince the school management and also the local authorities of the benefit of our action, as they had already seen a lot of NGOs and foundations which said they would help, but did not actually do so. Last but not least, we now had to convince our network and all the people we knew to help us, and explain why this cause we were fighting for – helping the underprivileged in Akouedo - needed to receive great support, and not only from our immediate network.

Our strategy was built around two main points: first, to ease the access to education for these children and second, promoting excellence. We conducted major refurbishment works in the school, offered round tables, school kits for children, and hygiene kits for the school. Regarding the promotion of excellence, for the second year in a row, we have been organising a math test where the best student can gain a scholarship to study in a better middle school. The outcome of our actions can be seen clearly with the results of the math tests we received for this year. In fact, we can see that thanks to our actions, more children are taking the math test and, as a result, a larger number of them passed the average mark. The school management team also told us that children aren't getting sick as often, as they are studying in a healthier environment, and they can definitely observe the children being more focused and enjoying their time in school.

As of today, and after 3 years of operation in Côte d'Ivoire, the Foundation has been able to offer around 500 school kits, 25 scholarships, around 100 school tables, 10 educational tablets, and it has fully renovated one school. We organised our first Christmas tree this year, where we offered 100 gifts to underprivileged children in Abidjan. Through our various activities, we have been able to reach over 1000 children since our creation. I am back now in Cote d'Ivoire full time dedicating 60% of my free time to guide the organisation forward whilst working my consultancy job. This experience is helping me better structure the organisation, think strategically about the way we should move forward and analyse critically the ways for us to expand our target and increase our impact.

In reflection, this experience definitely taught me several things, with one of the most important being that, if you have a goal, no matter how hard you think it is, you must pursue it, especially if you're looking to help others in your community. It also taught me the hardest part is taking the first step in order to start an action, but if you manage to do it, you will see that nothing can stop you and you will definitely be eager to do even more. Last but not least, I think my favorite lesson from all of this is that even if you think that what you are doing will have a small impact, you have no idea of how big the impact can be on another person's life. It is better to have this small impact locally, than doing nothing at all, or waiting to be big enough in order to do something, which might never happen.

Through this adventure, I've also learned more about humility, respect and tolerance and I continue to acknowledge how lucky and blessed I was to be in this position. Most importantly, I understood more than ever that it was my duty to do something in order to bring some change so that others can have the chance that I also had. And for the future, I only hope that we will manage to extend this opportunity and our actions to other underprivileged neighborhoods, children and families, across the whole of Côte d'Ivoire and maybe Africa one day.

Franck Kié is a Financial Advisory Senior Consultant at Deloitte in Ivory Coast, which he joined after completing various internships in finance and consulting in Abidjan, London, Paris and Dubai. He's really passionate about African history and politics but also about development, education, and environmental issues. Franck is also a political analyst contributor for Ventures Africa, the Country Chair in Cote d'Ivoire for Global Dignity and the past Curator of the Abidjan Hub of the Global Shapers Community which is an initiative from the World Economic Forum led by young people who are exceptional in their potential, their achievements, and their drive to make a contribution to their communities. He has a Master's degree in Politics and International Relations from the University of Warwick in the UK.

Mwalimu Musheshe
An African Rural University: For Women Only

When I was a young kid, about 12, my father was a Chief and we had a very severe drought. As things were at the time, we had a culture where people believed that we had people responsible for bringing in the drought or for making it rain. So they arrested and rounded up some people they thought were responsible because the drought was long. Cows and livestock were dying and crops were devastated. I woke up at night and went to one of the people who was tied up on the ropes, arrested on suspicion of causing the drought. I went up to him and said: "Are you God?"

He said: "No! I'm not God."

I remembered that at school they used to tell us that it was only God who makes it rain. So I said: "So if you are not God, why are you on the ropes, why have they tied you up for the rain?"

He said: "It is all lies; it is just because people believe in myths."

I repeated: "But if you are not God it means you are innocent, and it is just a myth!"

He replied: "Yes!"

I went into the kitchen, grabbed a knife and cut his ropes. My instinctive work for justice started then, and it has never stopped since.

From school days, even at university (for which I was imprisoned by the military and held incommunicado), and in the past 34 years, I have dedicated my life and work to creating education models for rural transformation and sustainable development by supporting change agency in local settings. With Ephrem Rutaboba and Silvana Veltkamp I founded the Uganda Rural Development and Training Programme (URDT) in 1987 to do this work. The URDT programme was founded to defy the status quo of aid distribution in Africa. We sought to address the missing link in development programmes:

the merger of truly functional education, training, and participatory action research with integrated rural development. Our thrust is the Visionary Approach - that permits genuine democratic participation by rural people and communities in development activities, thereby improving their ownership and leadership of the development process. In the methodology, people are accepted as protagonists in the development process. As such they: engage in determining what truly matters to them, their families, and community; formulate a clear vision of what they want to create in light of their current situations; and use the discrepancy between what they have and what they want in order to create structural tension and by its very nature, tension seeking resolution.

They then make informed choices to resolve this tension in favour of realising their aspirations.

We have worked with people as change leaders and organisations with a potential to become centres of excellence for rural transformation. Our commitment is to start with local government institutions especially the sub counties mandated with service delivery and cascade to villages, to work with all categories of leaders and organically roll out the Epicentre Strategy throughout Africa. The strategy is grounded in an understanding that a multipronged approach involving the individual, household, villages on one hand and Sub County level on the other, as change radiates outward. Our principle is to develop rural transformation specialists that are visionary leaders, creative, and systems thinkers so that we have great results. A simple example is that we have youth empowerment programmes and schools in rural communities. We take children from very poor backgrounds and bring them to the school and give them an empowering educational experience that allows them to realise what can be if they take their vision and turn it into action. We teach them leadership, empathy, values, team-learning, entrepreneurship, and how to work for well-being and prosperity.

We then take their parents, bring them to the school and help them work together (the two-generations approach to narrow information and skills gap between the child and the parents/guardians). We have seen transformation using this model, from poverty to relative prosperity in as short a space of time as two to three years.

Although establishing a rural university was one of URDT's objectives, it was not until 2001 that Ashoka recognised the idea of the University as a systems wide and transformational idea. Ashoka recognises and supports Social Entrepreneurs (www.ashoka.org) and I was awarded the Ashoka Fellowship. After 25 years of experience working with rural communities, the establishment of the university was finally fast tracked. In 2011, we were granted an operational license and the African Rural University (ARU) was born has continued to embed the roots of the URDT approach over the past 5 years.

There are many universities in Uganda. So what is different about ARU is that we focus on the critical element of agency and that it is an all-women's university. We decided to amplify the attributes of a woman as an organiser, as a teacher, as a leader, an all-round skilled resource – all those attributes that women have that have not been used as a strategic resource for development.

Why women? I get my inspiration from my mother. My mother nurtured me and demonstrates the characteristics and attributes we aspire to for development at ARU.

- My mother had the capacity to carry me for 9 months without complaining. As men, when we are given a load to carry even for a short period of time, we start complaining.
- The capacity to bear children and make sure that they survive, past the 5-year mark, is all up to African mothers.
- When I was ill, my mom will touch my forehead, know I am ill and in that case, be my doctor.
- She will go into the bush, gather leaves, pound them and put them in water, then she was my pharmacist.
- She would make sure I take my medicine, then she was my nurse.
- She would make sure I ate; she was our cook.
- She looked after me; she was my helper.
- She was our research officer.
- She knew what to eat and what to save, our household manager.
- She made sure the seed went beyond the season which means she treated them against disease and defect, then she was our horticulturist.

- She was our entomologist, keeping us protected from bites and stings.
- She was our marketing officer.
- She was our trader and business leader.
- She was the peacekeeper at home - she made sure she talked to our father.
- She was a counsellor
- She was a network, making sure our relationship with neighbours was harmonious

All these characteristics/attributes, though known, are never explained in a strategic way nor is the question raised about how we can use these for development beyond seeing the woman as only a compassionate, loving, and nurturing human beings. To me, a woman is very holistic in her approach and we miss that in our development approaches. And through our URDT work, we saw how much women advance development. I saw it with microfinance programmes. When we give men money, they drank it; if you gave it to women, they did what was needed for the household. Another observation that struck me about women's role in development came from my wife. She worked in the health sector. When she went for a workshop, came back and started explaining what she learnt until I have to stop her from talking. When I come back from workshops and she asks me about it, it doesn't take me more than a paragraph to tell what I learned. If someone can give you all the details of what they learned and why it matters, why not give them more opportunity to be teachers of change?

So we figured: what it would look like to put women in strategic positions and allow them to contribute beyond where they have been traditionally placed. We think about what it means to give women the academics and broaden their perspectives and status to women as leaders, managers, and women as integrators. And it has indeed been as they say: *If you educate a man you educate an individual, if you educate a woman, you educate a nation.* And then there's the scientific and statistical basis for our work. For example, if a woman is illiterate, her children will suffer the usual indices of absolute poverty, such as health impacts, poor sanitation, poor hygiene. If a girl has primary education, those indices are reduced by 25% for her children. If secondary-educated, the statistics are improved to 50%. If a woman goes to high-school, they are reduced by 75% and if a woman goes to college the poverty indices are

100% reduced. So, the education of a girl child is fundamental for transformation. Also, my observation is that in our culture when men are asked about education, they want to educate boys. When you ask women, they want to educate everyone at the household level. Thus, the value and sense of equity comes more from women. Men look at progeny and their own participation for their boy-child. The woman doesn't look at it that way. She looks at giving all children access to education, access to nutrition and that's why a woman is a good agent of change. So there is the scientific, emotional, and strategic reasons that made me think yes, let us promote women and start a university for women.

For me and team ARU (and URDT), *it is an opportunity to give women faith and opportunity to recognise the power they have within themselves so that they can express their highest hopes without being hindered by society or by rules and regulations.* We have the highest ideals in ourselves and if we can fully express them, that will define justice for everyone. And that's why we work for peace, equality, and agency for people. We ask people: "If the situation can be changed at all in your life, what would you like your life to look like. We talk about issues of values, virtues and principles and encourage people to live by their principles so we will have a just world. We want people to have confidence, to reach the highest in themselves.

The challenges have been many. First, is the cultural stereotype where people think men should be given all the opportunities, otherwise women are going to take over and oppress men. The other challenge is that we are transforming how people think as well as the education sector. We are not teaching single subjects and specialisations. We focus on a holistic programme, to build skills, intellectual knowledge and also be practical across the board. The main parts of traditional universities are still theoretical even in professional courses like medicine, engineering and technology and agriculture. I did agricultural engineering; I look back and say, did we really do farming or just the science of agriculture? That is different and we need to focus on the practical. So that's a challenge to look at the culture we have in universities and help people deal with the necessities of change. For example, people are not paying attention to climate change and this is a dialogue needed not only in the lecture room but in the community.

Another challenge is harnessing the wealth of wisdom out there. That is why we are looking, with ARU, at how to integrate what we have called traditional wisdom. When I am asked, "how many professors do you have?", I say I have one or two from the conventional university and the rest are from a lifelong learning university called the village. People are shocked and say: "professors from the village? what do you mean?" We have people from the village who are weather-beaten but hold a wealth of knowledge and information and skill, but they are never recognised except when interviewed as respondents. I want to bring those people into classrooms so that they can see what it is to have knowledge that is passed on from generation to generation. This can be a challenge when we are looking for funding and donors, familiar with western-educated models, are looking for the usual credentials.

So this paradigm shift has been a challenge but we are moving forward and seeing results that already tell us we are planting good seed. Based on our more than 25 years of URDT and now ARU work, we have touched over 30,000 people who have benefited. I have also now been asked to be part of the planning for Uganda's vision 2040, whereas when we started in 1995, we were visited by President Museveni at the time who said we were being idealistic. It is a good sign that Africa has moved towards vision-centred work like here in Uganda and in the AU. All the six states in the East African Community have long term national visions. It shows that there is an awakening taking place and we are moving in the right direction. For us in the URDT and ARU programmes our goal is to contribute effectively to the African Renaissance. That's why our motto is "Awakening the Sleeping Genius in Each of Us".

My vision for ARU is a centre for innovation in rural technologies. A centre which develops and nurtures women's leadership and capacities to influence change. A university that will give leadership in what it means to change the education system because the education system we have now is focused on specialised sectors instead of looking at development in a holistic way. That's why we have what we call Technologies for Rural Transformation - to help people think, influence mind-set change and create appropriate leadership and innovation in Africa as a beacon for change in the world. ARU will live her historic mission as *A CRADLE FOR LEARNING AND CREATING!*

24

Dr. Mwalimu Musheshe is Sr. Chairman, CEO and Founder of the Uganda Rural Development & Training Program (URDT) and the African Rural University (ARU), Kibaale District, Uganda. He has been a social activist since youth. Early on, Musheshe recognised the importance of education for himself, and the need for agricultural training for subsistence farmers. His pursuit of education was interrupted many times by political conflict. Finally, he achieved a Bachelor of Science in Agriculture Engineering from Makerere University, Kampala, Uganda in 1983. Then he studied Visionary Leadership, Systems Thinking and Strategic Planning in the United States and Canada. He proceeded to receive his MSc in Development Management from The Open University, U.K. In May 2009 he was awarded with an honourary Doctorate (PhD) of Environmental Citizenship and Leadership by Unity College, Maine, USA

Influencing people in his life: Harima Musheshe (his mother), Ruta Mutabazi Musheshe (his father) Silvana veltkamp, Robert Fritz, Peter Senge, Mwalimu Kambarage Nyerere.

Cecil Nutakor
eCampus: Forging a Path for the Pathless

On that Thursday, March 24th 1983, the most wonderful woman I have ever known – my mother – then a young midwife who had just begun practicing, delivered a pre-mature baby boy. According to Doctor Quest and the hospital's midwife Mrs. Ales Bleno the boy was only 6 months and two weeks old, and he would not survive without an incubator. Unfortunately, there were no incubators at the hospital. The best, professional thing they could do was to prepare my mother's mind to accept that her newly born first child was not going to make it. He might survive for a few weeks but he will not make it to two months. That pre-mature baby boy was me and the last time I checked, I have made it to my 33rd birthday. My mother, being a midwife herself, refused to accept what the experts were telling her. Instead she managed to create her own incubator environment and placed me inside it at home monitoring me day and night for 13 months and I survived. My father, who was not around at the time of my birth, had followed the mass migration of Ghanaian professionals in the 80s to Nigeria for greener pastures, but this would not end well for him. He did return for my naming ceremony but left back for Nigeria soon after, and my mother and I followed later when my condition was good enough to travel.

And so, my childhood started in Nigeria. Things were difficult for my parents. My father was still struggling to get a decent job, but my mother was able to use her midwife and nursing certificate to work as a part time nurse at various private clinics and she would work as a seamstress at home with her sewing machine. That was how my parents were able to put food on the table. I had to stay at home until I was five because my parents could not afford to send me to school. I learned from the other children in the compound when they returned from school, gathered around singing their nursery rhymes and songs. My father recorded them with his Walkman onto cassettes and played them back to me at home from time to time. That was how I learnt all the nursery songs without having the privilege of stepping foot in a classroom. According to my mother I could learn things very fast. I was able to speak seven different languages (Hausa, Isoko, Urhobo, Yoruba, Eshen, Ewe and English) at age six.

Not long after my father had finally gotten a decent job up north in Sokoto as a teacher at the state polytechnic, Nigeria decided that Ghana must go. All Ghanaian migrants were to leave Nigeria on the notion that they were taking the jobs meant for Nigerians. My mother took the lead back to Ghana with my kid brother and myself and brought us to our maternal grandmother in Ho, the capital city of the Volta Region of Ghana. My grandmother was the matron in charge of the kitchen at the Ho Nursing Training College and was doing quite well and food was not a problem. I got enrolled at Mawuli Primary School and my mother left back for Nigeria. Grandmom was so sweet; she took good care of us until my mother returned from Nigeria for good, and resettled in Ghana and re-joined the Ghana Health Service.

I did very well academically in primary school. I joined the Red Cross, Wildlife Club, and the Cultural Dancing group. I represented my school at competitions. My mother made the church a critical part of my life. I was active in the church even as a child and I acted a number of roles from the Bible during children's day celebrations – from the Prodigal Son, to Judas and even Satan. Before I turned 12 I had been initiated into the church choir, the youngest person to join the choir in its history. It got me the nickname Baby Choir. I was celebrated and appreciated by everyone I came in contact with in one way or another.

I saw my father again when I turned 13. All I could remember of him was pictures shown to me by my mother. When people talk about their fathers I had nothing to say apart from saying he was in Nigeria. When my mother told me that my father was coming back to Ghana, I was excited, but I was also confused because I didn't really know him. I was too young to remember him when we left him behind in Nigeria. From the day that my mother informed me about his return, I looked forward to meeting my father each day. Every day I would sit on the walls and look towards the main road for signs of him. The day he finally came I was playing football on the veranda with my junior brother. A tall dark man came towards us called our names and said in our local dialect," Can't you recognise me?" I remember asking him who he was, and he responded, "I am your father; I have come back from Nigeria." My brother and I started shouting "Dada, Dada, Dada, Dada!" I wanted all the other kids in the nurse's flat to know that my father was finally here.

It was exciting for me to see my father, but he looked ill and skinny. I wanted to know what he brought from Nigeria. I had wanted a television very badly so I was disappointed when he said he did not bring anything apart from a music player popularly known as a ghetto blaster. The truth is he had lost everything, sold his valuables to survive, and when it became unbearable he had to come back to Ghana broke. But truly, what really mattered to me at the time, was that my father was now here with us.

Within a year and a half my father got a job with the Kumasi Polytechnic in the capital city of the Ashanti Region in Ghana. He was given an official car, a three-bedroom bungalow with a big compound and boy's quarters. For the first time my kid brother and I had our own room. Things got better and I enrolled at the State Experimental Junior High School. Kumasi was good; we had a bicycle and a small football pitch at home. I had to learn a new language, Akan or Asante Twi, and make new friends both at school and within the community but I was able to settle in quite well. During my final year at school I noticed there was some kind of tension between my mother and father. They quarreled a lot more, and my father would stay out of the house for long hours with friends. Home was not interesting anymore to him, and eventually after my final exams in 1998 my parents divorced. I remember we had to go to the courts to choose between living with our father or our mother. This was a big blow to me and I did not believe it could be happening. Eventually the courts decided to put us, the children, in boarding schools so that both parents could have access to us. But my father never showed up again. At age 15 I was on my own. I was very angry and disappointed in my father for leaving. Not only did he refuse to send our up-keeping money to the courts, but he had left everything on my mother again just like it was when he was in Nigeria.

I tried not to burden my mother who was now working two jobs to take care of three children, but I was not easy. I used to rap and dance at events to earn some money but when I tried to give the money to my mother she would not take it. Instead she would get angry at me, telling me I should stop doing things for money and focus on my studies. I couldn't help it because I would see her sell all her expensive cloths and wax prints to pay for our school fees.

From that time in my life I knew I had to do something to support my mother. She wanted me to become a medical doctor, but senior high school was not as fun and interesting as primary and junior high school was for me and learning became more difficult, rigid, and unattractive. There was also limited access to reading materials and I had to spend hours copying chapter after chapter of text books in the library because it was expensive and I did not want to stress my mother with those costs. Eventually I failed my final exams miserably. My mother was devastated and disappointed in me. She made sure I registered to write the exams for the second time, but I failed again. For the same old reasons – lack of access to reading materials – and this time it was even worse because I was preparing to rewrite the exams as a private candidate and did not have the privilege of a school library or schoolmates from whom I could borrow textbooks and pamphlets of past questions and answers to practice and prepare with. I was on my own and the most painful part was this time around, I was actually more committed to making sure I passed the exams just to make my mother happy and proud of me again. But without the adequate access to learning materials and making do with my notes from school, I knew I was going to fail again. I could feel how under prepared I was but there was nothing I could do about it.

I became a complete failure in the family and I could notice and feel I was no longer an integral part of the family. My mother would not even allow me to play with my siblings when they came back home for vacation, saying that I would have a bad influence on them. I became lonely and isolated. I would stay in my room all day and I began to hate myself. I knew deep down that I was good, smart and intelligent. I keep failing because the educational system did not favour me and because I didn't have enough or the right learning resources at my disposal. Anytime I told my mother or uncles about why I think I failed they just made fun of me and told me to stop blaming the educational system and blame myself. "You are not the only student, so why do the others pass with flying colours?" they would ask. I became a laughing stock in the family and I felt I had lost my place and respect as the first-born.

I had to do something to earn the trust and love of my family, especially my mother. Clearly no university was going to admit me with those grades and so I turned to a newly found interest, computers. I started learning on my own by visiting Internet cafes, making friends with the hardware and network engineers and asking questions all the time. I needed to own a computer if I was going to make any headway. I remember waking up one morning around 5am to beg my mother to give me the last chance and buy me a computer. I promised her I would learn how to use that computer to create software that I could sell to big companies. To my surprise, she agreed and bought me an old Compaq and sent me to a computer-training Centre where I learnt the basics of how to use Microsoft Office. I was fascinated by how Microsoft Access worked and came to appreciate the power of databases. I regularly thought to myself. "What if we had a database of all the learning materials I needed to pass my exams on a computer?" Then I would have passed my exams and not have to be humiliated. In these conversations with myself I would think that maybe I should start that database, and would dream about what to call it. I played around with the words electronic and campus, and eventually settled on eCampus. That was how eCampus, today a world-class online learning platform and mobile app that literally puts the classroom in your palms, was born. The first prototype was ready in 2004. A year later, the President of Regent University College of Science and Technology, in Accra, the capital city of Ghana, showed interest in my work and awarded me a scholarship to study computer science, gave me a job, and the university became the first institution to deploy eCampus. This was profound for me because so far, I had no hopes of ever making it to the university. I couldn't wait to break the news to my mother. She was so happy for me; hugging me she said "I knew you were smart and intelligent." Regaining her confidence and pride in me felt so good.

In 2013, eCampus once again won me a scholarship, to pursue my MBA at the Catholic University of Milan. The MBA programme was bespoke and truly unique. You need to present a business idea to be admitted, then for 14 months you are challenged to improve the idea using research and scientific methods. My time at the MBA positively impacted eCampus significantly, especially the eCampus user experience of read, listen, watch, practice, play, and discuss was a direct result of the scientific research I had to do on how the human brain actually learns. This meant that with eCampus, you learn naturally and not the way the education systems force us to learn.

Nurturing and growing the idea and concept of eCampus into a usable product and service has become my life long mission. It has given me a purpose and a cause to live for, a much clearer path despite the seemingly pathless destiny that I lived right from my premature birth. It has pushed me to learn more about education, computers and technology. *Today, eCampus is the ticket to academic excellence for all who, like me, are struggling to make it through traditional school systems.* eCampus can be accessed on all smartphones and digital platforms with content to read, listen, watch, practice and discuss while earning points that let you know whether you are ready for an exam before you take it. eCampus is available in 7 languages – Arabic, Amharic, English, French, Portuguese, Spanish, Swahili – and is suitable for second cycle education, tertiary education and corporate training. After releasing the eCampus Mobile App on May 31, 2015, in just one year, there are 15 piloting institutions on eCampus, over 2000 downloads from the App Stores, and over 1000 registered users with free access to past questions from 1993 to 2014 for the West African Examination Council exams. And we are now working on taking similar tools to Eastern and Southern Africa. eCampus is incorporated in Ghana and Liberia. eCampus employs a total of 13 people and provides internship opportunities to university students each year. In 2016 eCampus was awarded the Education Startup of the Year at the Ghana Startup Awards.

Building a company has taught me the importance of passion, consistency, and expectation management. My life has become less and less about me and more and more about my employees and my customers, the students and employees of other companies, who use our products and services. I have also learnt to appreciate whatever happens to me and learn from it. Today it is easy for me to say to my father, "Thank you for not being there for me; it made me a stronger man." And most importantly, the experience helped me find my path in life; it gave me a sense of purpose that is so consuming that I wonder what other future there could have been for me other than putting eCampus in the hands of every student and corporate employee in Africa.

Cecil Senna Nutakor is a leading authority on the use of technology for self-paced education in Ghana. Combining a mix of self-taught technology innovation skills and professional training, he developed an ICT certificate programme in use by two universities. He founded eCampus, an online education platform, and is also CEO of E I L (Equinox Intercom Limited). Cecil holds an MBA in Global Business and Sustainability from the Catholic University of Milan, and a BSc in Entrepreneurship and SME Management from GIMPA. His work has made him a multi-award winning social entrepreneur, VC4Africa named him Africa's Most Promising Entrepreneur in 2013.

Chinyere Nwabugwu
Community Development at Ireti Primary School

I obtained my PhD in Electrical Engineering from Stanford University, USA in June 2014. As a patriotic citizen, I returned to Nigeria for my National Youth Service Corps (NYSC) in August 2014, with the ultimate goal of modelling leadership through service and by example. The year of national service includes: (1) an Orientation Course, (2) a Primary Assignment, (3) Community Development Service, and (4) Winding-up/Passing-out. The objectives of youth development through shared experience, participation in nation building, responsiveness to the country's needs, and the empowerment of future leaders that will be committed to the development of Nigeria while fostering unity are of paramount importance.

With the above in mind, I got involved in my special NYSC community development service (CDS) project. As a Christian (of the Anglican tradition), service is part of my call and I strive to incorporate the art of positively affecting the lives of people in my community into my life. Also, I am passionate about the development of children and providing access to quality education, both of which will lead to individuals who can positively contribute to society. As such, when I came across Ireti Primary School, Lagos (a public school) and its dilapidated learning infrastructure, while I served as Presiding Officer for the 2015 Nigerian general elections, I felt a resolve to do all I could to help. My hope was that this would result in a more conducive learning environment for the pupils at the school, and improve the quality of education delivered to them.

According to a study by the United Nations Educational, Scientific and Cultural Organization (UNESCO) published in 2012, Nigeria has the highest number of young people worldwide that are out of school. Given our population growth trajectory and economic instability, the number of kids that are out of school is expected to keep growing to the detriment of our national development. This statistic is traceable to a variety of factors including poor schooling conditions that act as disincentives for kids to remain in school. Furthermore, methods of instruction at these schools are usually archaic (especially for the government-owned schools) and present significant learning challenges and gaps considering global digitization. I wanted to do my part to keep the children of Ireti Primary School in school.

I started my CDS project in April 2015;Following the elections, I made several visits to the school and met with key stakeholders to assess their needs. The head teacher, assistant head teacher, and pupils of the school, as well as the corps members serving at the school, voiced several concerns, such as the need to renovate the school buildings; provide boreholes for drinking water, educational supplies, and whiteboards; acquire school buses; and employ additional teachers. Many schools have adopted the use of whiteboards in classrooms due to the numerous benefits they provide over chalkboards. Some classrooms at Ireti Primary School did not have blackboards and in some instances, the walls were simply covered with charcoal to form blackboards. In addition to finding out about the needs of the primary school, I discovered that a majority of the pupils were displaced children from Borno State due to the Boko Haram insurgency. Being a big supporter of empowerment through education, I was determined to improve the learning environment for the pupils to encourage a positive attitude towards learning and increase academic success.

After I analysed the needs that were raised and defined the scope of my project, I sought funding and vendors. My focus was on changes I could make at the school that would be sustainable and beneficial to the school children. Using the funding I secured, I renovated the dilapidated classrooms in the school by painting the classroom walls and fence and repairing all the broken-down ceilings. I also provided whiteboards, magnetic dusters, marker pens, notice boards, wall clocks for all the classes, and educational supplies (pens, pencils with erasers, sharpeners, and books) for the pupils. In addition, I instituted a vocational skills training programme for the pupils. I trained the pupils in bead-making and provided refreshments. Bead-making was my skill acquisition and entrepreneurship development (SAED) training during my service year and I was excited to be able to teach others!

In seeking funding for this project, I spoke to many (over 50) potential sponsors about my CDS project and was fortunate to have a good number share my vision to transform Ireti Primary

School. The key to getting sufficient funds was talking to many individuals and corporations. My employer (place of primary assignment), Execution Edge Limited, was my major sponsor. I also received financial support from several generous individual donors.

In addition to financial support, I had a number of people who accompanied me to the market several times to speak with vendors and make the purchases. There were people who came to the school to take pictures and others who stayed at the site to monitor the progress of the work. I sincerely appreciate the support rendered to me as I undertook this project that impacted the lives of close to 200 children.

I faced several challenges during the course of the project that I was able to overcome through careful planning and navigation. First, during the course of executing the project, the scope changed. The head teacher informed me that there were nine classrooms that needed renovation and not the eight of which I had previously been made aware. Second, despite agreed upon contracts and subsequent renegotiations with the addition of a classroom, having the work completed was a challenge. This was frustrating as it necessitated the cutting of costs on some aspects of the project to accommodate others and resulted in lower quality of work in those areas. Third, rain delayed the painting of the fence and careful planning had to be done to maximise productivity on the days that it did not rain. Finally, I was promised sponsorship by many but not all the sponsorships came through. I overcame this challenge by seeking sponsorship from over 50 people so that the fraction of sponsorships that came through ended up being enough to cover the project cost.

The resources expended for my CDS project were certainly worth it. The objectives of my project were to:
1. Provide quality whiteboards for every classroom
2. Provide a conducive learning environment for the pupils through the painting of the classrooms and fence, and the repair of the ceilings
3. Encourage the pupils to stay in school by improving the quality of education
4. Empower the pupils through skills acquisition by teaching bead-making skills I acquired over my service year
5. Contribute to the welfare of the community

My CDS project was a success, which was extremely rewarding. It was a privilege to receive commendations from the head teacher of the primary school, my employer, my local government inspector, and my zonal inspector. I was also honoured with a first-place award, out of the entire Batch B group of the 2014-2015 National Youth Service Corp (NYSC) set in Lagos State, for an outstanding CDS project. The best part was that the pupils were very pleased.

The children and staff of Ireti Primary School were so appreciative, which made all the effort I put in worthwhile. When the children saw the transformation to their classrooms, they were leaping for joy. I heard comments such as "this aunty really tried!" and "you have made our school to be like Corona." To put the latter comment in perspective, on the same street as Ireti Primary School is Corona School, a private school that is very well maintained, and the Ireti children could see that the transformation of the school made it as nice as Corona school. The pupils (and teachers) also really seemed to enjoy and benefit from the skills acquisition training. In addition, they prayed for me during their assembly.

I was thankful to have been able to complete my project before the end of my NYSC service year. While the project was an individual CDS project, it would not have been possible without the support of several donors and members of the community. The support of my sponsors and the community showed me just how much can be achieved when people work together towards a common good. I was further encouraged that "I can do all things through Christ who strengthens me" (Philippians 4:13).
I believe that Nigeria is repairable and we are better off attempting to piece her together than resign in despair and hopelessness, and that my revitalisation project is a first step of many to achieve this vision.

Over the years, the NYSC CDS platform has enabled corps members to engage in community service programmes aimed at improving community welfare through education and skills acquisition. I feel fulfilled having been able to support this cause through the execution of my project at Ireti Primary School. It is my first step towards many to help transform and build a better Nigeria and stronger Africa.

Chinyere Nwabugwu, PhD is from Nnobi in Anambra State, Nigeria. She was raised in Nigeria and the Netherlands. She has a double major in Electrical and Computer Engineering, and minors in Computer Science and Mathematics (summa cum laude honours) from Louisiana State University, USA. In addition, she has a Master's degree in Electrical Engineering and a Doctorate degree in Electrical Engineering, both from Stanford University, USA. She held numerous leadership positions during both her undergraduate and graduate studies, including being the Founder and President of the Graduate Students in Electrical Engineering (GSEE) at Stanford University. She has worked for Chevron North America Exploration and Production Company (a Chevron U.S.A. Inc. Division) as an Automation Engineer, Facilities Engineer and a Petrophysicist. She is currently a Medical Image Analysis and Machine Learning Researcher at IBM Research - Almaden, California, USA. Her hobbies include singing and playing the guitar.

Yeniva Sisay-Sogbeh
Called to be an Educator

While growing up in the US, my parents always talked about moving back "home" to Sierra Leone. With this in mind, each time I visited Sierra Leone in the 1990s, I was carefully connecting the dots of my existence and discovering who I am. It is the one place in the world where I felt connected and had a strong sense of belonging. And at the end of each visit, I returned to the US feeling incomplete – like little pieces of me were missing. I realised that being in Sierra Leone felt like home. It was in this way that the burning desire to return to Sierra Leone was planted in my heart.

On one of our visits during the Christmas holidays, I remember bringing up the subject with my mother and grandfather. I announced: "Mom I think it would be a great idea for me to move to Sierra Leone and go to school. You have always talked about moving home and I could live here with Grandma and Grandpa and go to school with my cousins. It would be so much fun!" My Mom looked at me with a puzzled look on her face and then gave me the side eye. "You are too young" she said. My Grandfather looked up from reading his newspaper and said "Yes Yeniva I am sure it would be very fun and I am sure you would have just as much fun getting into a reputable university as well. The value of education is not just about fun. You can't compare the education in America to that in Africa. As a woman, you have to fight twice as hard; here you won't even have a head start." His statement took me by surprise and it lingered in my head long after he made his declaration.

I first went back to Sierra Leone again in 2002 right after the war. I couldn't fathom what had become of the beautiful country that I loved so much. I had so many unanswered questions; Why? What was the reason behind the war? And most importantly, how could we make sure it never happened again? I knew I had to do something, anything, to make a difference. So I started collecting things to send: clothes, toiletries, school supplies, books - anything that could help. I began by setting up my own NGO and joined different Sierra Leonean organisations – all to try and contribute to the rebuilding process and make a difference. I made a trip to Sierra

38

Leone at least once every year and while things were changing, many things stayed the same and although these were valuable experiences, I still did not feel like my efforts were making the necessary impact. This was extremely frustrating.

This was around the time of the emergence of blogs – a time where humanitarian workers from all around the world were in Sierra Leone working in different agencies. I would read about people's experiences, perspectives, and perceptions of Sierra Leone. While I was excited to read about their tales of growth and potential, I knew it was just that; their stories. It was very important that Sierra Leoneans tell their own stories as well and that we shape the future of our nation by ourselves.

In 2007 I finally decided to move back to Sierra Leone. I felt like it was important to stop talking about change and it was time to actually be a part of it. With my passion for education, I saw the similarities between young people in my classrooms in America and the youth I worked with in Sierra Leone. I wanted them to have the same opportunities.

One of the many things I learned throughout my educational path is that education gives options and the power to make choices. The ultimate benefit of education to me is the ability to share thoughts with others, challenge and develop ideas, and blend them into contributions and solutions that can transform. These realisations led me to my calling of being an educator. I am an educator because it is my passion to assist others in their journey of uncovering the power of education. With that motive, I began teaching at underperforming schools in the American school system where each day I battled to capture student's attention as issues of poverty and gang violence surrounded their home life. Also, very few expected them to complete high school and if they made it to college, they would be the first ones in their family to do so. I was pleased to have been able to help them overcome these challenges and enter some of the top universities and colleges around the country.

With that experience, I returned with the belief that the future of Sierra Leone lies in the hands of the youth who are our future leaders. It was not long before I thought constantly about what it would take to get our "at risk" youth in Sierra Leone into colleges and universities of their choice, not only in Sierra Leone but around the world. I moved home to embark on a mission to change the way education is presented in Sierra Leone. This gave birth to the EXCEL Sierra Leone.

On July 21, 2008, the EXCEL Education Centre opened its doors at 9 Dillet Street to our inaugural class. EXCEL has endeavoured to reach some of the most promising young people in Sierra Leone to participate in collaborative educational activities, programmes, and support services. Our goals are achieved through the EXCEL Sierra Leone Programme model, which develops students in three core areas: Educational Excellence, Community Empowerment, Leadership, alongside a normal academic schedule. Since 2007, we have inspired, motivated, and supported over 500 (aged 14-30 yrs.) young people to reach their full potential.

Our successes include; delivering the first ever "Money Matters for Kids Workshop" with United Bank For Africa, UBA; and being selected as the recruitment representative in Sierra Leone for the "African Leadership Academy" in South Africa. Through the programme, seven students from Sierra Leone have successfully graduated from the academy, providing enrichment and WASSCE support, resulting in five of our participants receiving the top scores in the country and district (1st and 2nd places in 2008- 2009), and the "EXCEL Scholars Internship" Programme where students were given on- the-job training and employment opportunities, etc. Our biggest success by far is that 31 EXCEL Scholars have gone on to enter four year colleges and universities in Sierra Leone (IPAM Fourah Bay College, College of Medicine), the United States, England, Russia, Ukraine, including the University of Rochester, Colby College, Morehouse College and The United World College, Singapore. In 2016 we celebrate our tenth EXCEL Scholar's graduation.

While these achievements mean that more students have access to greater educational and life opportunities, I realise that even these efforts are not sufficient enough to fully address the critical needs left by gaps in the Sierra Leonean educational system. My quest for success was not met without trials. In the beginning, it was difficult to get cooperation from the Ministry of Education. An education enrichment programme for secondary school students did not belong to any specific category; it didn't tick any of the boxes outlined by donor partners. "We need more technical training institutes," I would hear from officials. But I pushed on. Even when I applied for funding, most NGOs focused on education were interested in funding primary education or building rural schools. I went from office to office, meeting to meeting with no luck. It was a harsh reality to find out I could not get funding for the programme. My daydreams about the creation of the programme were nothing like this. There were many days I was so frustrated! Fortunately for me, I reached out to my friends and family for support. Their constant encouragement has been a source of inspiration for me.

Today one of Sierra Leone's biggest challenges, and in Africa overall, is youth unemployment. Consider for instance that over 20 per cent of Africa's population is aged between 15 and 24 years, and over 40 per cent is under 15 years of age. This means that the challenge to develop and retain emerging leaders with the potential to meet the demands of a globalised environment is set to escalate even further. Unemployment amongst urban youth is extremely high. The employment challenges of youth in Sierra Leone are closely linked to the effects of the 11-year civil war. More than half of the youth population – who constitute approximately 80 per cent of the total population – are illiterate. Finding jobs in the formal economy is difficult. Access to jobs for young women has been especially challenging. While there has been a keen focus on job creation for youth, we need to be thinking well past the short-term solutions and engage in long term planning. In order to compete at a global standard and meet the demands of a growing and developing Sierra Leone, we need to nurture a culture of high achievement and quality education. Once deemed the "Athens of Africa" for our high education standards, education in Sierra Leone is simply not the same. The influx in the demand of education has caused overpopulation of schools, overcrowded classrooms, high student- teacher ratios, and an overwhelming amount of outdated, untrained, unskilled, and unqualified teachers. Education in Sierra Leone has declined to a point where even some of the students ranking at the top of their classes pale in comparison to their peers in other African countries not to mention peers all over the world.

Many educated young people do not see the worth of staying in Sierra Leone. Their hope is to find solace in other lands, most popular being America or Europe, resulting in significant brain drain. Many of these young people end up in poorly ranked universities or low income jobs because their education in Sierra Leone was not well rounded enough. While I can say that some schools are working tirelessly to meet the demands of students and parents, they cannot do it alone. Education should be our country's most coveted asset. There is a dire need for modern and innovative programming that addresses Sierra Leone's educational inequities, while promoting high academic achievement.

High-quality education in Sierra Leone is the foundation for success and growth. There is a need for empowered teachers, strong school leaders, better curricula, and the ability for students to connect with one another and the rest of the world.

I therefore set out to contribute in my own little way together with the help of many other fine people whose tireless contribution brought about the successes outlined above. EXCEL seeks to pioneer the transformation of the education system in Sierra Leone in order to develop a culture of academic excellence. We believe the best way to build a stronger society is by bringing youth together across the social spectrum, and equipping them with the tools, knowledge, skills and building abilities, required to lead, achieve academic success, and demonstrate exemplary character. We hope to inspire youth to lead change in their communities through their actions.

While education and unemployment are real issues, our goal is not to fix them, but to be a part of the larger ecosystem of solutions in Sierra Leone because at EXCEL we believe that youth leadership development is a mechanism for positive social change.

After spending time with EXCEL, we want our participants to be socially and personally aware, and for that awareness to provoke a sense of urgency and personal responsibility for change. It is our goal to develop a culture of academic excellence and empower the next generation of leaders, creators, innovators, thinkers, and change-makers who are not only inspired, but act to define Sierra Leone and create the change they want to see.

Yeniva Sisay-Sogbeh (M.A. Ed) is a Value Creator. With over 17 years of experience as a trained and qualified teacher, leader, mentor, coach, Yeniva has developed a portfolio of diverse skills and experience across private and public sector in the United States and Africa. She is the founder and Executive Director of EXCEL Sierra Leone which provides academic enrichment, character and leadership development to youth in Sierra Leone. In pursuit of her passion to develop, build and transform the continent through her work, Yeniva continues to create value as a consultant providing training, project management, branding, communications and events. Bringing vision into action in many areas of development in Sierra Leone, Yeniva has been a midwife in the birth of a range of projects and organisations such as, *The Ma dengn Beach Festival*, Sierra Leone's first luxury resort *"The Place,"* and she is the co-founder and Founding President of Sierra Leone's notable women's network, *PowerWomen232*.

Modupe Taylor-Pearce
Star Trek Starship Africa: Winning the Leadership Development Battle

("Boldly going where no Africans have ever gone before...")

In the first half of 1990 I joined the Republic of Sierra Leone Military Forces (RSLMF). It was a largely ceremonial army, and its lack of preparedness for combat was illustrated by the fact that I never once fired a gun or rifle during RSLMF basic training. In the latter half of 1990 I became the first Sierra Leonean to be admitted into the United States Military Academy (West Point), a school of leadership. The purpose of West Point is to "produce leaders of character who will serve the common defence". At West Point, we were exposed to a plethora of leaders – leaders with whom we interacted on a daily and weekly basis – captains, majors, colonels, generals, and of course, our fellow cadets. We were thrust into leadership positions – leading individuals, leading teams, leading squads, and leading peers. We were graded on leadership every semester. *I saw leadership quality ranging from good to excellent at West Point.*

Barely 4 months after graduating from West Point, I was thrust in the middle of civil war in Sierra Leone. (I often wonder whether, if I had known this, I would have still agreed to join!) The RSLMF, unprepared for the war, was struggling to deal with a rag-tag band of mostly under-age and under-trained fighters that constituted the Revolutionary United Front (RUF). During the war, I saw a whole new range of leadership quality in the RSLMF: from good to absolutely horrible. I saw leaders steal from their soldiers, refuse to show up to work, and get drunk while on duty. One of the memories I will never forget is having to personally bury six young soldiers in my battalion who were killed by friendly fire due to the incompetence of their company commander who, in a drunken stupor, had foolishly led his men into a night ambush set by soldiers from another company in the same battalion. *I learned that when leaders are derelict in their duty, it is the people they lead who suffer the most.*

It was during the war that my own personal leadership was tested and that I would learn the rewards of the leadership standards I had learnt at West Point. On Monday January 15, 1995, my unit and I hastily marshalled 12 miles north of the town of Masiaka in Sierra Leone to respond to news of a pending RUF attack. I attempted to outflank the rebels by a wrap around them with three of my men. While crossing the 'dead zone' I was hit by two bullets. One got me in the elbow, making me unable to return fire and the other hit me in the pelvic region, leaving my right leg paralysed and me helpless in the grass. With a voice now feeble with pain, I struggled desperately to organise my troops, fully conscious that with each passing minute, the likelihood of making it out alive was getting slimmer. There was constant chatter of bullets, yelling and screaming of orders as I faded in and out of the fog of memories from West Point and my ordeal. I heard voices of members of my unit shouting as they braved unrelenting fire to literally pull me out of the jaws of death to safety. After I recovered, I asked them why they had risked their lives to save me. *"You were always good to us, sir; you are our leader, and we could not leave you behind," was the reply.* I didn't realise the full extent to which I had impacted the lives of my men through my leadership until that moment. In contrast, many unit commanders lost their lives not to enemy bullets, but to the wrath of the men they had wronged.

A decade after leaving the army, I had returned to the USA, completed a Masters and was flying around the world, working for a management consulting company that specialised in turnarounds (helping companies that were struggling financially or operationally to achieve rapid and significant improvements in performance). Invariably the interventions we made were focused on leadership. Whenever a company was struggling, there was something that the company's leader was doing (or was not doing) that directly related to the poor performance of the company. *I saw once again the manifestation of the quote by Professor Stephen Adei: "Leadership is the cause; all else is effect".* Aside from learning how to quickly and proficiently analyse and diagnose companies based on their operational and financial key performance indicators, I also became adept at diagnosing leadership challenges and opportunities and found that I enjoyed the process of developing leaders. I was given the opportunity to train leaders from every country in Europe and North America, and enjoyed an exciting and rewarding mini-career in this field.

In the mid-2000's an African-American pastor friend of mine challenged me with the simple question: "Modupe, what are you doing in America?" He asked me this question while we were on a short mission trip together in Sierra Leone (his first trip to Sierra Leone). I was momentarily stunned by the question, because this was not just a getting-to-know-you question from a stranger; this was a penetrating question from one of my closest friends who knew me well, and knew what I did for a living. After I mumbled an incoherent answer (that he probably did not hear), he expounded on his question: "I mean, you are needed so much more here (Sierra Leone) than you are needed in America. What are you doing in America?" I realised that he was right. Here I was, an African, the recipient of world-class training and education in business leadership and management, plying my trade in taking coal to Newcastle, while my country and my continent were suffering from energy and capacity deficiencies.

It did not take long for me to convince my family to move with me to Sierra Leone, where I established a leadership and management training company (CTI Ltd: www.cticonsulting.sl) to develop and train leaders, taught an MBA class part-time at the local university, coached executives, and trained thousands of students and underprivileged people in the fundamentals of good leadership through a non-profit company that my wife and I established (www.leadersofgodlycharacter.org). My goal, when I left the USA to return to Africa and Sierra Leone in 2010, was to create a million new jobs for Africans in the next 20 years, and 100,000 jobs for Sierra Leoneans within the next 20 years. My vision was not to create those jobs directly by establishing companies that would hire a million people, but to indirectly create the jobs by training, developing, educating, and equipping the current and future African business managers and leaders who would then create the million new jobs in Africa.

Six years after returning to Africa, I found myself running significantly behind schedule in my goal to create a million jobs. I had developed Sierra Leonean business leaders and enhanced the capacity and education of a growing number of Sierra Leonean business professionals by leading executive training and coaching services, teaching MBA classes, writing a leadership book featuring successful Sierra Leoneans, and taken many other leadership training and development initiatives and actions. But I had accomplished these things *in Sierra Leone*. I had not yet moved the needle on impacting the rest of Africa, and I was lagging behind on my objective of creating one million jobs for Africans.

It was into this context that Fred Swaniker and ALU (African Leadership University) showed up in my life. The vision that Fred shared with me was almost identical to mine. ALU was born out of a recognition that: (1) Africa needs a significant number of leaders of competence and character to change the narrative of Africa, create the enabling environment for economic growth, and create jobs; and (2) the current crop of African political leaders cannot be relied upon to be the ones to develop or cultivate these leaders of competence and character because it is not in the interests of the current leaders to develop the continent's future leaders. Here I was, sick and tired of hearing about Africa in a negative light, patriotic to the bone, being invited to join an army of educated, passionate Africans determined, against all odds, to change the trajectory of Africa and turn our tales of woe into stories of possibility and action through the miracle of quality education. Access to quality education, this fundamental human right, has been denied to millions of Africans for the past century, first by slave masters, then by colonial masters, and then by *their own people.* It was clear to me that ALU was the engine that would enable me to achieve the vision of creating a million jobs in Africa by 2030. I jumped at the opportunity to become the inaugural leader of the ALU School of Business (ALUSB).

How is ALUSB (www.alusb.com) going to create a million (and more) new jobs in Africa by 2030? By solving a significant problem that businesses operating in Africa all share. All businesses / corporations in Africa are hampered in their growth by one common problem: an inadequate pool of competent business leaders at all levels of the organisation. By "business leader," I do not mean "Managing Directors"; I mean people at ALL levels of the organisation, everyday leaders. Imagine a small Ethiopian clothing manufacturer that has successfully established and gained market share in Ethiopia and wants to expand to Kenya or another African country; what does the owner of that company need? It needs a business leader to send out to establish a new branch. What about a Tunisian IT hardware supply company that recognises an opportunity to expand into IT services; what does the Managing Director of that company need to make it happen? A good business leader! The inadequate supply of competent business leaders of character forces many African companies to abandon visions or eschew opportunities for expansion despite the market need, simply because the owner or manager has nobody that can be entrusted with the responsibility, and he/she has only 24 hours in a day and cannot afford to stretch himself/herself too thin.

As such, companies do not grow as fast as they should, and without such growth, they cannot create the jobs needed on the continent. I believe that the business leadership we need in Africa is developing business leaders who are effective managers and inspiring leaders. Good business leaders are good at controlling and managing the resources that are under their control to achieve a goal (management), and they are effective at successfully influencing resources (people, capital, energy, etc.) that are *not under their control*, uniting them towards a common vision (leadership). *They are both effective managers and inspiring leaders.*

Today, I am proud to be the first Dean of ALUSB, to work towards achieving this vision for Africa. We have designed a first-of-its-kind, pan-African Masters in Business Administration (MBA) programme that is world-class in its content, distinctly African in its application, current in its delivery method and learning methodology, and invaluable in its pan-African network. Students admitted into this programme benefit from instructional programmes provided in collaboration with online learning platforms from Harvard Business School, Wharton Business School, McKinsey Academy, and The Drucker Institute. All of this is augmented with specific modules about doing business in Africa, delivered by the stars of African business and business education. The students receive this benefit without having to take a sabbatical from their jobs, and without having to break the bank – the cost is a fraction of the cost of attending many of the comparable premier business schools in the world. We are also pioneering Executive Education for African businesses, using the same world-class methodologies.

What we are doing at ALUSB has never been done before in Africa. Like the commanders of the starships in the Star Trek series, we are 'boldly going where no one has gone before' – into the frontiers of education and leadership development. The journey to make this vision a reality is fraught with risks, and is not for the faint-hearted. There are significant obstacles to be navigated, and the solutions to those obstacles require the use of some resources that are not within ALUSB's sphere of control. However, this is exactly why I am here – at ALUSB – leading the charge. I do not have all the resources at my disposal. I do not even know all the resources that will be needed over the next few years. However, I do know that we have a phenomenal team of competent, passionate professionals, dedicated to making this vision a reality; we are adding to the team every week, as more professionals (Africans and Africans-at-heart) recognise the need to be a part of something greater than themselves. In this vein, all of us at ALUSB are leading Africa. And I am honoured to have the opportunity to lead one team of brave leaders into another battle. This time—a battle for the continent's future prosperity.

Modupe S. Taylor-Pearce is a scholar and practitioner of organisational management and leadership. Born in Sierra Leone, and raised in Sierra Leone, Ghana, Kenya, and the USA, he is currently the Managing Partner of CTI Ltd (www.cticonsulting.sl), a management consulting company that specialises in leadership enhancement and crisis management. He earned his BSc degree at the United States Military Academy (West Point). After West Point, he returned to Sierra Leone, where he served in the Army during the Civil War. He later returned to the USA to complete his Masters in Engineering and Manufacturing at Cornell University. He also holds a PhD in business leadership from Capella University. With his business and military leadership background, he has successfully led the financial recovery of various companies in the USA, Africa, and Europe. Modupe is married to his bride of 18 years, Renee, and they are blessed with three children. He enjoys reading and playing the piano.

II. Social Entrepreneurship, Change & Policy

Adewale Ajadi
Pioneering Strategy for the Horn of Africa

This story started on August 1, 2011 and ended in 2012; however, it is still being implemented today. My name is Adewale Ajadi.

These days my specialty is simply systems or systematic change. It is a description of an organised approach to make change, a structured learning and improvement effort for an entire system. I suppose being trained as a Barrister from the University of Ife, now Obafemi Awolowo University, helps to focus one on systemic change. However, no one goes to university to learn about change. In fact, aside from qualifications like creative writing, the only other major qualification I have is an MSc in International Business Economics. My love of the process of change now seems so clear when I look back, but that is what happens when you look back. It became clear that change is what I was up to as the founder of Equality Foundation and the pioneer of the first Diversity Standard called the Framework of Excellence for Equality and Diversity (FEED).

Through the Equality Foundation, we started the process of translating Total Quality Management which was often used as a corporate tool to frame proposals for inner city development, called Quality in the Community. It was the first experiment using the Positive Action provision of the 1976 Race Relations Act of the United Kingdom. This pioneering attempt made it possible for many young African, Caribbean, Asian, and minorities to be given training in areas of established exclusion like: broadcasting, engineering, and management situations. This prototype in Bristol was widely replicated.

My cognitive awareness of systems thinking as it relates to Africa in general and Nigeria in particular started when I was a student of Dr. Heifetz and Marty Linksy, pioneers of adaptive leadership and professors at the Harvard Kennedy School for Government. I became aware that Africa is currently an epicenter of adaptiveness, a characteristic that will define the 21st century. The regularity, speed, and complexity of change was an area I had been working on in Diversity, Urban Regeneration, and Leadership without really recognising it. This meant that my involvement in the Adaptive Leadership and follow up course with Professor R. Kegan on the Immunity to Change (four column method) was the first time, in the early 2000s, that I started pursuing understanding and engagement with Complex Systems and Change. I took my next step at the New England Complex Systems Institute with Professor Yaneer Bar-Yam. I combined my work in Total Quality Management facilitation, which I learned from the late John Marsh, with the use of visual recorders and facilitators. I then had a complement of skills and a network that would help me turn sustainable change into a framework of social technologies. In fact, by 2009, I was able to complete a self-funded foray into strategic planning for the City of Ibadan, Nigeria, which culminated in a visually facilitated city meeting that was quite revolutionary.

In 2010 while working in Nairobi, Kenya with the African Leadership Centre, I was introduced to this incredible man, Dr. Martin Kimani. By this time in late 2010 I had developed a deliberate practice. I had seen Dr. Kimani twice and I automatically thought rugby player as well as Wall Street, both of which turned out to be somewhat right. We got along very well and right from our introduction we started talking about major African challenges and how to address them. I showed him the visual facilitation brochure for the work we did in Ibadan as well as the subsequent work on mitigating election rigging in Lagos, Nigeria. As Director of CEWARN-IGAD, he was quite intrigued and, unknown to me, he was looking at how a strategy could be created that would be participatory and live up to the purpose of his organisation. CEWARN (Conflict Early Warning and Response Mechanism) is a co-operative initiative of the eight IGAD (Inter-Governmental Authority on Development) member countries. The IGAD countries are the Horn of Africa countries of Djibouti, Ethiopia, Kenya, Somalia, Uganda, the Sudans, and Eritrea. It is to his credit that he took a risk with this stranger and asked me to develop a process for him for this strategy.

The strategy sought was a seven-year strategy for the organisation. We agreed that my process would be subject to staff of his organisation who were from at least three countries. It became clear to me that we needed to give the staff participatory opportunities to inspire them so that they would be a critical part of the design and own it. We had a three-day retreat at Hawassa, Ethiopia, which started on the 1st of August 2011. Quite simply, without them we could never have achieved what we imagined.

It seemed like ages before the 1st of August but even on the day we travelled from Addis Ababa, Ethiopia to Hawassa, it was like a dream. How could we expect such a major initiative, to evolve a strategy for the next 7 years, to rest on the participation of stakeholders across 8 countries?

Strategies are usually designs of the executives framed by reams of paper and multiple projections of the likely terrain. I was asking Dr. Martin Kimani to take a punt on a participatory process yet to be practiced by anyone we knew. If he was worried, it did not show. Such was his leadership that once he decided I was his man for the job, little would sway that. The staff were interesting with their own skepticism; the idea of eating an elephant one bit at a time was quite the attraction. Dr. Kimani and I seemed to have a good-natured pact whereby he would use his authority to clear the path and I would facilitate a participatory design and implementation. We would crowd source a strategy using the wisdom of multitudes across Kenya, Djibouti, Ethiopia, Uganda, Somalia, South Sudan, and Sudan. Eritrea, the 8th country, had suspended all IGAD Activities. We would work across Pastoralist Communities and war affected regions. And so, we started with a staff retreat.

Haile Resort, our home in Hawassa, was quite the place. After hours of travel, we settled into mapping expectations and exploring what success would look like at the end of the event. We had come loaded with magazines so that the language of our interactions would be conversational, visual, and based on group-work using collages. The staff were enthusiastic contributors and we not only bonded, but expressed the framework of what values we needed to have in this work. The staff gave me their endorsement as I facilitated and they responded like an orchestra practiced in the art of strategy design. We came to agreement on a three-stage process starting with a local phase in identified clusters of the CEWARN operation, where local facilitators trained by me and supported by a facilitator's guide would take some key strategy questions to communities. The design sense was that they would find spaces in markets and community gatherings to ask very simple strategic questions such as: what would they expect by 2019? how would they measure that expectation? how often would they expect feedback? what role would they want to play as well as expect CEWARN to play? We confirmed that we would do this across 7 countries and many clusters. We did not, however, anticipate that the numbers we would interact with would be in the thousands.

The local facilitators, as we termed them, were incredibly enthusiastic and knowledgeable. I had a vision of local facilitators certified in the best western skills, guided and imbued in local facilitative wisdom, trained in communities across the land as creative peace enablers. By this time, we had connected with my regular collaborators on the visual facilitation side - Group Partners in the UK who were recording their visual magic. However, the work brought tensions from its pioneering nature and my naivety working as an individual consultant. We captured the results of local facilitations with pictures and sometimes Martin and I attended the dialogues. For example, I remember Djibouti like yesterday, where we sat in the boiling heat, enamored by the commitment of participants as they opened their hearts and minds during the Dikhil cluster of operations dialogue. The challenges of ethnic conflict and future prospects opened all participants to a new creativity. Whether Turkana, Karamoja or Dikhil Clusters, local people were vocal, clear, and took ownership.

The next stage was to aggregate their feedback and put this before the CEWERU, which are units of local / national CEWARN operations. These workshops were now in a fundamentally new direction as clearly the agenda was set by the thousands of local people. Despite initial resistance and skepticism, the local events were powerful platforms of consultation and engagement. I was at the one in Kampala, Uganda and the voices of the women representatives struck a deep and memorable tone that shaped the way forward, similarly, in South Sudan, Sudan, Kenya, Djibouti, Ethiopia, and Somalia. The emergent draft strategy now demanded that we should have an agreement of the critical path for the way forward.

The regional meeting which gave the stamp of approval was held in Addis Ababa with National Governments, IGAD, and our support group partners. It was quite an impressive expression of the work so far - Group Partners had been aggregating feedback in the tens of thousands, as well as establishing the hundreds of organisational and community network data. The regional meeting in Addis Ababa was a prelude for official ratification. Our work developing a strategy through active participation across 7 countries of about 4,000 participants, over a two-year period, involving many different organisations culminated in the CEWARN Strategy. It has guided the organisation since 2012 and possibly will continue as planned till 2019.

The leadership of Dr. Martin Kimani in using his authority to translate official policy into action, create the holding space for this pioneering work to be done in spite of official skepticism, risking his reputation for an unusual architect, and supporting a more complex and expensive process, exemplifies what is needed on the continent. The need for original thinking rather than a pale copy of prior western approaches is fundamental. I believe I offered a complementary leadership approach embodied in the design, development, and facilitation by challenging social engineering assumptions that have been the bedrock of many 'paper' strategies. We pioneered replacing past approaches with adaptive social technology that is embedded deep in my work around the Omoluwabi system. Omoluwabi is a term from the Nigerian Yoruba language, meaning good character. The Omoluwabi system I have developed is a new generation of Social Technologies and transformative systems based on our Pre-Colonial African culture of excellence.

Even though Dr. Kimani left shortly after the development of the strategy to greater and more challenging responsibilities in his home country of Kenya, the result has been owned by subsequent Directors and teams of CEWARN-IGAD. The visual facilitation contributed by Group Partners rounded the pioneering work so that it was accessible to all contributors and stakeholders. Aside from the use of the strategy, the vision we had for a new community of facilitators progressed. On the 31st of August, 2016 CEWRAN-IGAD granted 33 local peace facilitators, Certificates in *Peace Studies and Conflict Resolution*. The journey of many possibilities continues in the Horn of Africa especially in Pastoralist Communities. It is humbling to be part of its inception, design and development. In all the challenges, *I am honoured to create spaces for the genius of our people so that their wisdom builds the future for their children and their children's children.*

To end, I include a reflection of the work we did sent by Dr. Martin Kimani about this process and work:

> Thank you Adewale! Your account is far too kind to me, but accurate in the accounting of what we set out to do. I will just add a few points that build on some of what you have said.
>
> 1. The prospect of asking people to identify simple facts, impressions and hopes about their lives BEFORE doing the same to government officials was a powerful moral driver of the way the process played out. So often popular participation, and the agency of our people, is praised but it rarely ever gets in the way of the hierarchies of power anywhere in the world. This was different and because of that it was difficult - and remains difficult - to build quickly on it. But such was the power of the ground up process that it created consensus within seven governments that can rarely agree on much. That the strategy is now slowly being implemented is testament to this moral power it had.
> 2. On the ground, our teams found people exhausted of being 'studied' (their impression) by multitudes of NGOs and international organisations. That we were not giving any money as per diem added to the strangeness and the challenge of the process. However, in almost every stop (in social halls, fields, village centres and towns) people responded powerfully, and positively, to the difference.
> 3. What did I learn? That transformation is possible but that it needs the kind of people like Adewale who embrace social innovation. To this day what I learnt about listening, challenging our people to push harder and patience has stayed with me.

Adewale Ajadi is a creative consultant, leadership educator, change agent, and storyteller. Born in Ibadan, Nigeria, he has over twenty years' experience working with people, organisations, and communities on issues that transform human interaction in the direction of meaningful dialogue, authentic interaction, and empowered value creation. He is currently the Country Director, Nigeria at The Synergos Institute. His book, *Omoluwabi 2.0 - A Code of Transformation in 21st century Nigeria*, offers guidance on achieving African excellence through values-based transformation. A barrister, Adewale has an MSc. in International Business Economics; he has also studied Leadership Education at the Kennedy School of Government, Harvard University and Complex Systems Theory in New England Complex Systems Institute, MIT. Ajadi is also a successful playwright, and his play, Abyssinia has toured the UK.

Ajarat Bada
Advocating for SDG16: Promoting Peace for Development

I can still feel the goose bumps as I write. I remember what I was wearing: a trench coat I bought from H&M, a green scarf my best friend gave to me, and the best pair of brown boots I have ever owned. I remember where I was standing: two rows behind the first; I towered 5 feet and an inch above those floors, in some room at the Excel Centre in London. The year was 2010, the month February, the date, the 8th and it was somewhere between 7:30 and 8.00 pm. That was the very moment that changed my life. I was 24 years old. I remember taking a hold of myself, connecting my heart to my mind, realising that if what I was feeling was indeed real, my life was never going to be the same again. It was real. It was the inaugural One Young World Summit and, as a new One Young World Ambassador, I had just finished listening to the most incredible and inspirational speeches that I had heard in my life. The words of Archbishop Desmond Tutu and Bob Geldof supported by the vibrant energy of 823 young changemakers would change the course of my life.

One Young World is a unique platform created for the world's most forward-thinking young leaders. It creates a meaningful opportunity for them to engage in the world's most pressing problems by offering unique solutions. There are many talk shops around the world – events that tokenise young people – but this was different. A paradigm shift, an energy buzz, an awakening that lit a bulb deep within me. Bob Geldof challenged us to be 'unreasonable,' to dare to do something different to save our world from us. Something had to change about my engagement with the world; I had to do something non-traditional, something very different.

A strong message from John Kerry also hit home: "Whenever you feel a strong sense of right and wrong, talk out of turn, the world will listen." The very next day, I gave a speech on the evaluation of the United Nations' Millennium Development Goals (MDGs) where I spoke of the progress with those goals and the loopholes that were preventing us from meeting their targets. This was the "what" that society demanded from us all; a critical look at the agenda that charted the course of our existence. The summit agenda discussed amongst other issues the importance of interfaith relations particularly relevant to a world where the reverberations of 9/11 still echo loudly, even today, 15 years later. After the summit, I felt the need to do something to catapult those discussions to where it mattered. The world's global development agenda, the MDGs were eight in number but none of them spoke to the opportunity cost of war and conflict on development. Resources, both human and financial, that would otherwise aid development were consumed by conflict, many of them with religious drivers, overtly or otherwise. Ending violence in the name of religion had to be part of any serious global development agenda, I reckoned. I suggested that this was indeed missing from the UN's list of eight, and like that the Missing MDG initiative was born.

This advocacy initiative, calling to ensure interfaith collaboration for peace, was targeted at the United Nations' Millennium Development Goals. This initiative spoke to the crisis facing religion whereby political agendas are advanced by propagating religious intolerance for political aims. This is particularly the case in my religion, Islam. Advocating for the addition of this goal mattered to me as a Muslim and it mattered to me as an African. The opportunity cost of war, armed conflict, violence and injustice are too great around the world and continue to rob Africa of some of its promise and prosperity.

A few days after the summit, I pitched this policy recommendation to my fellow One Young World Ambassadors; our new title of *ambassador* very apt as we were now supposed to carry the inspiration to the rest of the world. With the support of this group, particularly Catherine Peter (a South African) and Bogdan Gogulan (an Estonian), we took the campaign all over the world. We started in Rio de Janeiro, and went to the United Nations Alliance of Civilisation Summit, an initiative of the governments of Spain and Turkey in response to the 9/11 attacks. The campaign eventually made its way to the United Nations Headquarters in New York, with internships attached, affording us the opportunity to share our thoughts with our prime audience: global decision makers. It made its way to many university campuses, non-governmental organisations and to media outlets around the world. It afforded other bright young people the opportunity to champion a cause that also resonated with them.

The cause subsequently became larger than us and we proportionately rose to its merit. It became my full-time job, Director of the Missing MDG initiative. In 2011 in Zurich, at the second One Young World Summit, we were able to get the physical commitment of world leaders, including Archbishop Desmond Tutu and Sir Bob Geldof, the original inspirations for the cause. We also gained the support of Professor Muhammed Yunus of the Grameen Bank, the Crown Princess Mette Marit of Norway, and virtually, through signatures, thousands of other global citizens contributed to a petition that we presented to the United Nations. The sense of fulfilment was palpable even from our photographs. I still get chills looking at some of those pictures. I am still living this reality. It changed the course of our lives.

As for me, this sense of purpose and its fulfilment became much larger than my childhood dreams of becoming a doctor and I declined to start medical school the following year. I found that our voices made a meaningful difference to the cause and I wanted to give it my all. The campaign opened me to a world I did not know existed. I found a sense of purpose in the connections I was making and particularly in the places I was going; I was representing not only myself but also a demographic that was not the norm in some of those spaces of power and authority. Sometimes, I was the only black person in the room. More often than that, I was the only black woman and more often still, I was the only woman with a Hijab – the Muslim headscarf – on my head. Once at a closed meeting of global business leaders in Venice, Italy, the issue of the association between the 9/11 attacks and Muslims came up. One of the attendees, a global business leader, stated directly at me that Muslims should categorically not be allowed to build mosques in the vicinity of the World Trade Centre. This was in response to an outcry in the United States about building what was termed "The Ground Zero" mosque. Many people blamed Muslims in general for the attacks and to them it was unimaginable that such a proposition would even be allowed the light of day. I was invited to speak to that audience and it was liberating to get the opportunity to defend my religion from such grave misunderstanding. It is this misunderstanding that has resulted in and continues to result in the massive loss of lives and properties 'war' on Islam and Muslim majority countries.

From that same audience, I met Unilever CEO, Paul Polman, an amazing global leader extraordinaire. Paul, as he would prefer me to call him, has been very open in his support of the cause. When he speaks to audiences he cites us and our campaign for the Missing MDG, as an example for other young leaders to follow. He has been phenomenal in his support of the Missing MDG and his personal mentorship over the years has been clear proof that I made the right decision by shifting my perspective to embrace the world of advocacy and political activism. *I have represented women, African women, Muslim women and young women. Above all, I have represented myself and my own strong convictions in my role in the global peace efforts in many conferences, summits and spaces of influence around the world.* During the campaign, I met many Nobel Laureates, Presidents, business leaders and everyday citizen warriors who share this sense of purpose and with whom I have collaborated to nurture the dream of adding the missing MDG to the list of MDGs.

However, we eventually discovered that a call to "*Ensure Interfaith Collaboration for Peace*", the missing MDG, could not be added to a development agenda that was 10 years old when we started. UN member States had worked hard to implement the MDGs and their progress reporting mechanisms were solidified. Adding another goal at the time would have proved chaotic at the least. At that moment, my enthusiasm met with reality. I had come to learn a lot about the global policy process and now knew it was much more difficult than it seemed and that our order was very much taller than we had imagined; however, there was hope. There was a new development agenda, in gestation for the next five years that had room to accommodate more causes than the ones to which the eight MDGs catered.

The consultation process for the post-2015 global development agenda, the Sustainable Development Goals (SDGs), was launched in 2012 and as soon as we heard about it, we got to work. At the time, we believed we had successfully influenced other advocates or perhaps we were simply more aware of other similar causes. 'Sustainable Peace for Sustainable Development' was the motto going forward and we worked even harder on the campaign trail, hosting our own sessions at conferences and being regulars at the policy discussion fora at the United Nations Headquarters in New York. I got the opportunity to be a part of a select group of civil society leaders who contributed to a final round of negotiations for the SDGs in March 2015. And then finally, in September 2015, the SDGs were formally adopted and SDG number 16 bore testament to our hard work, six years in the making:

> SDG 16 – **Promote peaceful and inclusive societies for Sustainable Development, provide access to justice for all and build effective, accountable and inclusive institutions at all levels.**

The target was to strengthen national institutions and build capacities at all levels, in particular in developing countries, for preventing violence and combating terrorism and crime. This was where all our hard work had culminated and paid off.

I was at the launch of the SDGs in New York in September 2015 and felt a deep sense of accomplishment for SDG 16. It took six years and countless personal sacrifices, including family gatherings, lost wages from giving up my day job, and perhaps the prospects of a career in medicine, but the sense of fulfilment is immeasurable. I have absolutely no regrets and on the contrary, I feel an immense gratitude for the opportunity to make those sacrifices to contribute to a part of history. Through this journey, I got the opportunity to discover another part of me, the activist in me. I took active roles in advocating on behalf of my peers in high school, when I voiced many concerns on behalf of the student body in editorials as a member of the Press Club. However, I never knew that activism would particularly seek me out as a career. I am happy to be on this path.

In the next coming months and years, as the implementation of the goals take form, I continue to be involved in the dialogue around its implementation, impacting the lives of many all around the world. This is much broader than the demands of the campaign for the Missing MDG and has had me engaging the World Humanitarian Summit consultations and the review of the programme of action for developing countries. So far, all these engagements give me a strong sense of fulfilling of my purpose: to represent myself where I am most needed.

Ajarat Bada is a nurse by training. She received her Masters degree in Public Health from Loma Linda University in California and another Masters in Public Policy from the Qatar Foundation in Doha. Her academic and professional experiences span Africa, Europe, Asia, the Americas and the Middle-East including Brazil, Mexico, Austria, Switzerland, Italy, Nigeria, Philippines, South-Africa, Ethiopia, United Kingdom, Ireland, Qatar, Turkey, and the United States particularly through her advocacy with NGOs and international organisations including the United Nations. She speaks four languages. She has also successfully pursued her interest in writing and editing most recently of a book on *Innovating South-South Cooperation* (forthcoming Uni. Ottawa Press) and is invested in bringing to reality a unique perspective on Millennials and their engagement with organised religion. She balances her life's purpose between Los Angeles, California and Lagos, Nigeria.

Veronica Fynn Bruey
Deadly Voyage: Africans Crossing the Mediterranean

Despite the fact that some of the fastest-growing economies in the world are in Africa, and that Africans on the continent and in the diaspora are perfectly capable of telling their own stories and transforming their own societies, the White Saviour framework lives, like some prehistoric literary insect that has managed to survive the ages without having to evolve. And just when you think the world has made at least some progress in beginning to exterminate this trend, a big, fat, multi-legged #WhiteSaviourInAfricaStory crawls into the mediasphere. Good intentions allows for one to view Africa as one dark blob of violence, poverty, jungle bush and disease instead of a continent of 54 countries, each with a unique history and cultures. Linton manages to imply that she was somehow more at risk for African violence because of her whiteness, while reminding the audience that with her "angel hair," she is literally heaven-sent to Africa and the central character in the story, not the Zambians.[11]

Louise Linton, a Scottish actress now living in California, is the author of a controversial[12] 290-page memoir: *In Congo's Shadow: One Girl's Perilous Journey to the Heart of Africa*. On July 1 2016, Linton introduced her memoir (now pulled from shelves) in *The Daily Telegraph's* "How my dream gap year in Africa turned into a

---

[11] Karen Attiah, "Louise Linton Just Wrote the Perfect White-Saviour-in-Africa Story," *Washington Post*, June 16, 2016,
https://www.washingtonpost.com/posteverything/wp/2016/07/06/louise-linton-just-wrote-the-perfect-white-savior-in-africa-story/.

[12] Gena-mour Barrett and Hannah Jewell, "How My Dream Gap Year In Europe Turned into A Nightmare," Text and Pictures, *BuzzFeed*, (July 5, 2016).
https://www.buzzfeed.com/genamourbarrett/how-my-dream-gap-year-in-europe-turned-into-a-nightmare.

nightmare."[13] Following Linton's article in *The Daily Telegraph*, which describes her missionary work as a high school student in Zambia, was a series of backlashes, including the above quotation extracted from Karen Attiah's piece, written in the *Washington Post* on 6 July 2016. For example, Zac tweets: "How @Louise Linton a 'white skinny girl with long angel hair' is 'the central character in a horror about African genocide' is beyond me."[14] Days after much fury across many social media fronts, 34-year-old Linton apologises for distorting her "white saviour complex" experience in Zambia. Edgar Lungu, President of Zambia gives the "last word" in the saga:

> Ms Linton presented to the world a savage Zambia, at war. It is a historic fact that Zambia has never been at war but rather has been home to thousands of refugees fleeing wars from other African countries. (…) Those who work in the area of HIV and AIDS understand the need to respect the confidentiality of the people they work with. Clearly Ms Linton does not seem to take this into consideration nor does she seem to understand that freedom of expression comes with responsibility. The overwhelming condemnation of her falsified memoirs by both Zambians and friends of Zambia worldwide attests to the fact that many have seen through her intentions to tarnish the image of a very friendly and peaceful country. We join many others who have taken time to condemn the stereotyping of Africa and Zambia as a backward country in a jungle, thinking which is not of the 21st century.[15]

With the revolution of the Internet, gone are the days when Africans helplessly watched the Western world disseminate negative stereotypes and false beliefs about the continent. Nevertheless, in spite of technological advancement with social media enabling Africans' ability to confront twisted ideas about

---

[13] Louise Linton, "How My Dream Gap Year in Africa Turned into a Nightmare," *The Telegraph*, July 2016, http://www.telegraph.co.uk/women/life/how-my-dream-gap-year-in-africa-turned-into-a-nightmare/.

[14] Zac, "@ZacSpeaks," Tweets, *Twitter*, (July 5, 2016).

[15] Staff Reporter, "Zambian Embassy Slams Louise Linton Memoirs," *The Scotsman*, July 12, 2016, http://www.scotsman.com/news/zambian-embassy-slams-louise-linton-memoirs-1-4174540.

the cradle of civilisation, the painful reality is hunger, disease and violence still plague the continent in record number and we have work to do.

One of the issues that needs to be addressed is the perilous journey taken by many Africans across the Mediterranean as part of the global refugee crisis.

This is the story of why I have become an academic, policy advocate, and activist for African migrants making the deadly voyage across the Mediterranean. And it is my story, because I have made that deadly voyage.

Once upon a time, I was a forced migrant caught up in Liberia's bloody civil war. On 24 December 1989, Libyan-trained rebels led by Charles Ghankay Taylor, former president of Liberia, invaded the northern part of Liberia near La Cote d'Ivoire. Thereafter, a violent civil war ensued, which lasted for 14 years. Approximately 250,000 Liberians died and an estimated 700,000 were forcibly displaced internally. Amidst a chaos heightened by relatively high prevalence of rape, forced conscription, disease, and hunger, my mother sought to protect her eight children by securing a space on a Ghanaian Peacekeeping vessel. The fateful evacuation journey began 2:00 am on 18 July 1992 and ended four days later at the Port of Tema in Greater Accra. From manoeuvring through a condensed crowd, while tossing each of my siblings on to a dangling container held by a crane, to lying on the deck of the ship in a corner with a rusty perforation that was used for urinating and defecating throughout the journey, my siblings, mother and I held onto our dear lives. Arrival in Ghana was not without challenges. Starved of food and water on the open sea for the duration of the journey, our lifeless smelly bodies, dried from whatever drooping tatters were left of seasickness, rain and human excreta, we were finally allowed to disembark. Tema Port security inspected our sagging "refugee bags" bearing scant, yet tattered belongings. Representatives from the United Nations High Commission for Refugees registered us and gave each of us a ration card as we proceeded to locate our family and friends in Ghana. In spite of the ordeal, we were simply happy to be farthest away from indiscriminate blasting of missiles, rocket propelled grenades, mortars and unending crackles of the AK-47, Beretta, Uzzi and General Purpose Machine Guns.

Having survived three years of being internally displaced in Liberia, followed by nine years of living as a refugee in Ghana and 13 years of being a single immigrant in Canada, I vowed to commit the rest of my life to fighting for justice and equality for those caught in violent conflicts, especially children and women in Africa. A traumatic reminiscence of my own treacherous journey at sea in July 1992 not only strengthens my resolve to persistently advocate for African migrants crossing the Mediterranean, but it also sustains my passion for engineering social change on the continent. Through the process of migration, I have assessed and reassessed the purpose of acquiring education, equally yoked with a moral responsibility to ignite social change, fight for justice and promote equality. As a black African woman, I see nothing wrong with non-Africans feeling the need to "help" Africa as long as it is a genuine and well-thought idea. With particular regard to African migrants making deadly voyages across the Mediterranean, I suggest that the most important question to ask is not only who have desires to "help" Africa, but who will lead African migrants safely and humanely across the Mediterranean? If not "Angel Hair," the European Union, or Italy, then who?

The United Nations High Commission for Refugees estimates that in 2015 "more than 300,000 refugees and migrants have used the dangerous sea route cross the Mediterranean...with almost 110,000 landing in Italy."[16] The International Organisation for Migration's Missing Migrant Project recorded 2,933 people missing and dead between 1 January and 13 July 2016.[17] In *Mediterranea*, a documentary film written and produced by Jonas Carpignano[18] the experiences of Ayiva, played by Koudous Seihon, and Abas, acted by Alassane Sy, exemplify every day trauma, pain, and suffering endured by thousands of African migrants crossing the Mediterranean sea – provided they survive to tell their stories.

---

[16] Melissa Fleming, "Crossings of Mediterranean Sea Exceed 300,000, Including 200,000 to Greece," Text and Pictures, *UNHCR News*, (August 28, 2015), http://www.unhcr.org/en-us/news/latest/2015/8/55e06a5b6/crossings-mediterranean-sea-exceed-300000-including-200000-greece.html.

[17] IOM, "Missing Migrants Project," Text and Pictures, *Mediterranean*, (2016).

[18] Jonas Carpignano, *Mediterranea (Official Trailer)* (NDM Ventas Internacionales, 2015), https://www.youtube.com/watch?v=qaALVBbde_A.

There is perception that the European Union (precisely Italy, Greece and Turkey) is solely responsible for African migrants' fatal journey across the Mediterranean. After all, it is European borders and seashores that dead Africans are awash. This belief is authenticated by factual illustrations. For example, as of 25 May 2016, the Italian Coast Guard had rescued approximately 37,000 migrants in that year alone. The next day, 26 May 2016; baby Favour, a nine-month-old Nigerian girl, survived yet another shipwreck, where up to 30 people were feared dead. The most fascinating aspect of Baby Favour's story is not only that she was found in the arms of her dead pregnant mother, who was seriously burnt due to a petrol leak in the ship's engine, but also that her story precipitated numerous adoption offers from Italian foster families. Ironically, in Africa, stories of migrant crisis are either vaguely discussed because it's all too prevalent or they are narrated with a different focus in the media.

In her article of 26 September 2014, Sede Alonge asserts that the African Union appears to be doing so little to "secure its borders and prevent smugglers from transporting thousands out of the continent, often to their deaths, and should encourage those Africans who feel forced to leave their countries, or who are displaced, to choose African destinations rather than European ones."[19] On 31 October 2013, the African Union declared a day of mourning for victims when a boat carrying some 545 migrants mostly from Somalia, Eritrea and Syria sank off the coast of Lampedusa, Italy, drowning approximately 359 migrants.[20] In the press release, the African Union Commission affirms its commitment to "advocating for international protection and human rights of all migrants, regardless of their status" and that the Commission "will continue to work with Member States, Regional Economic Communities and Partners in promoting the rights of migrants." That was almost three years ago. In November 2015, during the Euro-African Summit on Migration, the African

---

[19] Sede Alonge, "The African Union Must Take Its Share of Responsibility for Migrant Deaths," *The Guardian*, September 26, 2014, sec. Opinion, https://www.theguardian.com/commentisfree/2014/sep/26/african-union-migrant-deaths-europe-illegal-migration-africa.

[20] AU, "Public Notice on the Day of Mourning for Victims of Lampedusa Boat Disaster" (Directorate of Information and Communication of the African Union, October 31, 2013), http://www.au.int/ar/sites/default/files/Press%20Release_Memorial%20Service%20for%20Lampedusa%20Victims.pdf.

Union Commission Chairperson Nkosazana Dlamini-Zuma restated concerns that even though "less than 25 per cent of migrants caught up in the current crisis are African,"[21] yet they represent the largest number of casualties.[22] Many are frustrated with the African Union's inability or unwillingness to move beyond sheer utterance and take action in addressing the continent's migrant crisis. Assumpta Lattus of Deutsche Welle's English Department laments that the EU is complicit in supporting Africa's neglect of its role regarding the migrant crisis on the continent:

> What I find strange is that hardly anyone, at least in Europe, seems to expect African governments to take part in a solution to this crisis. Europeans often say they need to find solutions, they need to make the places these immigrants come from better. But they don't ever seem to hope, or expect, that African governments will help them find that solution. Maybe EU leaders think it is enough to have the head of the African Union Commission (23.04.15), Nkosazana Dlamini-Zuma, speak at a one-day annual bilateral meeting, during which the migration crisis was just one of the topics on the agenda. No, that is not the way we have to work to solve the problem. Africans don't need European pity, what they need is to be expected to step up to the plate. [23]

Even after somehow managing to disregard its obligation to address African refugees' problems,[24] protect and assist internally displaced persons,[25] and safeguard human and peoples' rights,[26] on 12 November 2015, the African Union, financially supported by the European Union, launched the European Union Emergency Trust

---

[21] Liesl Louw-Vaudran, "Fortresses in Our Midst," *ISS Africa*, November 27, 2015, https://www.issafrica.org/iss-today/fortresses-in-our-midst.

[22] Ottilia Anna Maunganidze, "Time to Get Real about Migrant Deaths," *ISS Africa*, January 19, 2016, https://www.issafrica.org/iss-today/time-to-get-real-about-migrant-deaths.

[23] Assumpta Lattus, "African Governments Ignore Migration Crisis," *Deutsche Welle Online Top Stories*, January 5, 2015, http://www.dw.com/en/african-governments-ignore-migration-crisis/a-18423414.

[24] *Organization of African Unity Convention Governing the Specific Aspects of Refugee Problems in Africa* 1969

[25] *African Union Convention for the Protection and Assistance of Internally Displaced Persons in Africa (Kampala Convention)* 2009

[26] *African Charter on Human and Peoples' Rights* 1981

fund. The Emergency Trust Fund is a €1.8 billion project to tackle root causes of unprecedented levels of irregular migration in Africa.[27] Countries identified as the most fragile and affected by migration include Burkina Faso, Cameroon, Chad, the Gambia, Mali, Mauritania, Niger, Nigeria, Senegal, Djibouti, Eritrea, Ethiopia, Kenya, Somalia, South Sudan, Sudan, Tanzania, Uganda, Algeria, Egypt, Morocco, Tunisia and Libya.[28]

Among the countries listed, Libya appears to be the gateway to the migrant surge in Europe as thousands of Africans from the south fleeing the vestiges of wars, famine and climate change, funnel through the Libyan coasts. One may ask then, how about other countries such as Ghana, Nigeria, and Senegal, which appear to have relative peace and stability yet a high number of migrants dying across the Mediterranean? Once again, the African Union is dead silent on the issue of the African migrant crisis across the Mediterranean. Apart from Human Rights Watch and Médecins Sans Frontières, it is almost impossible to find information about individual Africans or grass-root organisations on the continent that are prioritising the agenda of African-Mediterranean migrant crisis. I strongly believe the courage to write this chapter is an initial effort to engage with the issue head on, at least on my part. The ultimate goal is to bring more awareness to the topic and explore the possibility of contributing towards finding a lasting solution.

---

[27] EU, "President Juncker Launches the EU Emergency Trust Fund to Tackle Root Causes of Irregular Migration in Africa" (The Directorate-General for International Cooperation and Development, November 12, 2015).

[28] EU, "The EU Emergency Trust Fund for Africa - International Cooperation and Development - European Commission," Text and Pictures, *International Cooperation and Development*, (July 15, 2016), http://ec.europa.eu/europeaid/regions/africa/eu-emergency-trust-fund-africa_en.

Veronica Fynn Bruey is an award-winning international interdisciplinary author and scholar. She has conducted research studies, consulted on projects and spoken at international conferences in over 20 countries across Africa, Australia, Europe, Asia and North America. She has held teaching positions at Tubman University, Australian National University, Cuttington University, York University, and the University of British Columbia. She has authored over 19 publications including two books, several book chapters and peer-reviewed journal articles. She is also the founder/editor-in-chief of the Journal of Internal Displacement and the founder of the Law and Society's Collaborative Research Network: Displaced Peoples. Currently, she teaches at Seattle University School of Law as an Adjunct Professor. In her spare time, when she's not blogging, she's either dancing, biking, hiking or running half-marathons. Fynn Bruey is a born and bred Liberian war survivor.

Chris Mulenga
Friends of Street Kids[29]

Meet Benson Komondo. Ben is now 24 years old. His parents divorced when he was only 7 years old, and his father took him from his mother who was living in a town in Northern Zambia (Mansa) to another town on the Copperbelt (Mufulira.) He has not seen her since and he has very little recollection of her. Life with his father was difficult. He was not allowed to attend school, and he was mistreated by his own father and step-mother. He was once locked in a small room. He managed to escape and went to his step-sister for help but she refused to take him in. He resorted to living on the streets in 2000 in order to survive and started sniffing insolvents (a mixture of glue, gasoline and other substances) and smoking marijuana.

In 2001, He was discovered by *Friends of the Street Children (FSC)* and he was invited to stay at Piano House, which was a boys' centre in town then. In 2003, he was enrolled at Matete Basic School in grade 7. School life was difficult for him after experiencing street life, but he adjusted and got used to the school routine. Benson completed Secondary School in 2007 and in January 2010 he entered Cavendish University in Lusaka to study law. He was expected to be at Cavendish for four years but unfortunately, he discontinued because of lack of sponsorship.

However, with ongoing support from FSC he is currently pursuing a Bachelor of Education in Natural Sciences (B Ed NSc) in the school of Natural Sciences at Mukuba University. Benson looks forward to

---

[29] Part of this story excerpted from Interview with Christopher Mulenga when he won the International Service Human Rights Award for Defence of Human Rights Children. Retrieved, October 29, 2016 from
http://www.internationalservice.org.uk/includes/documents/cm_docs/2009/i/1_interview_with_christopher_mulenga.pdf

becoming a Science Teacher after his studies.

***

In most African cultures, a child is child till death. This is true of Zambia, where there is a saying in our language that 'the armpit will never be above the shoulders.' This means that a child will always remain a child to his/her parents or elders. In this era, children who are forced to go on the streets, go against all codes of the community by deciding to live on their own despite being African children. However, for my colleagues and I in the organisation I co-founded called Friends of the Street Children (FSC), we see these children as some of the strongest members of the community. *They are resilient, intelligent, courageous, brave and daring. They survive on their own without any adult supervision. Our interventions are designed to not only empower them but help to uplift their standards so that they can be recognised for their strength and contribution to the community.*

My work with Friends of the Street Children is driven by faith. As a Catholic, I have been driven by a strong sense of purpose and social justice to care for street children in Zambia. Before I started FSC, I remember I was in a group with my friends at a church rally sitting under a tree. I watched a street child bypass everybody and come to me to ask for food. He must have bypassed thousands of people and came only to me! I saw this as my calling. Another time after I started my work, I remember coming from Tanzania Airport and noticed a boy in rags and tatters coming to me. He just came straight to me ignoring the rest of my colleagues and asked for help. I feel that this work follows me wherever I am. How do these children find me? And when I am with them, I feel freer. They embrace me; jump on my back, always joking. And when they see me, they have a good happy face. I always feel happy with them.

I am one of the two founding members of FSC and the other founder is a priest. I was working as a coordinator for the Prison and Distress Ministry and one day I went to the street with my colleagues to find out what brings children there so I could tell my church members. That was the day some people started developing an interest in what I was doing. One of them was a Congolese priest who then came to my home to ask why I wanted to do this work. He said he was ready to support me and introduced me to a Filipino priest with whom we then went out to the streets together. We then started inviting our friends and colleagues, and we formed FSC to try and get a better understanding of why this is happening.

We started FSC to work with and for the children found on the streets in the Copperbelt region of Zambia in 2001. Our goal was to respond to the growing number of children living and working on the street and to challenge the community to rethink their response to these street children. For example, "Friends of the Street Children" was the named coined in response to harassment of children by the community around them who looked at them as public nuisances. Therefore, the name Friends of the Street Children came as a positive response to the turmoil in a community that felt street children brought shame on them. With love of children, the organisation in its initial stages worked hard to sensitise people to the reality of these street children. We engaged the community through print and electronic media to change the perception of the community towards children. This was also done through meetings with community gatekeepers, church leaders, and people working in markets.

In order for children living and working on the street to flourish and be assisted to shape their destiny, different interventions were put in place to address the needs of these children who were swelling in numbers. My colleagues and I also worked very hard to change the perception of our staff, so that our service delivery could meet the actual needs of children as opposed to perceived needs.

To-date, our work has included three programmes. First, the Street Outreach (Emergency interventions for children already on the streets), through which we cater to the basic needs of the children on the streets and provide general counselling. This programme is designed to provide daily contact with the street children, getting to know their background information, establishing the reasons for their coming to the street, and planning solutions and possible interventions for their needs. The programme also provides recreation and educational activities to arouse the interest of the street children in social development with regards to education and rapport with other members of society.

Second, Family Outreach (For possible family reunifications). This programme provides unification possibilities for street children with their relatives, parents, caregivers, and/or foster placement or care. The staff in this programme explore the possibilities for the street children from the first day of meeting them on the street. Under this programme, children are linked with their families and relatives to provide possibilities of formally reuniting them. Time and again, reunion meetings are planned such as weekend visits to the family of a child with a view to familiarise the child with the family and establish a solid link. Other needs such as education support, life skills training and continued visits are provided to reintegrate children. Some families are provided with capital to help them start a small business and enable them to provide at least a meal a day for their own children.

Third, Children's 'Rehabilitation' (Temporary residential care). This programme provides home environments for the street children who have been identified through the Street Outreach programme and taken to our boys' or girls' centres for rehabilitation. The children are also provided with life and survival skills in the centres to prepare them for their future.

My vision and that of FSC is a society where every child, including children who have either taken agency or found themselves on the streets unexpectedly, grows and lives in a supportive family environment. We envision a society in which children are enabled to achieve their full potential by growing in a secure, stable, caring and loving atmosphere that ensures adequate nutrition, good health, physical and emotional security, and the opportunity to develop physically, intellectually, emotionally and socially.

We believe that every child has a right to be supported to be part of a loving family and community no matter the circumstances that landed them on the street. Some have been abused or may suffer from HIV/AIDS, STI or other illnesses. Every child has the right to be supported through these trials and receive love and care. We exist to protect children against all forms of abuse and help street children become responsible and happy members of society.

We are values-driven. In our work with the street children, we are respectful, non-judgmental, inclusive, innovative, forward looking, inspirational, and socially responsible. This is fundamental for us as the founders and for our whole organisation. For example, my co-founder priest took to sleeping out there on the streets to get a feel of what goes on. In my case, I took in a child from the streets as my own. I wanted to encourage many others to take in a child and I wanted to find out what street children are really like. My wife and I didn't yet have children of our own, so Adrian Mustaffa became our first son. He was 12 years old when I took him home as my boy. I gave him love and asked my wife to love him.

There were dangers. I discovered that the boy suffered a lot of rejection from his family so he wanted to fight back. As a result, his behaviour at school wasn't impressive. The teachers were labelling him a 'street-child' and he was using defensive mechanisms by venting anger on his fellow students. I changed schools - the same thing happened. Then he started stealing from my home. I realised it's a psychological problem that he had. He was fine with me at home but when he was going out I didn't know whether I would find him locked-up in police cells. That's how the children are destroyed; they suffer mental trauma. They see so many people rejecting them and don't trust many adults. So it can be easy to get jaded about the child, and maybe start blaming them and thinking the child is bad. Children can start doing things that are unpalatable. I realised the most important duty I had was to convince my family and peers to accept this boy unconditionally, and to embrace him like my own child. Whatever he did, after all his stealing and all the bad behaviour, we always accepted him back. That's why I always advise our staff not to be carried away by the trouble these kids get into because it might affect their work and their perception. There is a temptation to switch off and become negative.

It was also challenging for us because of lack of resources. It was very difficult to send Adrian to school because we live from hand to mouth (pay check to pay check), but I managed with the help of our organisation. After Adrian was with us for a while, we had our first biological child and I asked Adrian to look after our baby. I gave him that responsibility in spite of the challenges we had with him because after three years, he had changed. My plans were then to send him to boarding school so he could spend three months there, and one month in my home. But one day his sister came. She said she was there for him and I was happy because I managed to reunite him with his family. We are not there to prevent these children from being with their families. And the good thing is, when I removed him from the street - he never returned to the streets.

Our work has helped many street children in our African setting to make informed decisions and decide what they really want to do with their lives. Our role as an organisation is to facilitate the transformation of these children by raising their self-esteem and enabling them to claim what will help them become better citizens even from their former street situation. Those that have adjusted to this call have seen summers and winters on the street but have gone out with a positive attitude towards life and the community they live in. This has been the result of our value not to judge them but walk along with them out of their situation. We give them skills to survive on the street; and support them through the process until such a time they think they need a shift in their lives. It's up to an individual child to make a decision whether to hang on to the street or move on to other sectors of life. It's vital to understand that some street-connected children make decisions to leave their families based on their conviction that life is better on the street than in homes. And that is also our entry point in our programming so that children are first appreciated for their ability to survive on the streets against all odds.

Since 2001, we have helped over 6,548 children return to families and homes; 90% have never gone back to the street. Through our effort, there has been a transformed attitude of people towards street-connected children. The police service of Zambia that used to round up children were also engaged in a training called 'Walk the Walk' which was designed to help people understand street children. After the training, some police officers became agents of change by taking the training to their meetings and advocating for the protection of children. More still, some of the street connected children came from the homes of police officers. It was quite evident that even police officers were affected by the problem.

I am a Catholic and, although I am myself poor, Catholic work is known to support the poor. In the biblical story of the Widow's mite you see that the poor help the poor. My inspiration comes from the teachings of Jesus helping the poor and answering their call to save other peoples. It's also part of the way I was brought up - we were always receiving strangers in our own home. We felt very free at home and my family was outgoing and would embrace every person in the community. That helped me develop in terms of social responsibility. When I began, I didn't know that it was the start of such big work with international recognition. In 2008, I was awarded The International Service Human Rights Award for the

Defence of Human Rights of Children. I was nominated for the Consortium for Street Children's 'Street Child Champion Award' 2012. But I did not do this work for the recognition. From my family's perspective, we were just helping people. So that drives me forward. And getting closer to a prayerful life has made me realise it is part of my vocation to save the children.

Christopher Mulenga is co-founder of Friends of Street Children, Zambia. He and his organisation have been able to offer a peaceful haven for youngsters to learn and develop. Christopher and FSC's advocacy also received commendation and International Awards. In 2008, he received an International Award for the Defence of the Rights of Children in the House of Commons. In 2010, he received the Presidential Award in June as a best practice NGO in Zambia. In 2012, he was Recognised by Consortium for Street Children in UK as the Champion for Children's Rights.

Sal Muthayan
Strengthening the Roots of Leadership in the African Public Service

This story depicts the roots of my passion for working towards sustainable development in Africa. In 2006, I was privileged to realise this lifelong dream through the Regional Capacity Building Programme (RCB)[30] which has impacted leadership development of the public services in Rwanda, Burundi, South Sudan and South Africa. The innovative design of the programme was embedded in participatory and decolonising methodologies. The project continues to inform international discussion, debates and policy making around South-South cooperation and models for sustainable development involving local expertise and ownership. To this day, I remain committed to and involved in the work of African leadership capacity building rooted in the philosophies of Ubuntu and indigenisation. My belief is that the tree of development of African society can only be spread and deepened when capacity development initiatives are informed by local ethos and content. Story telling is a powerful teaching and learning tool in Africa and hearkens back to the oral tradition of recording history. So to tell the story of my leadership development work on my beautiful continent of Africa, I must first tell you a little bit of the story of me and how I came to my passion.

I was born in the Eastern Cape city of Port Elizabeth, South Africa and raised by parents who were very concerned about the plight of Black Africans in the country and the inequities and inequalities that pervaded our daily lives. I remember after dark visits to our house by political activists who were involved in the struggle against Apartheid. Although I was only about 4 or 5 years old, I had been warned by my mother not to listen in and, worst yet, not to repeat anything. The mere mention of the names of Nelson Mandela and Robert Sobukwe could result in arrest. Already then, I knew of the ANC and the PAC; organisations that were banned. Yet, I was aware that these were good people. Perhaps it was because

---

[30] The RCB, funded by CIDA and implemented by South Africa, was an early example of both North-South and South-South partnerships to build the capacity of public services in post conflict countries.

my father always explained to me how wrong the Apartheid government was in the way they treated people. I recall clearly that I understood it was wrong to treat black people as inferior. It was not just an understanding. It evoked in me an overwhelming sense of the injustice being perpetrated, that it was morally wrong and that there was an acute need to overcome this.

As well, father took me into the black townships in Port Elizabeth, (which was prohibited by law at that time), to distribute buns and milk at primary schools because there was no government feeding system for poor children who arrived at schools with hungry stomachs. By witnessing this dire poverty right in the midst of a big rich city, I remember feeling shocked and deeply sad. My father also took me to the rural areas of Transkei (former homeland) and Kwazulu Natal where I came face to face with how poverty stricken South Africans lived. This also exposed me to the music and dancing of African people which my father loved and respected and under whose spell I too fell. My father spoke fluent isiXhosa, the local African language and also knew isiZulu. This inspired my deep African roots in a country where people were racially and ethnically segregated.

So when I grew up, I was committed to making this country a better place for all the people who live here and particularly for those rural Africans who were the most marginalised. Every single aspect of our lives, from birth to death, was determined by the heinous Apartheid policy; it determined in which hospital you could be born and in which cemetery you would be buried. Even in terms of the allocation of education subsidies there was a chasm between what whites and other races received. However, education was the cornerstone of the repressive policy

I decided that the best way to overcome the system was to teach young children that everyone is equal and should be treated as such. For me, change needed to take place in education first, through the curriculum and teaching. So, I prepared myself to become this kind of teacher in the 70s amidst great upheaval in the country.

I determined that through majoring in English, (as well as Politics and International Relations), I would be exposed to the post-colonial literature of Ngugi Wa Thiongo, Achebe and other African writers who were rewriting Africa's history. Ngugi's *Grain of Wheat* was exemplary in this respect. Later, I became enamoured of his seminal book, *Decolonising the Mind*. I learned about the great African liberators such as Kwame Nkrumah and Julius Nyerere. I was influenced by the politics of the 70s and the Black Consciousness movement headed by the late Dr Steve Biko during the height of repression where states of emergency and curfews were the norm. I excelled in my courses and I determined that this literature and history could be included in the school curriculum under a new South Africa. My fervent wish was to change the curriculum before I had children and before they would attend school!

Years later, in 1993, as we prepared for the birth of the new democratic South Africa, I was both happy and surprised to find myself participating on a number of structures working towards a democratic education system for South Africa. One of these structures was for writing policy for the early childhood development sector which was published by the World Bank and later became the Government White Paper on Early Childhood Development. The dream I had as a child was within my reach, I was assisting with the design of a new school curriculum for my country.

Then there were my leadership lessons during our landmark democratic elections in 1994, which was also the first time in my life that I would vote at the mature age of 36, double that of citizens of other countries who are eligible to vote from the tender age of 18. I recall how when we received voter education in preparation for the big event, I trembled, and cried because I was experiencing voting for the first time in my life. During this time my husband, a reputed human rights lawyer, and I threw ourselves into serving our country to see the end of the apartheid regime both through our respective jobs and as activists of the liberation movement. I was the Director of an NGO, a training centre for preschool teachers from poor townships and rural communities. The Apartheid government never provided preschool education for black children and over 50% of black children were found to have "failed" grade one in the early 1990s thus limiting the potential of blacks in the country.

As the first free elections approached, we even halted our work and devoted ourselves to serving the party of the government in waiting - Mandela's ANC. We had young children aged 9 and 12 and my mother or aunt assisted in caring for them; thereby freeing us up to spend entire days and nights at the ANC's Command Centre for the elections. I was the ANC Party Liaison person with the Independent Electoral Commission (IEC), a neutral agency established by law for conducting free and fair elections. As an Advocate (barrister), my husband was tasked with interpreting the new Electoral Act, and other relevant law to prepare legal responses to the infringements by the Apartheid government or other political parties. When I was not in attendance at the daily electoral commission meetings, I assisted my husband to research the law and draft written responses. This experience of working side by side with a legal expert empowered me to cite the law with confidence in contesting the reactionary forces at the IEC meetings. But my authority also came from knowing I was representing Mandela's party and that I was on the side of the right, of justice, equality, and freedom! The challenges included white farmers using force to prevent the farm labourers from voting. There were incidents of sabotage where ballot papers and ink were destroyed or stolen.

My NGO was among other organisations conducting voter education for local communities. A month before the elections, I, as Director, consulted the staff and moved that we suspend other training programmes except for voter education in order to reach the large numbers. Whilst the white staff were historically liberal and had devoted their lives to serving the poor, suddenly they were not happy with my decision and felt that I was supporting a party with communist leanings. I was surprised that people I trusted could feel this way. Our mandate was to uplift communities through the provision of early childhood education and the development of communities. What could empower these largely illiterate communities more than educating them to exercise their right to vote for the first time? The management and mainly white Board informed our funders, who were American, of my affiliation with the "communist" ANC. As director, I had increased the funding significantly even to buy a new building for the institution. Eventually I resigned my position to prevent the institution being negatively affected through a loss of funding. I had learned the hard way that liberation comes at a cost.

A pivotal leadership moment happened for me on the eve our election day in 1994. Towards the late afternoon, I decided to go home from the Command Centre to spend some time with my children, who had seen little of their parents over the past month.

Furthermore, I was going to be intensely busy over the next 4 days overseeing a voting and then counting station for the ANC. To make up to my children, I took them out for ice creams. I drove past the police station to show them (and check on) where the containers of ballot papers, ink and other voting equipment and materials were being stored for the following morning's elections. This was historic and I wanted my kids to see this. Across the country, we were gripped with a mood of joy at the prospect of finally being able to vote but our joy was mixed with fear: fear of a bloodbath, that Mandela's negotiated settlement for a peaceful transition would go wrong. The tension was palpable. Many of us would not sleep that night as we rose before dawn to exercise our vote for the first time in the history of the nation.

The (white) police station where the containers with the voting supplies would be kept overnight was in a conservative white suburb and was one of the areas where the ANC anticipated there could be sabotage. Earlier that day, we took a decision at the command centre that all containers had to be moved to safe holding inside the local prison premises because of the threat of sabotage. The police were agents of Apartheid. They could turn a blind eye to any act of sabotage.

As we drove up past the police station a large tow truck had just delivered the last of about three huge steel shipping containers and was about to drive away. I approached the driver and Indicated that these containers were to be moved to the local prison. I informed him that this had been the decision earlier that day and that his company office had been instructed to do so. He knew nothing about this. I tried contacting someone senior at the command centre to clarify matters with the trucking company office as it was the end of working day. They were all in an urgent meeting and not available to take my call.

All I was intending for were a few moments to relax with my kids. But alas, the situation was too risky for me to ignore. The risk of those containers with all the ballot papers for the city being bombed was very real. I took a split decision to drop my kids off with a friend who lived nearby whilst I rushed back to the site.

As a Black woman of Indian descent, I knew the stereotypes the driver, an Afrikaner male, might hold of me. I represented the ANC whom he regarded was going to take away his privileges and way of life. Arguing with him in an open field as it was getting dark was risky. But at that moment, I was not concerned about my life! Eventually, I, a disenfranchised black woman persuaded him to move the containers to safekeeping! This was perhaps an instance of what Nelson Mandela once defined leadership as: it always seems impossible until it is done.

After the watershed elections, I continued my efforts to change the education system of South Africa into the post-apartheid phase. In 1996, the first Minister of Education of the new democratic South Africa appointed me onto a Task Team of 15 persons to develop the new School curriculum for grades 1 to 9. When my first child was born 15 years earlier, I had cringed at the idea that he would have to receive an inferior education. Imagine my elation that finally this heinous tool of Apartheid was to be dismantled and I was playing a role in this.

The Ministerial Team comprised education stakeholders across the spectrum of society. We expected the Afrikaners to protect the Calvinist curriculum but the biggest resistance came from liberal whites who hid behind the cloak of having always resisted Apartheid. They were imbued with the arrogance that they alone knew what was best for a new education system because of their expert skills set - the result of white privilege.

One story of the resistance we encountered from the liberals was against my attempt to include the African philosophy of Ubuntu in the curriculum. I was working on the learning area of human and social sciences where history could be re-authored. Ubuntu is related to the Xhosa saying: Umtu Umuntu, Ngabantu meaning "a person is a person through people." Ubuntu means that when we affirm the humanity of others, we affirm our own humanity. My suggestion was rejected by the mainly white team. Their argument that the term was communist dumbfounded me. This was the new democratic South Africa. I escalated the matter to the higher committee pointing out that consensus on the team was farcical because centuries of white privilege meant that they were overrepresented on an education stakeholder team.

It is against the backdrop of these and other similar experiences, that I took on the role of Head of International and Special Projects at the South African Management Development Institute in 2006. In this role, I had the opportunity to design a truly participatory project, the Regional Capacity Building programme for the capacity development of the public services in Rwanda, Burundi and South Sudan. The programme was funded by the Canadian International Development Agency to the tune of CAD $10 million over a five-year period. The innovative approach in this programme was not just about building the capacity of individuals, but also of their institutions to achieve greater sustainability.

In this role, I realised that central to my work with the RCB programme, was my early work with rural indigenous African communities in the Eastern Cape Province where I had developed the knowledge, understanding, and skills for authentic participatory approaches in working with local communities. I was blown away by how erudite and full of common sense these largely illiterate communities were. Most importantly, I learned to respect and value that these communities not only know their problems but, if given the opportunity, could also come up with the solutions. I also learned that these communities had a knack or intuition for differentiating between genuine and exploitive intentions of different development workers. *The key, I found, was to work <u>with</u> them and not <u>for</u> them; and to conduct any needs analyses or research related activities <u>with</u> them and not <u>on</u> them.*

So with the RCB programme, a participatory approach was adopted from the very beginning. During the initial bilateral meetings between my South African public service organisation and similar organisations in Rwanda, Burundi and South Sudan, we sat down jointly with our counterparts to discuss areas for mutual collaboration. From the beginning, I pitched this as learning from each other rather than with South Africa assuming a "know it all" approach. I was very aware that they should be involved in determining their needs and in designing the possible solutions to their problems. Thus, we worked under the theme of "African solutions for African challenges." The project sought not only to train some 6,000 public servants across the three countries but more importantly to build the institutional capacities of the three management development institutions within those countries so that they could continue to develop the public sectors of their respective countries beyond the lifespan of the project.

Some of the lessons I learned from the project include:

1. Confirmation that participatory approaches, where the so-

called beneficiaries (I prefer referring to them as partners) of the development project are also the researchers, designers and implementers of the project, lead to successful and sustainable results;

2. In fragile or even developing countries where strong institutions do not exist, process based management is as important as results based management;

3. Consistency in leadership of the project from conceptualisation to closeout is important for the realisation of the intended project goals;

4. Protocols for working with communities include mutual trust, respect, and accountability, which should come from all parties concerned including the donors;

5. In fragile countries where there are constant changes in political heads, strong administrative heads for the project is important for timely completion of the project;

6. Sustainability is dependent on capacity development rather than capacity building, that is, focussing on individuals as well as on institutions;

7. Ensuring that local communities benefit from development projects is crucial to meaningful and sustainable development; and

8. Building a strong and confident civil society sector is critical to development of all societies, especially those in need of empowerment and development.

The impact of the project related not only to benefits derived by the partners with regard to improved capacity and systems in baseline, training needs assessment, curriculum development, and the delivery of programmes, but also there were wider benefits in terms of policy for international development. An early indication of impact was that before we had moved to the curriculum design and development phase, our partner in Burundi was being contracted by their government to conduct needs assessments and training for local governments across Burundi. This showed a transfer of skills and capacity early on which contributed to the long-term sustainability.

The example of both triangular cooperation between the donor, CIDA, the implementing agency, PALAMA in South Africa and the beneficiaries as well as South-South cooperation between South Africa and the three partner countries of Rwanda, Burundi and

South Sudan attracted the attention of the international aid and development community. This project was selected as one of the best practice cases not only from Africa under the auspices of the New Partnership for Africa's Development (NEPAD) programme of the African Union but also as a best case from the South. It was showcased at the Busan High Level Forum on Aid Effectiveness in Korea in 2011. Busan was the first instance where the focus moved from aid effectiveness to development effectiveness. I had contributed to the development of the African strategy for Development Effectiveness (NEPAD) which was put forward at Busan. For the first time, the voices of the South were being heard not only in terms of governments but also from civil society organisations.

Subsequent to this initiative, the World Bank along with other partners supported the establishment of South-South networks and research on other South-South development programmes. In other words, this led to expansion and acknowledgment of more authentic examples of South-South cooperation. As a result, I worked on a research study of CABRI, (Collaborative African Budget Reform) initiatives in 2012. There were also calls for the establishment of a South-South Think Tank consisting of a network of academia, development practitioners and civil society stakeholders. I was a founding member of the Network of South-South Think Tanks (NEST) for Africa which was established in 2014 and continues to play a key role in research and studies in South-South cooperation.

More recently, I had the opportunity to pick up on a project which had not taken place as planned. Namely, the design of a curriculum for the development of trainers or facilitators on the Art of Facilitation. Often trainers focus on content rather than on innovative methodologies for teaching and learning which then result in a limited transfer of learning from the classroom to the workplace. I have spent the past three years leading the conceptualisation, design and development of a Lead Facilitator Development Programme: *Art of Facilitation* for the National School of Government[31]. I introduced the philosophy of "know, be, do" – integrating head, heart and hands with a strong focus on "being" (presence and authenticity) and "doing" (or application). The topic of African leadership, including Ubuntu, has been

---

[31] Formerly PALAMA.

brought into curriculum for the public service of South Africa. This course is being delivered by me and my team. It is based on the view that before one can transform the public service, you need to begin with yourself. Hence the focus on self-reflection and self-transformation. This programme has received praise from the executive to junior level public servants. It has potential to be used in other African countries as well. As one participant claimed: "It has truly empowered me. I feel like a new person."

Dr. Sal Muthayan is a South African who has 20 years of experience in policy development, governance and capacity development at the international, national, provincial and local government levels. She has a passion for African development and the reconstruction of post conflict societies. Dr. Muthayan also initiated South-South Cooperation between the Management Development Institutes of India, Brazil and South Africa to harness innovative, indigenous best practices and models in response to local challenges. Dr. Muthayan, who is also an Executive Coach, has a PhD from the University of British Columbia, Canada and a Master's Degree in Education from Rhodes University, South Africa.

Daphne Nederhorst
Sparks! Spreading Local Innovations from Africa to the World

I grew up playing in the red African soil of rural villages and urban areas of Tanzania. That's where my story starts. So, where is your home, people often ask me? Even though I was born in the Netherlands, I feel more African than Dutch. I was nine months old when my family moved to Tanzania. My parents worked in the diplomatic and international aid sector and we travelled across Tanzania, and East Africa. We didn't live in poverty but we certainly travelled in communities where poverty was prevalent. As a child, I started noticing very quickly the difference between where we lived among diplomats in luxurious housing and the poverty-stricken communities that we visited. I strongly feel that I was born with a deep passion to care for others especially those that are suffering. It was due to this combination of growing up in a setting where I saw suffering and poverty and my inner drive to create an equal and just world for everyone that led me to begin building a grand vision to help humanity.

Three significant things from growing up shaped where I am now and what I do. First, even though I witnessed extreme poverty, I also experienced an enormous amount of culture and warmth and energy from the people in those settings. Everyone, although marginalised, seemed so alive. Second, my upbringing taught me a deep respect for local cultures. My motto is that when you go to new places, not only do you need to respect local ways, but know that in every community there is a leader or leaders that already know the solutions needed in their communities. Third, I witnessed poverty and sometimes severe poverty not only in East Africa but all over the world. Travelling reinforced for me that everyone has a right to be free of suffering and to have dignity. I also saw that in every community you can find locally-created solutions that already exist, done by the people and run by the people.

Therefore, since I was very young, I had a deep desire to work toward a world without poverty, led by the people living in it. That passion never left me. In fact, it only grew and now here we are. I founded Sawa World officially in 2007. Sawa World is now a globally

92

awarded NGO that uses a unique approach to lifting people out of extreme poverty with their own ideas and solutions.

Before Sawa World, I initially worked for a range of different international aid organisations, governments and the private sector. I hoped that within the system I could change the limitations of international aid work. I have seen and assessed dozens of aid projects around the world. Although mostly well-intentioned, they generally do not work. I make an exception to this when it comes down to emergency aid and some health interventions. They have contributed an enormous amount of positive impact. However, in general, aid projects don't work because when you impose an idea on someone that isn't theirs, you take away their opportunity to do things themselves. You take away their dignity and their innovation. When I was working with NGOs or doing international research for my academic degrees, I realised that the system of international aid is ineffective and conservative. Working within the sector felt like running into brick walls. I knew there was a more effective and dignified way to solve extreme poverty for millions.

I believed that there was an untapped recourse that could bring permanent local solutions to poverty in Africa and other countries. We simply needed to look at locally created solutions that were already working and collaborate to grow these. With this deep vision in mind, I resigned from my fulltime job in 2007. I was working in local government as an environmental consultant. I set off to shine a light on all the beautiful and selfless people I had met in poverty who radiated hope and resilience. I'm not claiming that only using local solutions can solve global poverty but it certainly is a powerful and immediate way to self-empower large groups of vulnerable people. The local inspiring leaders that I refer to are beacons of light (Sparks) that already know what works, but they are most often overlooked in the search for answers to eradicate poverty. The exciting fact is that such Sparks can be found in every community all around the world. They hold and demonstrate valuable lessons on how to mobilise vulnerable communities with local resources instantly.

For example, I did a pilot project in Colombia to test the idea and ended up finding Marlene Gomez, a Spark. She was a single mother who had very little money but had a passion to help abused and abandoned streets kids in Bogota. She was able to help 113 children and teens single-handedly. She gave them shelter and education, hope and love. When we were with her something clicked within me. It was as if my whole life from Tanzania to all my travels and adventures around the world came together in a split second. I thought: *this is it, I am going to start an organisation that will highlight and connect and self-empower millions of people to use local solutions, founded and owned by the people that are already working and having an impact.* I was driven to get these stories of success to others in adversity so that they could get themselves out of poverty. That was Christmas 2005. By early 2007, I had resigned from my corporate job. And that is how Sawa World was born.

Sawa is a Swahili word. Sawa can mean okay, but Sawa also means equal or unity. So, for us, "Sawa World" means an equal world where nobody lives in poverty and people living in poverty can lift themselves out it. Sawa World helps people use locally-created solutions, resources, and ideas around them that are already working. From 2007 to now, we have operated programmes in 11 countries including Haiti, Vanuatu, Solomon Islands, Cape Verde and Senegal. We tested and innovated our approach and although it has changed 360-degrees from where we started in 2005, the concept of "solutions from within" is still the same. It is local solutions, found by local people, that can inspire others in that same adversity to change their lives instantly and lift themselves out of poverty. That's always been the mission, but our approach continues to evolve. We are really good at letting things go in our projects and programmes that don't work and then readjust with what does.

In 2007, our focus was looking for inspiring grassroots people - "bright lights" in communities and making short videos about them. We then connect them with global partnerships that would allow them to grow their already successful small-scale project. We connected them to medical schools, media companies, or individuals that could 'mentor' them.

As the programmes started growing, we realised that our model wasn't the vision we had and neither was it sustainable. It was starting to look like a typical aid approach where local people living in poverty were receiving mentorship from outside. This charity model was exactly what we didn't want. We wanted these extraordinary people living in extreme poverty to teach us, the rest of the world, how incredible they were in terms of living in adversity and still being able to make a change for others in their communities. That's a valuable lesson for all of us. So, when we came back from Haiti in 2010 we reassessed our approach. We wanted to create a systemic movement among people living in extreme poverty so they can lift themselves out of poverty while also sharing their valuable knowledge with the rest of the world. We went from being in 11 countries to focusing on one. So instead of scaling up, we scaled down in order to scale up again to a global level. We decided to innovate our approach in one country by listening and working even more closely with the communities that faced extreme poverty. We wanted to innovate an effective eco-system to become a permanent gift for the rest of the world, and that is what we did.

We selected Uganda as our focus country. We started our programmes in Uganda in 2011. The scaling down decision was a gift. We have grown through scaling down, by trial and error, and listening to the people and leaders within the communities (Sawa World Sparks). We now have established local teams of youth who run the entire approach on the ground. They find the Sparks who have already found simple and local solutions to self-employment and improved livelihoods. We then facilitate the sharing of their solutions on a large scale by hiring them to do practical workshops which also gives them income. We also offer "how to" videos and learning posters and annual events to spread the local solutions to thousands of vulnerable youth in Uganda and East Africa.

Our team of youth have become conduits on the ground to spread the local solutions. For example, they found an extraordinary woman called Nulu in one of Kampala's slums. She uses organic waste to make fuel eco-briquettes. The briquettes produce no smoke, burn twice as long as charcoal and are highly marketable. Our team now spreads this innovation through practical workshops and community events, and the selling of videos and posters of her solution. This allows 1000s of vulnerable people living in extreme poverty to gain access to her innovation and use the skills to start a business or use it at home. At the same time, it allows Nulu and her team to gain more exposure and earn extra income.

Over the last five years we have trained over 40,000 marginalised youth in Uganda in local solutions primarily through practical workshops delivered by Sawa Sparks. Impact tracking is central to our operations. We found through our monitoring and evaluation in 2016 that 63% of the youth we reached had replicated a solution within one month of learning it. We aim to reach a replication success rate of 80 percent over the next two years. What happens typically after that is that the youth raise their income from nothing or $1/day to $2-$4 per day, just by starting a simple and practical solution they've learnt from us. We now have over 30 solutions that can instantly inspire a young person to start a business and make an income. The instant change that we witness through our approach amazes us and motivates us to do so much more.

The other unique factor about our impact is that the start-up costs of the Sawa World Solutions are very low ranging from between $5 to $20. We encourage the youth to raise their own money or start savings groups to pool resources. For example, we have encouraged some of them to make different kinds of paper bags which are in high demand in Uganda, because the government has banned plastic bags. We teach them to make different types like paper bags for popcorn, or for other snacks such as Daddies which is the local sweet. The start-up costs for this solution is less than $5.

For the youth who don't start a business, because not every youth we meet is an entrepreneur, they often take the skills and change their lives at the household level. For example, the fuel eco briquettes made from organic waste don't cause smoke. That is a significant improvement over charcoal which produces smoke in the household. So, when they learn how to do this and take it home, it can also instantly change the health of the family as well as save money because they don't have to buy charcoal.

Last year, the Country Director of the Aga Khan Foundation in Uganda asked me: "so what is the most secret success component of your model?" I replied, "it's the Sawa World Sparks." The leaders who teach others. They are selfless and pure. They go and teach everyone in their community to do the same and they are not threatened by that. They see that investing in teaching others is investing in the wellbeing of the entire community. That is the most powerful part of Sawa World. We find Sparks in every community. It is their inspiration that motivates the youth, because when they see them teach, it makes it real for them. The youth see that the Sparks are from their same communities. They speak the same language. The youth often say, "if they can do it, I can do it". *The selfless local leader is the most powerful part of the Sawa World approach. When we start tracking the youth who are replicating solutions, it is beautiful to see that most of them are also training and teaching others. It is a ripple effect. It is a spark.*

I see arising challenges as gifts to getting closer to our bold vision. One of the biggest learning opportunities that we run against is the change in mindset that is needed among the youth living in extreme poverty. Most youth that we train ask what we are giving as a free handout: "will we get free t-shirts," they ask? "Do we get free lunch, notebooks and pens? Are you going to provide seeds or a capital fund?" We have learned that change in this type of mindset needs an enormous amount of patience because this idea of asking for things has been ingrained in our focus communities over the past 60 years as a result of unsustainable international aid paradigms. For most people, the way that we work is new. We encourage people to use their own ideas and efforts to lift themselves out of poverty. We tell them that if they want to transform their lives then getting free stuff will not get them there. For example, at our Solution Center in Kampala, we had 40 slum-dwelling youth come for a workshop, but someone had told them that they were going to get free soda and lunch. We told them that coming only for a free lunch and free soda is not the mindset that is going to help them become successful and selfless leaders. That shift in mindset will just take time.

I have learned valuable lessons on this journey both about the goodness and endless potential of humanity and also about myself. I am greatly humbled that I was able to just leave my full-time job, surround myself with top class mentors, and lead with my heart the change I want to see in the world. I am honoured that I can live the dream that I had as a girl every day! The power of the beautiful human spirit that you can find everywhere, especially where people are suffering - the hope, the smile, the strength, the creativity and innovation in places of adversity - is astonishing! It always touches me. We need to learn together to respect each other and allow all of us to live with dignity. We don't need to say the "global south" and "global north" but we need to find ways to equally collaborate as one humanity to share the solutions we already have among us.

Our vision is big - we want to impact a billion people by 2030 in 42 countries. The simple fact is that if you can see it or vision it, you can do it, not alone, but with a good group of people around you to do it. Nothing will stop you if you have something you want to do, even making systemic positive change globally. Put it down on paper, work hard, and constantly innovate your idea based on real experiences. If you can be humble enough to throw things out that do not work and then innovate, any vision, big or small, will become reality

Our Solutions Centre is in Kampala, Uganda and we run our main programme activities there. In 2015, we tested part of our programmes in Kenya, Tanzania and South Sudan, with local partners replicating our approach with their own versions of our Solutions Centre. In South Sudan, for example, a group of 100 ladies replicated three of our solutions and started 103 businesses. In early 2017, we started an ambitious project called the Sparked Women Project, an element of the DREAMS Innovation Challenge, partly funded by the Bill and Melinda Gates Foundation. We are working with four other partners in Uganda including Aids Fonds, Healthy Entrepreneurs, National Forum for People Living with HIV/AIDS Networks in Uganda (NAFOPHANU) and International Community of Women living with HIV Eastern Africa (ICWEA) to train and impact 15,500 girls to start their own businesses in rural communities in Central Uganda.

By the end of 2017, moving into 2018, we aim to have the Sawa World paradigm replicated organically by other countries. We will develop a franchise model, and train others to adopt the Solution Centre in their own countries. By 2019, we aim to have reached one million people in five other countries, and then at that point, we also plan to generate 100% of our own income. We will be a social enterprise versus a not-for-profit. Right now, we are about 15% to 20% social enterprise. Beyond that, we will create an eco-system, for humanity in general. We will highlight that the solutions are all around us and within us. The vision is that our approach itself will serve all humanity and the planet.

Daphne Nederhorst is nominated among the world's leading social entrepreneurs by Ashoka. She is the founder of Sawa World (www.sawaworld.org), a globally awarded organisation for its unique approach to empower vulnerable youth with local solutions to self-employment.

Global dignitary such as, political leader, Kofi Annan, peace activist, Emmanual Jal, and Richard Branson's Virgin Unite have endorsed Daphne and Sawa World for the exceptional leadership and innovative approach to ending extreme poverty among youth.

"Solutions from within" has been Daphne's motto to solve extreme poverty since Daphne was seven years old. This has been her life's mission for the last three decades. She grew up in Tanzania, witnessed extreme poverty from a young age, travelled to over 42 countries and lived in hundreds of communities stricken with crippling poverty. She listened and learned from the poorest of the poor, got inspired by their innovative spirit, encouraged them to live with dignity, and together developed new and inclusive paradigms to solve extreme poverty on a global level.

Ndidi Nwuneli
Rage for Change: Blazing Trails for Social Innovation

There are many sources of vision in an individual's life. I have had two defining ones that have fuelled my drive for development in Africa.

My first defining moment was my early encounter with Christ as a child. I was invited to church by amazing university students who would periodically invite children of faculty to Sunday school. Through their life's example and wonderful encouragement, I was drawn to the church and gave my life to Christ when I was thirteen years old. This early encounter shaped my outlook on life and pushed me to continually work to discover and fulfil my life's purpose.

My second source of vision is rage. This rage got me into trouble as a child, when I often lost my temper and lashed out at my siblings. As a middle child of 5, I was sandwiched between my two amazing older sisters, Dr. Adaora Okonkwo Ogbuefi and Prof. Una Osili who could do no wrong. They were my earliest role models and continue to inspire and challenge me today! I also had two younger siblings – a sister and a brother, who were simply adorable. That made me a freedom fighter at a very young age, always looking for a way to have my voice heard and expressing that through rage. My mother used to say I would end up in jail by 15 if I didn't sort out my temper. Thankfully, she taught me how to channel it into positive change. This anger has now propelled me to champion causes and establish institutions focused on development in Africa. It has given me Rage for Change, which is also the title of a publication from one of the organisations I have established - LEAP Africa.

I was born and raised in Enugu, in South-eastern Nigeria into the family of Professor Paul and Professor Rina Okonkwo. My parents, who are professors and worked at the University of Nigeria Enugu Campus were extremely devoted to raising children who were hard working, disciplined and ethical. My parents exposed my siblings and I to the concepts of patriotism and service from very young ages. Despite their Ivy League education, they both chose to devote their lives to teaching in the Nigerian higher educational system, fighting against all odds to ensure some level of excellence in their respective departments.

Following my primary and secondary school educational experiences in Nigeria, I enrolled at the Clarkson School, a bridging programme in the United States, and then the Wharton School of the University of Pennsylvania, and then joined McKinsey & Company, a global strategy consulting firm. I then followed the traditional path of enrolling at the Harvard Business School for my MBA, and returning to McKinsey as an associate. However, throughout this process of traditional schooling and career development, I chose non-traditional roles that expanded my desire to make a difference for Africa. For example, during Business School, I chose to take a summer opportunity to go to Ramallah, Palestine to work with the Centre for Middle East Competitive Strategy. The Centre was started by Michael Porter, with the ideal that if we could get countries to work together and trade, it will foster lasting peace in the region. One hot afternoon in Ramallah, one of the team members asked me: "Why are you here helping our country, when yours is such a mess?" It was a question that really rattled me. It was one thing for a fellow Nigerian to say Nigeria is a mess but for a Palestinian to say so, it rattled me. That had me thinking: "What am I actually doing here helping other people?"

I returned to Harvard to complete my MBA and initiated the first African Business Conference which drew students from across Africa who had an interest in Africa. The theme was: *reversing the brain drain.* I ended my speech with *my favourite African proverb: Do not follow the path, go where there is no path and leave a trail.* After business school, I went to Nigeria and worked for the Ford Foundation and worked on micro-finance projects. I ended up really angry that summer when I realised that the goal of helping the women get out of poverty would not happen because they were selling their products below market prices. It was then I decided to work on entrepreneurship and business development. Nine months later, I left McKinsey which had paid for my MBA, took a loan to pay them back and moved to Nigeria to serve as the pioneer executive director of the FATE Foundation in 2000 to help young unemployed people start successful businesses. We launched Nigeria's first School of Entrepreneurship, business plan competition, and incubator.

Two years later, my anger resurfaced again on a spring break trip with my husband's MBA class in Guatemala. I looked out and realised that in spite of Guatemala being one of the poorest Latin American countries, there was evidence that they had attributes missing in the African context: Leadership, Effectiveness, Accountability & Professionalism (LEAP). So, in 2002, LEAP Africa was born. The vision for LEAP Africa was inspired by God, based on the conviction that Africa desperately needed a new generation of visionary, ethical, creative, and disciplined servant leaders. I believe that a small group of people who shared the same vision could work together to change their communities, countries and indeed the African continent.

Another source of conviction for LEAP came from some of my earliest memories of Children's Day celebrations in Nigeria. These celebrations consisted of speeches from adults telling us children that we are the leaders of tomorrow. However, as I got older, I recognised some of the same faces from the 70s were giving this same message in the 90s, while refusing to budge from their positions to make room for the younger generation. I also noted that Africa was being left behind relative to the rest of the world and that some of the people who lead our world positively started leading in their youth. I sought through LEAP to start a non-profit organisation that would change mindsets about the word "leadership" - from political leadership to everyday leadership. We inspire, empower, and equip young Africans to lead positive change in their communities and countries.

Between 2003 and 2016, LEAP has worked across 26 states in Nigeria providing leadership training, and coaching to 50,000 entrepreneurs, youth, teachers, and community organisers. In all our programmes, we ask our young people: **'What makes you angry about your country and your community and what can you do about it?'** We encourage our people to use anger to do good. To be mad enough to make a difference. Our youth beneficiaries have launched over 1,000 change projects to improve the lives of others in their communities. LEAP has also pioneered curriculum and published eleven books on succession, ethics, governance and management. Young people who have benefited from our leadership training are 80% more likely to stay in school, retain jobs and excel at their careers, than peers who are not exposed to this training.

Our youth Leadership, Ethics and Civics (LEC) programme has been featured on CNN Inside Africa and as a finalist in the Financial Time (FT)/Citi Urban Innovations Award in 2013. We host our annual flagship event - The CEOs Forum - which was initiated in 2004. The CEOs Forum targets business owners and focuses on a theme relevant to building sustainable enterprises. We offer training workshops and resources on some of our core themes: business ethics, corporate governance, succession planning. To ensure that Nigerian businesses outlive their founders, LEAP Africa launched the Business Leadership Programme (BLP) in 2003 to equip SMEs with knowledge skills and tools. Since then, the BLP has trained over 3,000 CEOs and managers on leadership and business management. We have also established eLEAP which focuses on leveraging technology for social change by inspiring youth and entrepreneurs to be leaders through elearning/ mobile learning, apps, video and audio clips. We have very recently launched our eIntegrity course designed to raise awareness on ethics and empower Africans to resist corruption.

*My Rage for Change inspired me to also established NIA in 2002. NIA stands for **Ndu, Ike, Akunuba** which means **life, strength** and **wealth** respectively in the Igbo language and also **purpose** in Swahili. The goal of NIA is to help young women achieve their highest potential.* From an early age, I observed that most female university graduates focused on moving into a husband's home upon graduation and immediately producing a male child to secure their place in the marriage. This trend continues in spite of the high value placed on education for development in Nigeria and the fact that in South-eastern Nigeria, more women are enrolling in schools compared to their male counterparts. This has not translated into better socio-economic outcomes primarily because society still expects these women to achieve less! I established NIA out of the burden to stem this trend, and inspired by many of the Global Fund grantees that I met at the Association for Women's Rights in Development (AWID) Mexico Conference in 2002

Since our inception in 2002, the Global Fund has supported NIA's work on five university campuses – transforming the lives of young women through its core Leadership Institute which includes training on leadership and life skills, discussions on feminism as well as exposure to Nigerian women leaders who are often disregarded in academic and historical texts. NIA has launched a movie series on women's issues, held dialogues with male students, and hosted drama productions on sexual harassment to raise awareness on its prevalence in institutions of higher education. NIA has also provided career counselling and workshops featuring accomplished women entrepreneurs, professionals and politicians, which has encouraged the students to set career goals and exceed the limits placed on them by society. To-date, NIA has held 22 Leadership Institutes on university campuses and has graduated over 500 women from its programmes.

NIA has empowered young women to run for political office on their campuses, shattering stereotypes and enabling them to assume positions never before held by women in the student council, in the law and accounting associations, and in community groups! Through this engagement, NIA has helped young women advocate for change, by raising their voices and demanding a seat at the table.

NIA also runs a Big Sister Programme, managed completely by its alumnae, which brings NIA's leadership institutes to secondary schools offering girls a chance to be trained and mentored by female university students. Through this programme, NIA has reach thousands of women in four Nigerian states.

The most recent venture and evolution of my journey as a social innovator is the development of AACE Food Processing & Distribution Ltd. Unlike my previous ventures, AACE foods is a for-profit. I have come to realise that there is a place for non-profits, but that when you create a profit organisation, you create a sustainable enterprise that can employ many people and you can fund non-profits without being reliant on funders.

The passion and sense of urgency behind the creation AACE was motivated by three facts. Firstly, according to the 2008 Demographic and Health Survey, 41% of Nigerian children under 5 years old are classified as stunted and 18% are considered wasted. This contributes to Nigeria's high infant mortality and maternal mortality rates in our country. Second, researchers at the University of Agriculture Abeokuta estimate that 40-60% of the fruits and vegetables grown and harvested by smallholder farmers across Nigeria are wasted annually. Third, 90% of the processed food consumed in Nigeria is imported and this is true for most of Africa.

AACE Foods aims to directly address the high levels of malnutrition in Nigeria and capitalise on the dearth of local manufactured food products by processing and packaging nutritious food sourced from smallholder farmers within Nigeria, in partnership with community groups and non-profit associations. The company provides support to the farmers, empowering them with training and access to microfinance and storage technology.

Today, AACE offers 10 spices and seasonings – chili, ginger, garlic, pepper soup, suya seasoning (yaji), black pepper, turmeric, jellof rice spice, fried rice spice, yellow pepper, - herbs - moringa, and two complementary foods – Soyamaize, SosoNourish, as well as corn flour and beans flour. AACE Foods offers its products to both commercial and institutional buyers, including food processors, caterers, restaurants, hotels, wholesalers and retailers. Our products are sold in Nigeria's largest open air market, supermarkets, utilized by leading fast moving consumer goods companies for producing spices for instant noodles and most recently the company has commenced exports.

Beyond improving the lives of farmers, displacing imports and addressing high rates of malnutrition, AACE Foods is providing jobs for previously unemployed youth, engaging community residents, and helping create micro and small businesses run by women. Our biggest challenge has been changing the mind-sets that imported foods are better than local foods.

Through FATE, LEAP, AACE Foods and NIA, established between 2000 and 2010, I have experienced some moderate impact at tackling the serious social challenges for which they were established. However, they all desperately need to scale – to reach millions with impact, instead of reaching hundreds and thousands. This burden is shared by many social innovators operating in the private, public, non-profit and civil society on the African Continent, who struggle to move from successful pilots to large scale high-impact and sustainable initiatives.

I define success by the ability of many of these initiatives to transform social landscapes and become credible frameworks that are being implemented across and beyond the African Continent. For example, with LEAP Africa, I strongly believe that if the Nigerian and other African governments would successfully incorporate our Leadership, Ethics & Civics (LEC) curriculum as part of their core teacher training programme and high school curricula, this would ensure that millions of youth benefit from life and leadership skills. This in turn would enable them to make positive changes in their communities and empower them to enrol in higher education, get better jobs, and start businesses.

In order to ensure that more African social innovators are able to reach millions with impact, I invested in research over an 18-month period, interviewing organisations that have scaled, and creating a book to capture these learnings. The book is titled *Scaling Social Innovation in Africa: A Practical Guide for Scaling Impact.* This book outlines the critical steps required for building sustainable business models that scale, which are demand driven, low-cost, simple, engage the community, utilise technology, and measure impact.

It is my hope and prayer that more Africans will get angry enough about the social conditions in their sphere of influence and resolve to act like leaders to change their circumstances and those that affect others. As Aristotle said: Anybody can become angry, that is easy, but to be angry with the right person and to the right degree and at the right time and for the right purpose, and in the right way, that is not within everybody's power and is not easy. I also hope that more social innovators will infuse scaling into the DNA of their initiatives from the onset, developing appropriate business models, attracting and retaining talent for scaling, and ensuring that they are investment ready, in order to attract financing for scaling. *My call to action to the elite and growing middle class of Africans is to is stop talking, blogging and tweeting and start acting like leaders.* More importantly: *How do we ensure our children are not shielded from the realities of the work that needs to be done?* I am optimistic that collectively we will invest in and build cross-sector partnerships to expand our collective influence and impact to ensure lasting change. These efforts will ensure that we leave the Continent better for our children, grandchildren and generations to come!

Ndidi Nwuneli is the Founder of LEAP Africa, Co-Founder of AACE Food Processing & Distribution, an indigenous agroprocessing company, and a Director at Sahel Capital Partners & Advisory Ltd., an advisory and consulting firm focused on the agribusiness and nutrition sectors in West Africa. She started her career as a management consultant with McKinsey & Company, working in their Chicago, New York and Johannesburg Offices. Ndidi holds an M.B.A. from Harvard Business School and an undergraduate degree with honours in Multinational and Strategic Management from the Wharton School of the University of Pennsylvania. Ndidi was recognised as a Young Global Leader by the World Economic Forum and received a National Honour – Member of the Federal Republic from the Nigerian Government. She was listed as one of the 20 Youngest Power African Women by Forbes. Ndidi serves on numerous international and local boards including Nestle Nigeria Plc., Nigerian Breweries Plc., Globethics.net, Godrej Consumer Products Ltd. India and Royal DSM Sustainability Board, Netherlands. Ndidi is the author of "Social Innovation in Africa: A Practical Guide for Scaling Impact," published by Routledge in 2016.

Fatou Wurie
Healing as Building: The Survivor Dream Project

Touching became forbidden; the scent of chlorine lingered in the air as hand washing became the norm. Whether directly or indirectly, Ebola with a sense of abjection and pervasiveness affected every Sierra Leonean. The problems that Sierra Leone faced in 2014 were where catastrophe and need intersected with the call for innovation – a new and sustainable approach to building social structures from the ground up. It is often during desperate and chaotic situations that we try to redefine our place in the world and give birth to innovative solutions. This was precisely the case of The Survivor Dream Project (SDP) when Sierra Leone, Liberia and Guinea experienced the worst health epidemic to hit West Africa in recent history. This is a story of survivors. It is my story as a survivor of sexual assault, and it is the story of the inaugural group of the 20 Women Ebola Survivors who formed SDP. We are choosing to live by **Faith**, **Design** and the Possibility that we can **Change** our circumstances and our world.

The Survivor Dream Project (SDP) is an organisation based on community-generated solutions, dedicated to supporting women, girls and young men who have survived post-traumatic events. Our aim is to implement sustainable and impactful social change within our communities, where it matters the most. We've made use of holistic psychosocial, educational, and entrepreneurial cultivated spaces to support the reintegration of Ebola Survivors and build the capacity of the women in our programme. The nucleus of our work has been about using healing as a sustainable approach to rebuilding communities torn apart by Ebola. Our mission is: *Healing Bodies; Transforming Communities.*

SDP started with a group of 20 women who met on a bi-weekly basis. We organised 24 community-based healing and narrative therapy sessions where we made sure that each woman and girl in the programme had access to psychosocial support. Some of these sessions have been led by nutritionists, farmers, medical professionals, other health service providers, and even a BBC Africa journalist. As a result, the BBC covered the women's stories in a programme titled *Women Who Survived Ebola*. These provided opportunities for the women at SDP to tell their own stories and to narrate their own vision for the future.

My motivation behind founding SDP is viscerally grounded in my own survivor story. Once upon a time, I was sexually assaulted. I want to tell you about the day it happened and about the next day. About how I felt and the days after that when fragments of that day would spill in unexpected spaces and places. And the months after that when I discovered all the creative ways to not deal with or address "that day." And the year after that when I would eventually spill some more onto strangers and other friends who'd calmly, as calmly as they could possibly configure, politely ask, "Why did you go that night?" I want to tell you about how I'd fold into a thousand more pieces because my answer was so simple, obvious in its simplicity. I liked him. *I trusted him.* I want to tell you about what my body did and the ways it broke, bent, contouring itself into surprising shapes and sizes — repairing itself as our bodies often do, only for that progress to be halted by memories that would not repair as quickly. Maybe I should tell you about the bleeding, feeling decapitated, being frozen and shaken all in a single moment or in a series of moments. And maybe if I tell you about being unrecognisable to yourself and the feeling of departing from your very own body as you welcome shame to lay rest on your skin, in the crevices of your mind and heart, then 35 percent would mean more than a statistic to you.

Thirty-five percent. That's the proportion of women globally that have experienced that kind of pain either due to physical and/or sexual intimate partner violence or non-partner sexual violence. Millions of young girls and women either process or don't process this pain. And it is because I am counted among that 35 percent of survivors that I was moved to stand with other women survivors. In Sierra Leone this word survivor was being thrown around like confetti in 2014. Just another term for global consumption. A euphemism for scars, underneath which lurks the pain of the Ebola Virus Disease (EVD) outbreak that hit Sierra Leone. For those, especially the women, who have survived Ebola the real battle began after they had survived. They were left to pick up the pieces of their lives and I was drawn to their pain and trauma from my own survivor experience. I interviewed them to share the stories and their pain. I created space for their pain and healing dialogues.

As survivors of trauma we gravitate towards others. Extending understanding and empathy becomes part of who we have become. I choose to play my part in assisting women and young girls who have survived Ebola through art and advocacy with the hope that something good, something positive could grow. Reaping a positive harvest from an experience that dances with death. Survivors' stories help us understand their pain - to move from stigmatising them to seeing our common humanity in them. It shows us that survivors are more than the label of what they have survived when we hear their stories.

For example, meet Mamusu Mansaray. Mamusu is 30-years-old and animated. We sat across from one another as she described the paralyzing fear that came with her diagnosis of Ebola. "When I began to fall sick I got scared to call 117 (emergency service). We heard that those who were taken away by Ebola ambulances didn't return. And when I finally found myself in an ambulance and being taken to a treatment centre, I was so scared that I would die in the ambulance like everyone else. I was sure I was going to die, laying there in the ambulance with other people who were sick too." Mamusu reminded me that fear paralyses one during a crisis. This is what I recalled after my own assault. Fear nested in every crevice of my body. Fear paralysing the physical pain yet amplifying the experience enough for it to be forever etched in my memory. I remembered the feeling of becoming just another statistic. Then feeling calm in fleeting moments. But soon the tears would appear of their own accord. But for the most part, I remember feeling incredibly scared. The journey out of physical pain was a long and arduous one, with symptoms that until this day appear unexpectedly. The road towards emotional recovery? Well, it will take a lifetime. Perhaps.

Then there was Nurse Adiatu Pujeh's story, showing the strength of a survivor in spite of a health system that had failed her because of poor Infection Prevention Control protocols and training. Adiatu and four of her colleagues, all female nurses, contracted Ebola in November 2014 while caring for others. She is the only one who survived. Adiatu walks with a limp and a spark in her eyes. Meeting her for the first time you know that she is one who beats the odds every time. She said, "Three days after I was discharged and came out alive, I went back to work. I didn't want anyone else to suffer the way I had suffered. I went back to work. Look, I've survived a car accident and have a plate in my arm and I have survived Ebola. God clearly doesn't want me yet! So, even though it has been very hard, I am still here and will continue to do what I can to save lives."

Yet, in spite of her resilience, strength and daring to keep living and giving selflessly, Adiatu still feels stigmatised and shamed. This is often the survivors' plight, especially when they choose to speak up. A conspiracy of the discomfort and disapproval of others that keeps survivors silent. In spite of their pain and heightened social structural barriers, the SDP women are choosing to keep talking and acting to make a difference: "I filmed my story when I just came out of the treatment centre and after that, I could not go to the market for months. Every time I go to the market they call me the Ebola woman. Even at work, where I caught the virus, it's taken a while. I still get the looks". After my own assault in Canada, I was surrounded by resources, colleagues, and access to counselling that initiated the process of healing. In short I had many more privileges and access than many women in Sierra Leone will ever have. Even then, self-inflicted shame prevailed in social structures that either boxed me into a rape statistic or demanded I prove an unassailable narrative. But the experience to this day remains fragmented, culturally damaging, and personally dehumanising.

So our work with SDP is our way of exposing the hidden reality of 'surviving' which is the ability to pick up the pieces of life when all is destroyed. It is about designing a localised programme to assist in building capacity for women and girls who have survived Ebola to become economically empowered. To address the lack of access to quality health care services and to cultivate a safe space for heart-to-heart, skin-to-skin discussions. It is about supporting women and young girls garner strength to push through stigma and not be defined by Ebola, to not remain a statistic. Most importantly, to remind our policy makers and the world that we still fail our women, we still fail to cultivate social systems conducive to gender-based rights to dignity, social and economic growth, and empowerment.

We are nourishing the dreams of our women in the programme. Five years from now, where will the 20 women in the project be? What type of positive change would have occurred? In what part of their bodies and psyche will this trauma reside? These questions for any survivor are difficult to conceptualise without safe spaces and institutional systems dedicated to nurturing them, so that it becomes possible to envision a future where they did not only survive, but bloomed.

So what have we accomplished so far? SDP's community-based interventions are rooted in the belief that each woman who enters the programme leaves knowing that she has the capacity to aspire and realise her dreams, and design her own road map to success. So far we've achieved this by ensuring that five girls returned to school and thrived in their education. We've provided a space for semi-illiterate and illiterate women to take part in workshops providing basic business skills with the opportunity to tap into seed-funding. In addition, we've invested in each woman by helping her co-develop a business plan during the training on basic business skills for their classes on entrepreneurship. These women are constantly encouraged to drive their own change, to tell their own stories, and to shape their own dreams. This is an ethos that underpinned the curated photography exhibition *Through Her Eyes*, which was the first photography exhibition solely curated by the women at SDP. The exhibition was also featured on Pulse Ghana's digital news site. The proceeds from the photography exhibition were used to fund seed grants for each woman's business idea, making sure that each woman remained central to her own progress. The social workers at SDP never envisioned that their role would come to include personally advocating for the women in the programme. They have been called on to mediate family conflicts at the community level and sometimes in the workplace. Each time, they have had to re-create safe spaces for dialogue, education, reconciliation, and healing.

We've cried and laughed with these women and we've celebrated successes, like one of our student nurses who completed her nursing degree and our senior nurse who was awarded the Presidential Medal of Service by the President of Sierra Leone. We've also been present during the difficult times, such as when one woman was still homeless and others continue to live with varying levels of mental health illnesses including depression, anxiety, and post-traumatic stress disorder. We've also developed a more nuanced understanding of the barriers and the efforts required to drive investment in the psychosocial welfare of vulnerable groups of people in Sierra Leone.

SDP's achievements would not have been possible without the generous support of OSIWA and Africell Sierra Leone, who believed in the potential of our healing based approach to support the reintegration of women Ebola survivors into their communities. But we have only started. We have bigger dreams to open our programme to 50 more underprivileged women survivors of Ebola and watch them create change for themselves and their communities as they step out in faith and design their futures. We. Will. Lead.

Fatou Wurie has over seven years of experience in social-impact initiatives, health communications and policy advocacy having working for Options UK Health Consulting, UNICEF and UNMEER. Her passion for gender equity and commitment to building resilient health care systems led her to found the Survivor Dream Project (SDP), a local non-profit organisation aimed at providing holistic support to women and youth survivors of trauma in Sierra Leone. Wurie is an Abshire-Inamori Leadership Academy (AILA) International Fellow, a NEXTe Award Recipient for 'Young Professional of the Year 2016', a 2016 Illumessence Community Builder National Women's Award Honouree and TAB FUTURE 100 Influential Female Students in the UK. A proven leader, public speaker and advocate, she is currently completing a Master in Public Policy (MPP) at the University of Oxford as an African Governance Initiative Scholar and completed her bachelors in Gender Studies & Political Science at The University of British Columbia (UBC).

III. Arts & Culture

Bolanle Austen-Peters
Identity Through the Arts[32]

On the 21st of July, 2016, along with my cousin Gen, I went to watch a musical in London. This would typically be unremarkable. Over the years, I had watched several musicals with numerous friends and family, and quite enjoy the genre. However, there was definitely something different about this one. You felt it in the air, which literally crackled with excitement. You observed it in the almost party-like atmosphere, and it was confirmed in the pre-show announcements - "you can take all the pictures and video you want, feel free to sing along, get ready to make this your own experience, but above all else have a great time and enjoy yourself!"

Welcome to Wakaa the Musical, *runaway West End success. The first wholly Nigerian conceived and produced show to feature in London's West End. A long time coming perhaps, but then it would not even have happened without the sheer determination of Bolanle Austen-Peters.*

The experience of Bolanle Austen-Peters' Wakaa the Musical
Judith Okonkwo – We Will Lead Africa Co-editor

My passion is exploring African identity through the arts. However, even though I always loved the Arts, I started out life on the traditional higher education path that educated Nigerian parents treasure for their children. I studied law at university, and went on to have a career that spanned international law, refugee law, and development work for organisations like the United Nations. After working in this field for several years internationally, my husband and I decided to return to Nigeria in 2000. I intended to explore the

---

[32] Note: This story is based on an interview with Bolanle and quotes by her excerpted from the following online interviews and articles:
http://www.terrakulture.com/austen-peters-living-for-the-love-of-art/
http://www.vanguardngr.com/2015/08/93-days-the-ebola-story-needs-to-be-told-bolanle-austen-peters/
http://www.cp-africa.com/2014/11/06/terra-kulture-10-making-nigerian-art-culture-lifestyle-priority/

law profession here, but quickly decided that I would rather try my hand at something else, and my creative side re-emerged.

I had always done interior decor for my own homes, and given design advice to friends and family. I also loved nature and loved gardening, and watching seeds come alive. I love literature and history so, overall, I think I'm artistic. For example, when it comes to fashion and design, I can easily put together ideas for clothing, which came to serve me well in the ventures I've taken on. In addition, I'm an entrepreneur and being home made me realise that I had a growing desire to create jobs and do work that was passion-driven. These passions led to my desire to create in the artistic space, where I believed I could make a difference

In my travels around the world I had noticed a glaring gap in the Nigerian socio-cultural space. There was no arts/cultural centre that served as a contemporary gathering place for Nigerians to experience arts and culture. So, in 2003, I founded Terra Kulture and later BAP productions. This organisation has become an avenue for me to explore my passions of culture and arts, while creating jobs. The central idea behind Terra Kulture is Identity - how do you recognise a particular country? For me, you identify a country and its culture from food, art, literature etc., and this is what Terra Kulture is about at its core. Terra Kulture has created a visual arts gallery, bookstore, restaurant, language schools, theatre, and movie productions – all to showcase Nigeria and celebrate all things Nigerian, locally and on the international scene.

Today, Terra Kulture has been hugely successful in becoming the cultural centre of which I dreamed. We were one of the first to showcase Nigerian food in an upscale setting because for me, our cuisine is part of our art. Our visual arts also picked up quickly. The gallery is considered one of the best auction houses in the region. To-date, Terra Kulture has organised over 200 art exhibitions and auctions, over 90 plays, 500 book readings, and over 10,000 adults and children have attended language classes and excursions. We are a leading gallery in Nigeria with over 80% of the major and young artists exhibited at the gallery, including: Kolade Oshinowo, Abioden Olaku, Bruce Onobrakeya, Ablade Glover, Abayomi Barber,

Olu Amoda, Sam Ovraiti, Alex Nwokolo, Ndidi Dike, OluAjayi, Sam Ebohon, Lekan Onabanjo, Defactory Studio, Iponri Studio, the Guild of Professional Fine Artists of Nigeria, Diseye Tantua and Segun Aiyesan to name a few.[33]

We make our money from commissions on works that we sell here and also work with a lot of institutions who want to kit out their offices with artwork. Terra Kulture has begun exporting from the shores of Nigeria. I know some collectors that take this so seriously you wouldn't even believe it! I can tell you stories of Nigerian works that used to cost about N100,00 just 4 or 5 years ago, but are now worth well over N2 million or N3 million. Some of the pieces we have taken abroad in some of the auctions there as well, I mean Nigerian art pieces, have gone for over £500,000. That is an exception, but on the average, you find pieces going for £20,000 which you bought here for maybe less than £7,000 to £8000.[34]

BAP Productions continues to grow. Although BAP productions only started in 2013, we have done nine shows to-date starting with *Saro*, the musical and *Wakaa* most recently. *A Fela musical is coming next, which is where my inspiration for musicals started. I saw Nigerians trooping to see the Fela musical on Broadway, but for me, my thought was this is our story, we should be telling this story. That was the day I decided to start doing musicals.*

The experience with stage plays is what encouraged me to move into movie production. As a play Director/Producer, I have always worked with the best actors, dancers, choreographers, stage and set designers, costumiers, make-up artists etc. With this experience, venturing into feature film production became almost inevitable. It's been amazing to promote and work on *October 1*, then *93 Days* with Steve Gekas and International Directors Pemon Rami and Dotun Olakunrin. I chose to work on the Ebola story because we owe it to those who gave their lives to tell this story of how we combatted and won the Ebola battle, so for me its philanthropy. The cast included Nigerians Bimbo Akintola, Gideon Okeke, Bimbo Manuel, Adebola Williams, Patrick Dibuah and Somekele Iyamah and Danny Glover (USA) amongst others. It

---

[33] List of exhibitors originally retrieved Jan 18, 2017 from: http://www.cp-africa.com/2014/11/06/terra-kulture-10-making-nigerian-art-culture-lifestyle-priority/. List vetted by Bolanle Austen-Peters

[34] Paragraph excerpted Jan 18, 2017, from: http://www.terrakulture.com/austen-peters-living-for-the-love-of-art/

was time and resource consuming but productive, and hopefully at the end of the day our viewers appreciated our effort.[35]

Getting here hasn't been without challenges. We started very tentatively and no one believed the concept of Terra Kulture would work but yet here we are. For example, when we started BAP, a huge challenge was the high cost of productions. Theatre was dying out when we started—our theatre productions were mediocre; the quality was not great. I believe this was largely due to limited funding. We didn't have infrastructure. We didn't have the spaces or theatres and the skillset required to drive the process was also unavailable. So, we started coming up with ideas. We taught ourselves as we went and I did a directing course in the US. I wanted to focus on contemporary stories not old classics. The first production was *Saro*, the musical. We used established hands for production and directing, but it was difficult to translate my vision and interpret what I wanted to them. So for me, the production quality was not great, which was a discouraging result at first and the technology we used was poor. We were able to overcome all that to make *Saro 2* a success. By *Saro 2*, I began both directing and producing. Plus, I was making approximately 80% of the costumes.

Another challenge is the prejudices I have to deal with. The truth is there are prejudices everywhere in the world. When you are outside of Nigeria people look at you different because of your colour. When you are in Nigeria men look at you different in a particular setting and women do the same as well, so it depends on the context within which you are operating. People come here expecting to see a man running this. They expect to see most times an expatriate. They do not believe for some reason that a Nigerian woman can run this for 10 years successfully and maintain the standards. So there are stereotypes; there is nothing you can do about stereotyping. Are you going to live your life based on a stereotype? I just move on. They make their remarks, 'oh my goodness I thought you would be older' or 'oh my goodness, I thought you would be younger'. There is always something but I just ignore all of that and get to the point, why are we here? What

---

[35] Paragraph excerpted Jan 18, 2017, from: http://www.vanguardngr.com/2015/08/93-days-the-ebola-story-needs-to-be-told-bolanle-austen-peters/

are you here for? And let's get the job done...that's my attitude.[36]

Highlights of this journey for me include securing our initial partnership and funding with GTBank. At the time, this ground-breaking collaboration with a leading Nigerian bank began to challenge people's assumptions of the place/importance of the arts. I pitched the idea for six months with no success before I was advised to speak to the late Tayo Aderinokun, former Chief Executive Officer, GTBank. He was somebody who really loved the arts and he put his money where his mouth was, so to speak. So, when I met with him he said 'this is something I am interested in doing' and invested and that's how we started this institution. In time, I bought out GTB and regained full ownership of the business.[37] Other highlights include the phenomenal success of the restaurant at Terra Kulture, bringing professionalism back into the arts, building a theatre, and, in the theatre production business, breaking all the ceilings to cut across class for audiences and selling out shows.

Setting up Terra Kulture as an institution has been a most rewarding exercise often filled with adventure, frustrations and triumphs. Now, we can look back and thank God that the institution we started out with has been able to touch lives and create jobs and entertainment.[38] We also have a lot of interns over the summer holidays to build our capacity and teach the younger generation these skills. My inspiration for the creative process and everything I do comes from God. I often see scenes, typically when I'm exercising, which is something I do a lot. For the future, I see a lot of theatres. I see a talent pipeline – we are growing talent for the ecosystem. I see us creating more jobs. I am focusing on infrastructure now, although there is much else to do. People say: why don't you start a training school? Alumni who have been with us are doing well, such as the recent winner of The Voice 2016, Nigerian Idol 2015, and best female actress AMVCA 2016. We now have the technical know-how to do so much more.

We are creating exceptional pieces here, artistic pieces, we would

---

[36] Paragraph excerpt retrieved Jan 18, 2017, from: http://www.terrakulture.com/austen-peters-living-for-the-love-of-art/
[37] Retrieved Jan 18, 2017, from: http://www.terrakulture.com/austen-peters-living-for-the-love-of-art/
[38] Retrieved Jan 18, 2017, from: http://www.vanguardngr.com/2015/08/93-days-the-ebola-story-needs-to-be-told-bolanle-austen-peters/

like to showcase our works. We are looking for partnerships with theatre companies in Europe and America, and we need to export our own stories to a wider audience. And also, Nigerians are so talented, super talented, there is so much more we can offer the world. I want audiences to leave entertained but having learned more about who we are, so they can pass on the message.

To the world, I say, keep coming, come support our shows, tell people about it. The revolution has just begun.

Bolanle Austen-Peters has facilitated, organised, managed, and attended numerous workshops and seminars both within and outside the United Nations system on various issues. Prior to that, she had worked as a lawyer with the United Nations in Geneva, Switzerland, Ethiopia and Namibia. She returned to Nigeria in 2001 as Consultant to UNDP, Lagos. She also gives lectures on Entrepreneurship and has won many local and international awards. She worked as a Consultant to the Ford Foundation Lagos. She has successfully managed Terra Kulture, a proudly Nigerian organisation which has been in the forefront of the promotion of Nigerian art and culture and is the founder and CEO of BAP Productions.

Twitter: @Terrakulture @Bapproductions @Bolabap
Instagram: @Terrakulture @Terrakulturefoodlounge @Bapproductions @Bolabap

Liza Bel
Things Come Together: Tales of 4 Everyday African leaders

I vividly remember the weeks preceding my first trip to Africa, to Goma via Kigali. As I was frantically running around finalising jobs and visa arrangements, everyone around me was enthusiastically projecting their Africaphobia at me. "Don't shake hands with anyone – that's how you get Ebola!"; "Don't wear make-up or skirts – it's not the right place to do that!"; "Make sure you take loads of food!"; "Pack a first aid kit!" Nobody told me to simply have fun or be inspired.

I set off with the baggage of preconceived ideas that others neatly packed for me, a few bags of sweet-salty popcorn to go with cheesy airplane Rom-Coms, and my own story with empty chapters waiting to filled by what awaited me on the other side.

Being of dual Latvian - Russian heritage, I spent a fair bit of my adult life explaining to foreigners that I'm not registered on the Russian Brides website, I wasn't born in Siberia, my dad isn't a billionaire and my grandpa wasn't a WWII spy. As a journalist disillusioned with catchy headlines and hasty conclusions, I have also spent a fair bit of my adult life peeling off layers of cultural stereotypes to learn about deeper histories and practices. As a writer, I have grown to believe in the supreme power of narratives. In the world where technology has overruled the predatory ecosystem, the power belongs to the one who holds a microphone, occupies most column inches, and makes their story heard. And the ultimate goal of individuals and societies is to reclaim our own narratives, take control of them or become the platforms where they can be discovered and enjoyed.

Since the first moment when the inebriating heat penetrated into my veins in Kigali airport, I have been exposed to the most fascinating narratives across East Africa. That day, I was lucky enough to be in the car with a young man of my age, who was part-timing, driving strangers from the airport to the city. He gave me his book about hiding in a tree and surviving the Rwandan genocide. I was honoured with what could have been a fascinating TED-Talk, about courage, joy, and taking control of history through storytelling. Yet his story is not getting the same airtime because of where it is from.

For the three years that I zigzagged around the cities in East Africa, making friends, breaking bread, and finding new colleagues, many entrusted me with their stories. *These stories allowed me to have a peek into the continent, not in decline or on the rise, but in all its unreported ambiguity. The common thread that ran through all the stories was one of leadership and change making, not associated with slogans and banners, but driven by individual energy and determination to invent, change, and influence causes or communities.*

As an Eastern European frustrated with stereotypes, as a disillusioned journalist and lover of stories, my East African experience gripped me for purely selfish reasons. I couldn't bypass those fascinating accounts of individual power simmering quietly on the by-lines of global information flow. They need to be shared to empower each other, inspire or simply unveil our shared humanity in the times when we are focusing so much on what divides us and revert to apathy.

Hence in this chapter, I highlight the stories of four remarkable individuals I met on my journey that inspired me and tickled my imagination.

Story 1. Innocent Balume was born into a musical family and he propelled to fame at the tender age of 12 after recording and touring with American superstar Akon. I meet him when he's 18, dressed in fame, eyes covered by funky shades, and giving away generous smiles to the loving crowds who know him as Innoss'B. Yet behind the bling hides an acute sense of responsibility for the Congolese youth who look up to him and a surprising sense of focus for a soul so young.

How did Innocent Balume, a boy from Goma, become Innos'B, the star, singing duets with Kofi Olamide?

First of all, I was very motivated by the idea of being big and inspiring other young people to make themselves remarkable. In our Congolese music industry, there are not so many young artists shining and it makes our music lose freshness. And then, I have to thank my family because they helped me stay out of trouble despite all the things I went through because of fame at a very young age.

What is the meaning behind the #jeuneleader hashtag on your social media posts?

I use the jeuneleader hashtag on my social media only because I want to inspire young people. I'm more motivated being in this industry in Congo, with entertainment in general. I feel like not many young people are involved. Even if they are involved, they don't shout like the old folks. So, I always feel like if we have more young people in the game, we will have more fresh ideas, we will have quality in everything we will do in the future.

That's why I always want to inspire young people by calling myself the "youth leader." It's not about me, I want it to be a movement. Congo needs the youth, needs freshness and quality ideas and I know this will come from the youth. I always want the youth to understand we will be the ones making big decisions tomorrow.

What is the role of music and entertainment industry in shaping the image of Africa abroad?

The role of the entertainment industry is that it's finally showing the people outside that Africa has a life; Africa is creative; Africa is all about good vibes. It attracts people from the outside. You can't do entertainment in a bad environment. I know that to this day, a lot of people are confused, they think Africa is all about wars and violence. That side of the entertainment always reminds people that Africa has a lot to offer. It's not the negative that they put in the media. The entertainment industry has a huge role in shaping the positive image of our continent.

What does African mean to you?

I feel like it's my ID, it's who I am, it's a part of my name. Calling me African is like calling me by my own name. So it's not like a strange term. I cannot even explain it - I was born and raised here, and everything that I do, in my blood everything is African. It's just like calling me Innos'B and my family name is African.

What is your favourite saying, proverb or wisdom?

My favourite saying is that "change is not an event - it's a process". I love it because it always reminds me that I have to take initiatives. I have to start something from zero and hope it will get to a certain level.

Story 2. Walking through the perfectly ordered playgrounds and classrooms of Bright Kids Uganda, happy giggles echoing from the classrooms and cheeky smiles emerging from the notebooks, it's difficult to imagine that these children were victims of brutalities we hardly knew existed. Victoria Namusisi, the founder of the orphanage, is a mother figure to all of these children, a simple fisherman's daughter whose mission is bigger than life.

Do you consider yourself African and what does it mean to you?

Yes, indeed, I consider myself an African, born and bred in Africa. Being an African means a lot to me; I had to struggle for so many things right from the time I started studying, to this very day. Things other children call rights are a privilege to us in Africa. It's a right for a child in Europe to go to school, while even putting shoes on to go to school is a privilege here.

How do you see your mission as an individual?

My mission as an individual is to give an opportunity to as many kids as possible from underprivileged homes to, first and foremost, get an education. My motivation in doing this comes from my background as a simple fisherman's daughter who has shaken and moved society in my country. Because my father toiled hard to give me an education, I rose to the level of dining and wining with the mighty of the world. I know that out there, there are several intelligent kids who have not been given an opportunity to see the inside of a classroom because they were born in Africa!

When did this sense of mission come to you?

In my 20s, as one of the leading journalists in the country (1st Woman Sports Journalist in Uganda), I realised that the pen was mightier than any weapon, and I could use it to point the masses in any direction I wanted. Empowered with a sound education, I decided to use that tool to bring up several topics geared towards improving the welfare of the marginalised members of society. I believe this activism was the reason the Head of State appointed me a District Administrator in a District of more than two million people. From a simple fisherman's daughter to a District Governor!

I demonstrated leadership qualities and started leading large groups right from my school days so I believe I was born a leader; ironically, I have never written a job application in my life!

Your "reality" is not common for a lot of ordinary people. How does it shape your vision of society (particularly in Uganda) today and its future?

Unfortunately, the society in which we live is tribalistic, colour-minded, looks at people according to where they come from and based on their financial status. It puzzles me so much that form determines content everywhere you go.

It is interesting that although I can't see money in my bank accounts, I'm able to feed and educate the many kids who have passed through my hands. I'm blessed that I can see so many kids from poor backgrounds taking on the mantle of leadership in our country and moving and shaping the nation in a positive way benefiting all.

What was the biggest sacrifice you made on your journey?

The sacrifices I made in resigning from my President's office job included two cars, armed escorts and all the privileges which went with my title. I even sold my personal car and started travelling in public transport which made so many people laugh at me. However, those sacrifices made in order to run a Children's Home - including staying in night commuter shelters in Northern Uganda as I struggled to save children during the 20 years of the LRA War - were bearable because I grew up in poverty.

As leaders, what can women bring to the table towards the development and empowerment of society?

I believe women are best placed to champion development and the empowerment of others if they can fight for the education of the girl child, as education is the key factor. Women should focus on ensuring all girls are in school rather than simply fighting for equal rights and equal opportunities. Even if the governments offered equal job opportunities, who will take them up without the education required to run the offices available? You don't have to fight for equal rights if you are empowered by education. I have land, property, respect and much more without even asking for it because my dad gave me an education. It enabled me to get whatever I want without begging for it or belittling myself because I want something!

A lot of children who end up at Bright Kids Uganda go on to become successful. How do you educate for empowerment?

Most of the kids from Bright Kids Uganda end up successful because first and foremost I teach them to fear God, be hard working, always ensure transparency and accountability in their activities, and remember that in whatever they do there must be a human touch. "Never cease to be human!" I always tell them.

What is your favourite saying, phrase or proverb?

I usually end my speeches, especially during presentations at universities and other educational institutions, with the saying: "If you think education is expensive - try ignorance".

Story 3. Oyin Akiniyi has very short hair. She oozes coolness and femininity. She is a Nigerian born, UK raised founder of The Good Hair Club - that aims to change the black hair care industry. The club encourages women to accept their natural hair, liberating them from the shackles of ideals of beauty imposed by mainstream media. She walks me through the sensitive subject which my Instagram feed tells me white girls with straight blond hair, will never understand.

Do you consider yourself as African? What does it mean to you?

Yes, I do consider myself African. I also consider myself British and I'm proud of being British. Before living in Nigeria for a year and a half for work, I thought I was Nigerian first. Living in Nigeria gave me a greater sense what it means to have a dual citizenship and dual identity. Now I feel I'm equally both. I'm Nigerian, brought up and raised in London.

Being outside of Africa, gave me a different perspective as to what it is to be African; a privileged perspective. For example, I never had to question access to information; in Africa, you have to be in a privileged family or financial situation to access information. In

London, you can come from a working-class family and still have access to culture. I see the world beyond Nigeria, it gives me a rounded point of view.

You are championing the natural hair movement - what does it represent?

In our culture, hair is so important on so many levels. Through our history, it was a symbol of status: what culture you are from, whether you are married or single. It signifies so much! It filters down to everyday society. If you go back to slavery, the first thing slave owners did was shave their slaves' hair and thereby removing a big part of their identity. Now, the fashion media dictates the ways that we need to fit in and what is beautiful. The natural hair movement represents a contrary view of not being bound to the European aesthetic and an opportunity to own the conversation on our own terms.

What is interesting about the natural hair movement is that it comes from the ground up; loads of individuals across the world have the platform to celebrate who they are. As a child, I didn't have an opportunity to see others just like me, but girls now can realise that their hair is ok the way it is and they don't have to change or manipulate it.

How did you decide to shave your hair and what did it mean to you?

I shaved my hair in Nigeria where they value big hair: straight or wavy with a long aesthetic. I didn't shave my hair to make a statement, rather I was in a hot country and I wanted to be less hot.

In Nigeria, people had a lot of opinions – which are expressed whether solicited or not. In my passport, I have long hair and a guy at the passport control told me to go back to long hair because I didn't look good with short hair. Even my mum was put off by it and told me I don't look good with it; however, I also had amazing people who thought it was powerful and inspirational.

At the core, the idea of me cutting my hair was choosing to navigate the world on my terms. As soon as I did, it was weird and looking in in the mirror - there was nothing I could do. Nonetheless, as long as I could look in the mirror, the important thing is that it was ok.

What do you think women can bring to the table as leaders?

Collaboration is what I want to see from women. Men are very good at working together. Women don't have to do it on their own but they still feel they are weaker if they do something together. Women need to be collaborating and asking for help.

They also need to be holding men accountable. In African culture, women are held accountable but we should be holding men accountable for their actions, accountable to their society and not just excuse them because they are men. Men should be expected to work as hard for their communities as women.

Do you have a sense of mission with regards to Nigeria?

There is always a sense of wanting to make Nigeria great and live up to her promise; I'm resigned to the fact that it is really hard. I can't change it, but I can do my little bit by focusing on black women here, in Africa, or elsewhere to the best of my ability. I don't feel like I need to change Nigeria, I feel like I should be passionate about women, support and empower them all over the world.

The more I worked in Africa, the more I realised it's not up to western-based people to say they know her, how to fix her or try to change her. The best thing is to listen in those environments and support them and not try and change them because I'm western and I know better.

What is your favourite saying, wisdom or proverb?

A quote from Harriet Tubman, African-American abolitionist: "I freed a thousand slaves. I could have freed a thousand more if only they knew they were slaves". Often in our society now, where we don't have physical slaves, we think that we are free. We are not critical when navigating the world, we consume the information without questioning it. When I was in Nigeria, I saw a lot of people who would never question the leaders, or system but take it as it is. To change the system, it is necessary to be awake; you have to understand there is a problem. It took years to realise that there's a natural hair issue. We didn't realise there was a problem, but now we are awake and free.

Story 4. Salim Amin was at the wild age of 25 when his legendary father, Kenyan photojournalist Mohamed Amin, tragically died in a hijacked plane. Salim inherited a personal legacy of a man who reported all the social and political tribulations of the African continent in the 20th century and a mission to continue the development of African journalism. I meet Salim during a power cut in a hotel in Goma and I quickly learned that energy and charisma don't always require electricity.

What does being African mean to you?

For me, it's to be part of an amazing, vibrant beautiful, sometimes scary, colourful continent. To be part of a place where everything is a surprise. Coming from every corner, you see something new, something interesting that takes your breath away.

What was the mission behind your talk-show "Scoop"?

I launched "Scoop" purely because I enjoy listening to stories about Africans and the amazing things they've done. Well, I figured if I love those stories so much then I'm hoping a massive audience of young Africans around the continent will also feel the same way. I wanted to showcase the new Africa by talking to entrepreneurs, musicians, artists, innovators, techies...

What have you learnt about your continent and its people from all the exceptional people you have interviewed?

They were all inspiring. I don't think I had an interview where I didn't feel inspired. They were giving me a new perspective about what's happening on the continent and what has happened. I don't think many of them had been interviewed about their personal lives before and it was wonderful watching them reminisce on their childhoods and families. It was like being in the university of life - of the African life.

You have a very unique pan-African legacy inside your house. Your father has sacrificed his life documenting 20th century coups and disasters... in stills and on film. History lives within your family - how does it make you see contemporary Africa and its future?

My father mostly covered the bad things that happened on the continent. Personally, he also focused on the beautiful parts of the continent: the wildlife, the flora and fauna, amazing resources, the different tribes, how people made their way in a very difficult place. I use his legacy to try and make sense of what Africa is today, where we are going. To figure out our future, we need to know about our past - and that's what I spend a lot of time doing to see how the continent can live up to its potential.

With the growing global attention to Africa - how do you see the role of African-bred journalists?

We have to work against the stereotypes that western media still uses to portray this continent. That is our role; we can't expect the international media to come and do it for us so we have to do it ourselves. That's how I see the role of African-bred journalists increasing and expanding. It's telling more in-depth stories that reflect our way of life, a reality on the ground, giving more perspective and context to some of the news coming out in the international media.

The Positive African story is a new alternative media trend (especially through social and online channels). How is it challenging and affecting "traditional" reporting from Africa?

I am not sure if positive African stories are now trending. Social media allowed some positive stories to appear online and reach a much bigger audience but this has a limited and fairly small international audience. In Africa, traditional media is still the dominant way people consume news. It's not changing that fast yet. We need to teach our journalists to look for more positive stories.

What is your favourite Kenyan (or any other) saying or proverb? And why?

There is a Swahili saying that loosely translates as "when two elephants fight, it's the grass that gets trampled." There are so many conflicts on this continent, selfish leaders are fighting for power. They don't normally suffer, apart from small scars and bruises, but the grass that gets trampled - it's their own people.

Liza Bel was nurtured on Soviet lullabies, grew up in the spirit of the newly acquired Latvian independence, expanded her horizons at an ancient French academic institution and got into the media world on English soil. She started off as a radio talk-show host on French Radio London, jumped to the digital world at AOL, and went on to manage a peace building project in East Africa before joining Google UK, where she's rolling out a social development initiative. Liza is a founder of How is Africa - a platform for young voices from Africa and an education initiative in digital storytelling. She also blogs on Huffington Post UK.

Mina Girgis
The Nile Project

This is a story of the long, narrow, snaking river, that connects many peoples across 11 countries. The river literally represents life to the countries it connects. It has two tributaries. It is called white, where it starts in Lake Victoria and this white part of the river is surrounded by Uganda, Kenya, Tanzania, Rwanda, Burundi and the Democratic Republic of Congo. It flows into Uganda and South Sudan where it meets its blue twin coming from Ethiopia in Khartoum, the capital of Sudan. The conjoined twins then flow into Egypt and empty into the Mediterranean Sea. This is the River Nile.

My personal story working to connect the peoples along this Nile Basin happened because I grew up by this river in Cairo. I crossed this River every day to go to school. Yet I was never exposed, or interested, in the peoples and geography of this river that I lived by. It wasn't until I left this river to come to the United States 18 years ago, that the river began to mean more to me.

In 2011, after the Egyptian revolution I was invited to attend an Ethiopian concert in Oakland California. At that concert, I realised that we don't really get exposed to the other cultures that connect us on the continent, and especially the cultures of the countries along the Nile in Egypt. It made me realise that while I'm living here in the US, I have the privilege of being exposed to all the cultures of my river neighbours in East Africa. People in Egypt and Ethiopia are rarely exposed to each other's cultures and each other's music. So, I thought that connecting the Nile peoples culturally and viscerally through music would be an interesting way to spark that curiosity and spark interest in getting the conversation going to prevent the environmental conflict that was starting to take place. I realised I wanted to use my experience as an ethnomusicologist to allow people to develop a sense of goodwill and trust for each other before they have to face many of the emerging Nile watershed challenges. So, it was really coming from my work in ethnomusicology that the opportunity to work on the Nile Project became apparent to me. However, if I hadn't been an Egyptian who grew up in Cairo and who was connected to the Nile in both visceral and intellectual ways, I don't think this project would have become a reality.

As an applied ethnomusicologist, I've researched and worked mostly on developing trans-boundary musical narratives that cross multiple musical geographies to tell a story. I worked on the migration of the gypsies from India to the Middle East and Europe. And I've worked on a number of other similar projects. So, when the idea for the Nile Project came to me it seemed to make a lot of sense to bring musicians together from 11 countries, those sharing the Nile watershed. The goal was to get people to start seeing their environmental and cultural connections that have taken place over thousands of years within this environment. I wanted to shed light on some of the ways we can, as everyday citizens in any of these countries, collaborate with one another to address some of the challenges at the root of the water conflict that we are facing.

My goal with the Nile Project work was to figure out how to connect people culturally through music and simultaneously spark and move people to action. In my work researching and engaging with the music of the gypsies, I had learned that we can help audiences understand and appreciate the migration of people across centuries and continents through the music that is presented on the stage. However, one of my conclusions and paradoxes was that, while I thought it was great work, I was left wondering - why are we doing this work? Does it really help us understand these people better and if so how so? And part of the problem is usually that music producers put a lot of effort into creating a product and playing this music on stage so that people can see it and feel it. This creates the cultural curiosity and empathy that makes you identify with a lot of people and start understanding where they come from; however, that culture of curiosity is usually not followed by any experience that allows you to move from the ephemeral space into a more intellectual critical space. I became convinced that part of our role as ethnomusicologists and music producers is really to allow the audience to go from appreciating the music and appreciating the people whose cultures are represented on the stage to really asking questions and understanding better what are the issues behind the music. In the case of the Nile this became a very clear direction for me.

The Nile Basin represents one of the most severe water conflicts in the world. The Nile is the longest river in the world but it's also a very skinny river with very little water that is shared by 11 countries and a combined population of 415 million people. This population is set to double over the next 20 years so we're facing many serious environmental and political challenges in ensuring the sustainability of this system. Unless we all become part of finding a solution to this, not only the politicians negotiating a treaty but also citizens from all these different countries, I don't think we're going to get through this problem. We need to develop creative solutions to some of the challenges that the Nile is facing. So, to me, the music that we were creating was an engine for turning this cultural curiosity into environmental curiosity. This action will lead to learning and that will lead to dialogue which will lead to finding our respective roles as citizens of the Nile. Our goal is that in addressing some of these challenges, being inspired by musicians we see on stage, and developing these collaborations and dialogues we can come up with new projects of our own.

So over the past five years, we have been investigating what the Nile means to people from the Nile Basin as a starting point to this dialogue and solution-finding. What the Nile means is really hard to put in words and I think that's what music does so well. It expresses what the Nile means to us in a very open and less abstract manner. When you ask people what the name means to them they will say life or love or belonging or identity. When you look at Egyptian history, for example, and how intertwined the Nile is with everything there, the Nile is literally everything; it is the reason why Egypt exists. So, for Egyptians to wrap their heads around what the Nile means to them is quite a daunting task and, in a way, I think that is the realm of music: to express what we cannot express in words. Even for me, it's hard to say and that is where I shy away because I think I will be saying words which may not fully express what I feel. I would say, however, that part of what the Nile means to me is motherhood. That's definitely one I've been thinking about for some time - the gender of the river. The Nile for Egyptians is a very feminine force. It's a source of fertility. It's the source of life. The ancient Egyptian god of the Nile is also the ancient Egyptian god of fertility and life. The ankh which is the worldwide symbol of femininity is the Key of Life and key of the Nile. So, I think understanding what the Nile means has significance beyond Egypt or East/Central Africa to across the world. For example, the Nile was the ecosystem that inspired the idea of the afterlife and many of the ideas that we all live by today. So I think looking at how much the Nile has influenced and affected the whole world and the world's religions is quite important.

To-date, the Nile Project has established and influenced understanding and action related to the future of the Nile Basin and its peoples. We are a non-profit and have three programme areas. We have a music programme which is what most people know about us. Our first gathering was in Aswan in 2013, where we brought together Nile citizens from different countries to work on a common project. We brought together 18 musicians for 2 weeks and engaged in a number of music workshops. At these events, we taught each other not only about our respective musical traditions but also composed and wrote new music that combines many of these elements; we then performed this music live and toured and recorded it into an album. Every year since then, we've had an annual musicians' gathering that takes place in one of the Nile countries. Over the years, this collective has expanded to include more and more musicians representing more and more cultures in the Nile Basin. We now have 35 musicians in this collective which meets every year to tour. We have toured in the US, in Europe, and in Africa.

We also have a community music programme aspect to what we do. It's called the Nile choir and it's really allowing amateur professional musicians from different Nile communities to participate in the same collaborative. We wanted to create a more accessible opportunity for people who want to engage in the same music creative process, but are not necessarily professional musicians. These are people that we wouldn't be able to sponsor to fly out to a different country every year or pay them to create this music. We wanted to allow that access to the different communities so that there would be a way for ordinary Nile citizens who are really interested in expressing their relationship with their river to create this music with like-minded peers and experience a sense of community. So, we started this choir back in April 2016 in Cairo as a pilot programme. We brought together 35 amateur and professional musicians and over the span of two months they met twice a week; they collaborated on writing songs that combined many of the musical elements in the Nile Basin. We performed in May 2016 and we're hoping that this pilot will be replicated in many other cities in the Nile Basin so that we have multiple choirs across those cities. And at some point, these choirs will start exchanging some of their repertoires and some of their members.

Then there's our university programme. We try to change people's paradigm about sharing the Nile water from the zero-sum game that is usually attached to thinking about this conflict to a shared resource that we need to find creative solutions to. The question is, after we change this attitude where do we go next? I think that is one of the most defining questions that I've been looking to answer with this project. In this case, we decided to focus mainly on University students for this work because we are experiencing an incredible youth population growth in Africa. In most of these countries, our population is going to double in 20 years, so where are we going to find water? Where are we going to find food to support this increase in population? We are trying to think of these youth as people who will come up with ideas to solve many of these problems. It is conceivable that if we have double the amount of youth we'll probably have double the amount of ideas and double the amount of solutions provided these young people are properly engaged.

To respond to our youth population growth, we have started a series of programmes catering to University students this year. We have a fellowship programme starting with 24 students from six universities in six cities in the Nile basin. We are working with universities in Cairo and Aswan, Egypt, in Bahir-Dar, Ethiopia, in Nairobi, Kenya, in Kampala, Uganda, and in Dar-es-Salaam, Tanzania. These students in each of these cities will establish Nile project chapters on their campuses. These will be like student clubs that operate at the intersection of water diplomacy, environmental innovation, and cross-cultural dialogue. They will engage other interested students and work on projects specifically focused on the water-food nexus. They will work on food sustainability questions related to the Nile Basin to come up with local innovations in each of these different communities and work on it in coordination with one another. We are creating a network across these different countries to allow these students to think and act locally but also to put it in a watershed wide context. We want them to think about how these ideas will serve the local community and either be scaled across the other countries or how each country can benefit from the work that is happening in all these different Nile project chapters.

Thirdly, we have launched a collaborative network. It is an invitation only, exclusive network of experts, scholars, policymakers, CEOs of companies, and executive directors of NGOs working in various ways to address the food sustainability question in the Nile basin. It was started with our first meeting of Nile scholars, professors of universities in the Nile basin, that were looking at opportunities for collaborative research among the different universities. We are establishing a Nile Academic Association that will be producing multidisciplinary academic meetings; not just the hydrologists and irrigation people, but also a lot of work on climate change, on culture of food, on trade and so on. We are really trying to look at the large map that connects all of these different issues and find ways of developing the agendas for high-level discourse.

We are having different kinds of impact with this work. The music work and classes especially are having a pretty profound impact not just on audiences in the Nile Basin but also elsewhere. First, *I think the idea of the Nile project itself is a bit counterintuitive to many people. Most of the world thinks of Africa in a lateral geographic sense. When we think of Africa, we think of North Africa and sub-Saharan Africa and most people don't really think about Africa in a vertical way. So the Nile challenges that paradigm. It forces people, to rethink that paradigm and to see the validity of Egypt related to Burundi or Rwanda.* That is not something that we grew up with. I think that there is a lot of basic geographical misunderstanding overwhelmingly present in many of the countries in the Nile Basin, let alone the United States or Canada. Most people don't even know the names of the Nile countries that together make up the geography of this watershed. So I think that music is an interesting way to humanise the interest and to get people to start seeing the connections that are happening across all of these different countries. In that sense, I think that the project has had a pretty profound impact.

Second, over the past three to four years when we've seen some of the most severe water conflict moments and flash points in the history of the Nile, the Nile project has remained a voice of collaboration and of cooperation and dialogue. Citizens in Ethiopia, Sudan, and Egypt have been engaged in heated conversations about whose water it is. Who has the right to build a dam, and who doesn't? Ethiopia is building the largest hydroelectric dam in Africa on the Blue Nile. The Blue Nile is the source of 85% of the water that reaches Sudan and Egypt and is the only source of fresh water for those two countries. So in the case of Sudan and Egypt, there's a lot of survival instincts that happen when you feel like your water will be controlled elsewhere and you might not have the same amount of water that you rely on to survive. There's also a large amount of frustration from upstream countries whose development has been stunted by difficulties in accessing funds from former colonial powers to develop these dams over the last few decades. On the other hand, there are concerns by the downstream countries as they feel threatened by these developments. So that's a lot that needs to be healed, to be processed, and to be thought about in a new light. This will not happen from hydro-political arguments about whose water it is. That just doesn't get us anywhere. The work of Nile Project transforms that narrative to provide an alternative way of seeing the problem and seeing the possible solutions. It has been helpful for some people and that's really what the Nile Project is about.

Our impact can be seen in the growth of our projects, but with music the impact is so ephemeral. People come to you and they are crying and that's as concrete as it gets. People say, this is the most hopeful concert I have been to in the last five years in Egypt. When we had our first concert in Aswan, the Nubian community there was double the amount of people than the theatre could accommodate. People were singing our songs all the next day all over Aswan and holding posters and it was such a profound moment because the Nubian Community has been historically marginalised. The hydro dam that is being built in the south of Egypt to make space for the water reservoir is at the very location of their ancestral homes. To see that the Nile Project, this organisation that is about the Nile, has prioritised Aswan as the place where we started was a really important moment for them. Our impact has also been felt in California; during the drought last year we toured UC Berkeley, Stanford, and Los Angeles, which were addressing many of the same questions as we do along the Nile. This year well be going to North Carolina and talking to many of the universities there that are really concerned about questions of

African identity and the Black Lives Matter movement. We are looking at the Nile Project as a way to allow us to process many questions related to African identity and to what it means to be an African.

I have been doing nothing else the past five years and have learned a lot about the Nile itself. I've grown as a person in my ideas, the development of those ideas, and making them possible. I started with a crazy idea of creating a floating raft made out of plastic water bottles and using this raft as a stage to go up and down the Nile to play to these different communities who will come sit on the banks of the river, enjoying the music. It's turned into quite a learning process not just translating music but also translating complex environmental, historical, and political concepts to people in different countries. I was living in San Francisco and started a community World Music School there in 2009, but the main catalyst for starting on this path was the revolution happened in Egypt in 2011. I was really inspired by what was happening and I decided to close the school and go back to Egypt to see how I fit into the craziness of what was happening there. The Nile Project was a really interesting vehicle to allow me to engage in something very real that is always going to be relevant to Egypt, that has political dimension, yet it is also very close to what I do and very close to where I can apply all of my skills and experiences. The last five years have really helped me understand what it means to be an Egyptian and an Egyptian in the diaspora making a contribution.

I see the Nile Project maturing a bit more in the future. I think we are on our way to making the work stronger and more relevant. The music is just a spark that will get the inspiration going and get people to start looking at the Nile differently, but unless they do something different about it there will be no real change. I think that the university programme is the movement that will be sustainable beyond the music. This is the next stage that we are putting into effect to see if this can be self-sustaining. The proof will be in seeing if the work resonates enough with people in those different countries that they would be willing to put the effort into making it happen as opposed to a small non-profit based in San Francisco carrying this work and trying to spread this message across the world.

An ethnomusicologist with a background in hospitality , Mina Girgis explores new ways to cultivate environments conducive to learning, making, and experiencing music. He specialises in curating and producing innovative musical collaborations across diverse styles. Mina earned his bachelor in Hospitality Administration from Florida State University.

Ricardo Pinto Jorge
Pilot-Slash-Artist: We are all Kaleidoscopes

Who am I? I hope I don't end up sounding crazy as I am made up of many different people. I am Ricardo. I am Mozambican. I am a pilot-slash-artist. I am interested in many different things and I'm someone who enjoys and gets really engaged in what I do. I wish I could be more, do more, but with the limited time I have, I just try to do what I love, and love what I do. I hope to give you a feel for the many different parts that make up the whole Ricardo; and to give you permission to be a human with many personalities within you.

First, I would like to share my perspectives from flying. I fly professionally, which is amazing because I get paid to do something I really love doing. And although I think it is fun, I don't want to underplay how meaningful the work is to me. It isn't a walk in the park, and it has and continues to require dedication and sacrifice, but I really appreciate the opportunity to dedicate myself to something so magical and rewarding.

I've always looked up to my parents, and this all began with my dad – he is also a pilot and as a child I would see him come home and leave for work; I'd travel with him and was fascinated by all the people dressed in the same uniform, working together to get the plane off the ground. My first experience of a real cockpit was in a Boeing 737 when I was six. I watched the bright lights and switches, and out of the window of the plane I could see the stars in the night sky. It made a real impression on me to see the sky from a different perspective. It is still such a vivid memory, and now I fly that same aircraft, the 737; such a beautiful plane, so I am always reminded that I am now doing what I've dreamt of since I was a child.

I don't say this because it's the right thing to say, but this is truly what I envisaged for myself. I feel it's a privilege. And it brings me such perspective. I still love looking at the sky and travelling – I am enamoured with the concept of flight. Not necessarily moving from place to place, but more the idea of moving through space. The only thing that could top this would be to be an astronaut!

I decided I wanted to really do this at 13 – I was never a super bright student, but understood what the requirements would be. I negotiated with my parents that they would support me in training as a pilot, if I first got a degree as a back-up. I think that's a very common thing in our society to have a back-up plan, something solid in case the other plan doesn't work out. And although I now believe that back-up plans aren't necessary, and getting a degree wouldn't be my personal approach, I was not against it at the time. Everyone has a way of manoeuvring through life, we are all uniquely the same and different... and this was their way of doing the best for me. So, I agreed with them, applied to universities in the United States of America, to do a Business Administration course (it was just a generic choice) even though I didn't really want to do it, and although I got in, I didn't get a visa. So instead I applied and got into a marketing course at the University of Pretoria.

I did my first year of the Bachelors Marketing Management degree, but I was unmotivated to apply myself in the course and so after an unsuccessful first year I returned home and had a discussion with my parents about what I really wanted to do. And the answer was clear to me - fly. I wanted to fly. At this point I had gained high interests in art, but my childhood dream to become a pilot prevailed. And so my aviation journey began, I registered at the Escola Nacional de Aeronáutica in Maputo and was fortunate enough to pass the tests and be given the opportunity to be in a Cadet Pilot Programme, sponsored by the government. Meanwhile as I engaged more and more with aviation, I cultivated my passion for art and invested time in researching, reading, discovering, and started painting extensively during my free time. The initial part of the ATPL (Airline Transport Pilot License) course came to a halt in Maputo and we eventually headed to South Africa to complete it.

I spent 10 months at the 43 Air School, became a commercial pilot, and have flown two aircrafts professionally - the Bombardier Q400 and the Boeing 737 Classic and New Generation series - which has turned out to be an unreal experience. I think flying is amazing. There is so much going on, so much that comes together, in such a stunning way. When you study aviation you get to focus on such a breadth of topics: human performance (biology, how the human body behaves), meteorology, electrical, pneumatic and hydraulic systems, and so on. And everyday when you get up and go to work, all of it comes together. You constantly have to look at yourself and your environment: am I eating properly so I can be healthy in my career? What's the weather like today and how might that affect my flight? There are so many elements involved, even in a short one-hour flight from Maputo to Beira, to take people, mail, cargo from one place to another. Seeing all of the things I've studied come together is amazing – I see it come to life… and sometimes I think it's magic. One day you're in a classroom learning about auto landing, and the next day you're in the cockpit watching the plane land by itself. I really enjoy seeing that fruition of a belief.

Second, I want to share some perspectives about expression and exploring in my other life as an artist. It was during my gap year, before going to university in Pretoria, that my artist life began to converge with everything else. I had liked cartoons and graphics, and used to always sit next to people who could sketch in school. I wanted to do art for myself. From grade 8 I got introduced to graffiti – I. Was. Amazed. I'd never seen anything like it. During my gap year, I was also in a Dance Crew – you know, B Boys – and I used to do graffiti on all our gear. I had the urge to graffiti all over the city, but there was some fear in it so instead of walls, I did it on t-shirts, shoes, and so on. I thought, "I'll use myself as a canvas." And so I started thinking about starting a fashion brand.

I realise now that I have been fortunate enough to be exposed to many things as a kid, things a vast number of people in Mozambique haven't. Things like a good education, multicultural interactions, and easier access to information. So many of my friends are fountains of inspiration – and they are who they are due to the experiences and opportunities that they are given and with which they have been presented. Many people don't get to have that. For me, there's nothing better than having options. It's really unfortunate that options are a luxury; they shouldn't be, they should be a standard. You should be able to be whatever you want – a plumber, painter, mechanic, sculptor; it should always be an option.

I've always had so many options. My parents always asked me, "what do you want to do? Who do you want to be?" In this country not a lot of people get the opportunity of being asked that. *I would like to at least inspire that sense of opportunity in Mozambicans, especially children – to create a forum, an experience that allows kids to understand that if one thing is not what they want to do, or not what they are built for, or feel like, then they have the option to think broadly and do something else.*

I know a lot of kids don't get to experience art. When I was at my Mozambican primary school, we had Art as a subject but it was very formal and not very motivating. It wasn't until I moved to the International School and went into the art class that I had the real experience of art. So for me, part of being an artist is also that I want to expose kids to art, show them what it's about, and share my passion. Art is my outlet, where I share, where I express; I can't really do that in the cockpit. It's why I want to share art: for me, it helped and helps me, and it could do the same for others. A lot of people just work and don't do anything, don't have a place or an endeavour that gets them out of the one person they are or allows them space to process. So, I try to make art accessible to a broader audience. I like to share a lesson that I learnt from an instructor, Captain Tom Gladden, at flight school but I think is relevant in all parts of life: you have to use all your resources and all the resources available to you. Don't be embarrassed to use them; you might want to try and prove that you can do it without support, but really you are just using energy where it's not necessary. Ask for support and resources whenever you can and focus on the things that only you can do.

I want to do so much more, and I'm building the platform for it, especially for bringing art into the communities. I've done a mural in Mafalala, a suburb of Maputo, which holds a lot of cultural, political and social history of the country and from where a lot of historical events and affairs stem. It was part of an initiative by Ivan Laranjeira, for his association, IVERCA. IVERCA is a tourism, culture, and environment guild to uplift the community through cultural events, increasing education standards and bringing in teachers, musicians and artists of all kinds to inspire kids. I have also had workshop sessions with kids where we paint together and discuss the art.

I also use my exhibitions to express myself, in ways which I can't when in uniform as the tasks at hand require a certain posture. However, we are just humans too and so I try to be thoughtful and, in addition, I try to render things in a format that breaks the ice between the taboos of what you can and can't say, and express those things constructively. You're not the same when you are alone, with others, happy, sad, when staring at the computer or when staring at yourself the mirror. Everyone is multi-faceted.

These hidden or contradictory aspects of humanity fascinate me. I would love to study psychology. Why do we have a habit of not talking about the other side: like the side of you that sings in the shower, that thinks about sex, or masturbates. These are topics we don't want to go into, but they are all different sides of us. They add up to one, but I try to explore as many as positively possible. I don't indulge in darkness, but I do say, "let's talk about these things!" rather than stopping conversations halfway. That's why problems aren't solved, we start talking about it but then stop before we get somewhere.

So when I make art, in general my starting point is: What are we doing? Who are we? What's going on? My most recent exhibition, Heands Up!, is about the juxtaposition between our mind (emotions, logic, thoughts, all the stimuli we take in and process) and how we manifest it. Sometimes our bodies will tell the truth before we even know it. I know that to be true through my experience. We are living examples of cognitive dissonance. I had a discussion workshop with kids at the Cultural Centre exhibition space. I wanted to share my experience and my vision and hope that something will spark for them – hopefully it will lead them to become the next Maïsa Chaves, Gonçalo Mabunda, Mauro Pinto or Felipe Branquinho – and beyond that, I hope it helps them really find themselves. I think it's really important for people to do what they love and I'm just trying to share what I do and love, as much as possible. I don't want to be a reference point or for people to say, "Hey, I wanna be like Ricardo." I just want to be a part of the development of my society, my community, and I want to make sure that as many obstacles as possible get successfully tackled.

Luckily, I have had the privilege to work with some very talented, motivational and inspiring people, and they are contributors to the aforementioned development and growth that I would like to witness: Musicians such as Nandele and Chilled Vibes, as well as creatives like Antonio Macheve Jr. and Tavares Belarmino Cebola; I maintain an ongoing interchange with the intent to explore expression and spark fruitful dialogues in order to learn.

For the future, I have some thoughts but I'm focusing a lot on the present and on what needs to be done now. I really love the plane I'm flying and I've only just started so I really want to grow and deepen my knowledge, in order to one day be the best captain I can be. It might take me five to ten years to be a B-737 captain (or maybe a B-777 – another awesome plane). And then I want to pass that knowledge on. There's a lack of professionals in the aviation industry here, so I would like to contribute to that growth somehow. Maybe that means becoming an instructor.

As an artist, I want to keep painting – I would love to have a platform, an art centre, where we can help develop art in this country to standards that I have seen abroad and that can be a home for the budding artists. I also want to collect art, contemporary Mozambican art. The Mozambican youth are really finding themselves at the moment, searching for voice; there is a lot going on and I want to be part of archiving it. I don't think enough is being done to register what's going on here, and I want to help society archive it's emerging history, record it as it's happening. I also want to capture stories from our parents' generation as a way to preserve our heritage. I just want to share and gain and grow. That's the intent. We are such a young country, a young community. I want to be part of positive growth and to create more accessible, effective platforms for others to get involved. I want to be part of that movement. There's so much to do.

Born in Portugal in 1988 and raised in his Motherland, Mozambique, Ricardo Pinto Jorge is currently living his childhood dream as an Airline Pilot. He also engages in a slightly newer passion, the arts. Additionally, Ricardo works as an Art Director for the newly created magazine, Chinguirira, whilst investing his remaining time on solo projects such as Heands Up, his third solo exhibition, and his forthcoming artistic projects, Xapa100 and Bits of Maputo. Predominantly working with stencil and painting mediums, he is also involved in video art, graphic design and photography. Highly influenced by pop culture, contemporary Mozambican arts and his surroundings, Ricardo draws inspiration from life and nature. He intends to continue his never-ending quest for dialogue about existence by creating thought-provoking installations.

Simon Okelo
One Vibe Africa: Inspiring Youth through Music

I was born in a large polygamist family in Kisumu, Kenya, with a dynamic heritage, accomplishments, and controversies. Thus, I found myself in a complex situation growing up. When my brother and step brother passed at a young age my life became even more complex. I was stuck between the relationships of my parents because I became the eldest son. The work of an elder son in my community was to sort issues and take care of people in the family. However, outside our home I was caught up in the violent gangster lifestyle that had caused my brother's demise. I was also deeply involved in community service through Young Generation Centre, an orphanage home that my mother created to serve children orphaned by the HIV/AIDS epidemic in the 90s. I naturally began thinking of my place in all of these worlds that I found myself caught up in.

Sometimes I wondered if continuing to spend time with my peers at illicit drinking dens and causing chaos in the community was the life I wanted. I saw the mob lynching many friends I grew up with. I did not want to die like that so I tried other things like working with kids at my mom's orphanage, distributing milk and bread, or DJ'ing at reggae shows locally. During this time, I was physically assaulted for various reasons. For example, on one occasion I was assaulted while defending my younger sister from being robbed. I was fascinated and tormented emotionally, mentally, and physically by everything that was going on around me. As I observed these physical fights and deadly situations, I simultaneously saw the joy of having a chance to live through my work with the orphans in my mom's home at the Young Generation Centre. I began seeing that I had a special place and a role to play in this whole chaotic situation.

The realisation that I had a purpose no matter my situation made me think that I could change my story. While working at Young Generation Centre I was tasked with literally doing everything, from manual labour during construction projects like the demolition of an old dilapidated semi-permanent building to development of the current school building that also houses One

Vibe's programmes in Kenya. Even though the amount of work was overwhelming I felt needed and useful so I kept working. When the organisation that funded the school building needed someone to develop a similar project in South Sudan they approached me to execute it and before I knew it I was travelling around Africa assessing communities in need of schools and health clinics. I helped youth from Liberia to Malawi learn sustainable building technics and create social businesses to sustain the physical structures we had built. For example, the school we built at Young Generation Centre was surrounded by a trucking business, cyber café, tailoring, and other small businesses that created employment while generating needed revenue to sustain the organisation. These responsibilities helped me realise that everything I had believed I was were things that people told me, but not what I really was. For example, when people saw that my brother was a thug they said that I would be a thug too. In December 2007 after the elections in Kenya I travelled to Ghana and then Liberia. I had just voted and was following up the results through the Internet. By then, I was working for an international NGO as the Field Director for Africa. I was still working for my mother's orphanage, and touring cities in Kenya as a reggae DJ. My DJ group had a weekly reggae segment (on Metro FM, a National Radio Station in Kenya that has since been rebranded) on Sunday afternoons. Our radio show attracted a huge following, and when the election results were disputed and the whole country plunged into ethnic violence that cost the country over 1,200 lives, we used our influence to mobilise youth against violence.

We organised a concert and pushed it through the radio show because people of all ethnic backgrounds listened to it. The concert dubbed "Unite The People Concert" allowed youth, especially in Kisumu to put down their weapons. The success of this event inspired us to do another one and through such events we have been able to create awareness about youth empowerment, and we developed a robust Education, Music, and Art Programme in Kisumu, Kenya that has served over 500 youth. However, when you have been told so many times that you are thug, you almost feel obligated to become a thug and forget the other things in your life that do not equal thug.

I felt that I was going to die really young because I saw most of my friends die young. Some of them were proud of that. I started

151

looking outside of my neighbourhood of Manyatta to see what's going on there. I started trying to read newspapers and other stories to counter what I was being told. As I grew up I became creatively rebellious; I started trying to become independent because I felt that most of those that told me I would be a thug were relatives or people that we depended on in one way or another. My mother was a second wife in a polygamist marriage, and she was not fully accepted or embraced by my father's family. She also faced abuse in multiple occasions from the first wife's family, which forced her to leave our rural home in the lush hills of Nyahera on the outskirts of Kisumu city. That is how we ended up in Manyatta, the largest slum in Kisumu and how we got exposed to thug lifestyles.

When my mother settled with us in Manyatta, we became vulnerable, and we were forced to conform to the living standards of the slum, or seek an alternative. When I organised 'Unite The People' concert in 2008 April after the post-election violence, I realised that I was capable of doing more than I thought I could. That's when I started developing the idea of creating the first music and art centre that would give youth an alternative to drugs and violence, and hopefully help them develop their creative potential, get jobs, and become self-reliant. Today this idea has spread from Kisumu to Seattle, Washington where I moved to in 2010. In Kenya One Vibe Africa runs an Education, Music, and Art Programme, which provide classes in dance, visual art, music production, film production, theatre, and cultural preservation and mentorship workshops. In Seattle One Vibe Africa runs Madaraka Festival that's an arts and music extravaganza creating an international cultural bridge that allows collaboration between Kenya and Seattle while raising funds for the operation of One Vibe's programmes in Kenya.

The way I was able to develop One Vibe Africa's programmes and events in Kenya and Seattle was largely through collaboration, relationships, and financial support that came from individual supporters and grants from Prince Clause Fund and the Paul G. Allen Family Foundation. We have also benefited a lot from the support of small businesses in Seattle and Kenya, as well as artists who have dedicated a lot of time to support and perform at some of our events without a fee or at a significantly reduced rate. I have primarily relied on relationships to grow my vision for One Vibe Africa, and in the process, I have been able to start changing my own narrative. One technique that I learnt along the way was to tell my story within the first five minutes of meeting a new person, and share my vision for One Vibe, and my community as early as possible in any interaction to allow people I encounter to have an idea of my mission on this earth. I also learnt to ask for help, because asking is not being stupid, but an opportunity to learn.

The outcomes from the work I have done through One Vibe Africa have been tremendous. In Kenya, we have served over 500 youth through our Education Music & Art Programme. The programme immerses children and youth into yearlong hands on apprenticeship type of classes where learners train alongside professionals as they produce tangible projects together. For example, students in our guitar and vocals classes learnt how to sing through their instructor, and toward the end of their stint at the programme they collaborated with Nazizi Hirji, the first female rapper in Kenya, to produce over five songs and music videos. The experience with Nazizi allowed our students to work directly with a public figure that they look up to. They also learnt the production process from writing the scripts to raising the funds to finance a film project to marketing the final product.

We have held Madaraka Festival three times in Seattle since 2014, this is a huge accomplishment since the event has attracted over 2,000 patrons and reached over 3 million people digitally. The event is also known to be the only African oriented event in the Pacific Northwest that has brought together artists from the African Diaspora and African American communities. We have also managed to facilitate the travel of over 40 innovators, filmmakers, and artists to Kenya from Seattle to collaborate with their counterparts.

One Vibe Films, part of One Vibe Africa's sustainability strategy, has created over twenty music videos, educational video content, and a documentary. Our hope is to grow toward producing content for TV stations as well as build sustained programming by continuing to produce original content.

The experience of building up One Vibe Africa has taught me to be humble, honest, and open to collaboration. The work is difficult and challenging, especially in the last six years when I've been based in the United States. I am working a full-time job, raising a daughter, and running One Vibe Africa that continues becoming complex as it grows. The biggest challenge we continue facing is consistent funding. *We have strong hopes of earning a substantial amount of revenue for long term sustainability when our initiatives like One Vibe Films, and One Vibe Studio become stabilised, but until then we will continue working hard. Whether I sleep early or late, my goal is to always ensure that I do some One Vibe related work daily because that's where I get fulfilment.*

I see myself working fulltime for One Vibe Africa in the future and collaborating with like-minded organisations and institutions in the continent and diaspora to scale the One Vibe model to other communities. My hope is that as we find ways of changing the narrative about us as African people from the slum in Kisumu, Kenya. We can grow and use the same approach to help other people from our backgrounds discover themselves, get inspired and empowered to develop their creative potential, and also become self-reliant.

Simon Okelo founded One Vibe Africa. Raised in the slums of Manyatta in Kisumu, Simon discovered his own potential in art and music, organising "Unite the People" Concerts in Kisumu in the wake of the 2007 post-election violence. Simon honed his skills in the non-profit business as director at Young Generation Centre in Kisumu, Field Director for Africa for Solace International, and Associate Director for MED25 International. Simon started One Vibe to establish a Music & Art Center in Kisumu as a platform to encourage its citizens to participate in critical engagement of culture, art, music, technology, and education to inspire youth to realise their full potential, avoid drugs and violence, and create a sustainable future.

IV. Healthcare & Wellness

Toks Bakare
On Autism in Africa: Ask Toks

I was only here for two months and I was supposed to be on holiday. I was supposed to be taking a break from it all but it wasn't as simple as that. The parents were waiting for me. They would call me, they would tell me their stories of how they had travelled the world to find treatment, they would ask my advice, they would beg for an ear, they would ask me to meet their friends, and promised to connect me with this or that person. Almost everyone I spoke to in those months of "holiday" admired my line of work; they all had an opinion about how my career path ought to go. They all knew someone who needed me urgently and had one hundred and one reasons for me to move back.

"Move back," those words fell so heavily; it was like an inevitable transition, but one for which my entire life abroad could not have prepared me. The simple daily challenges of no light, no water, petrol scarcity, misunderstandings with security guards and drivers, and traffic jams made Nigeria seem like my return would be a certain failure. So as good as it felt to be needed by Nigeria, I felt at the time that my life was in England.

This story is about me; about how I only know how to follow my heart and about finding purpose, and finding a way back home.

In England, I stood on seven years of work with children with neurodevelopmental disorders like Autism and Asperger's. I was an experienced Applied Behavioural Analyst (ABA), consulting with clients that missed me every day and colleagues that inspired and guided me through my work. I knew my place in the organisation I worked for and got great pleasure from my work. Every day I took home stories of the mini milestones we had achieved in the day's session, milestones sometimes even the parents didn't notice. And I knew that I was making a difference to these lives. I knew that each day I spent with these children, I was unlocking a potential that very few people had the nerve to even conceive. I was happy in England but I felt like there was something more.

Then one day my boss called and said she had a new client for me.

A client that only I could take on. She knew how busy I was at the time but this was important and I was the only consultant to whom she would give the job. She was giving me a client in Nigeria.

I remember my first flight out. It was my first business trip back home. I had done many trips within Europe so that was nothing new and I'd flown home before, but this felt different. As the plane took off from Amsterdam I was overcome with the overwhelming certainty that this was a pivotal moment in my life's journey. I was both proud and nervous about returning home. It was time to use everything I had learnt in England, back home in my country to help a little boy whose parents had flown over 5000 miles around the world to find *me*.

For two years, I would fly in and fly out of Nigeria working with this little boy and his family, training a few local graduates to implement the procedures and techniques while I was away. Each time I would hear of another family, another parent, another child that needed me. Each time I would refer them to my organisation in England but it never worked out; they needed "someone on ground." It was heart-wrenching to have to leave each time with no advice for these parents about who was on ground to help them. So, I started to do my research. I spoke to friends, acquaintances, related professionals like teachers and doctors who also interacted with children with special needs through their line of work. This all helped me begin to understand the system in Nigeria and to identify the need for specialist services. I spoke to doctors, for example, who could diagnose children but then couldn't refer them to anyone for treatment. In many cases, they could do nothing but advise parents to go abroad. Just this group of professionals alone was desperate to have someone in the country that they could refer patients to.

By the time I returned for my two-month "holiday", it was more like a research and discovery tour. I got deeper into the real life experiences of children with special needs in Nigeria. I visited centres and schools, and tried to understand more about the situation and was disappointed and heart-broken. The quality of what I encountered in those schools and centres was awful, in some cases almost harmful to the children. All of a sudden, everything I was doing in England, my career, my ambition to further my studies, seemed pointless. It didn't matter. The need was so much greater here. England didn't make sense anymore, it just didn't make any sense to continue doing what I was doing in a country that already had so much.

The reality that I encountered was this: 15% of African children have a neurodevelopmental disorder yet only 35 of the 54 countries on the continent officially provide services for this population. There is nowhere for these children to go and there aren't enough skilled professionals to educate them. The prevalence of conditions like Autism is on the rise according to the Centre for Disease Control and Prevention (CDC) and is the fastest growing developmental disability. Despite this, South Africa is the only country currently offering a university level course that teaches about autism.

So, it was without much difficulty that I said goodbye to my life in England. I just left. I packed up my things, gave up my job and "moved back." I contacted all the people I had met over the last few years, and just like that I started providing ABA treatment services for children with neurodevelopmental disorders in Nigeria. The organisation I now work for is my own and is called asktoks.com. It was set up with the idea of creating a world that understands autism, Asperger's, Down's Syndrome, and all the other neurodevelopmental disorders out there. I believe that we can achieve change if I can show people the same things I see when I meet a unique child like the ones I work with. I can show people the potential stored in each child. We can educate more people about autism (and related disorders) and show them every child can learn, even when learning happens at the child's individual pace. If we can do this, we can change the way they understand the world and the way people react to disabilities and we can become a society that understands.

Here I am, two and a half years after my return and still as excited as the very first day. I feel blessed to be in my country serving my people. I feel blessed to bring meaning to the lives of people who may have been lost without it. I am honoured to meet and work closely with talented teachers who have the patience to keep trying, matrons whose goodwill nurtures, and with doctors, nurses, priests, and parents who are consistently doing the best with the little resources they have. I couldn't do what I do if it weren't for the ecosystem of people around each child and I'm grateful for it.

Interestingly, in the time I have been here, the enthusiasm from others about what I do hasn't wavered. Almost everyone I encounter has a story to tell about a relative or someone they know with symptoms of a developmental disorder of some kind.

There are now more schools that offer some support for children with special education needs, cooperate programmes and advocacy campaigns that shed light on the issue throughout the year, and training courses are beginning to become available through private institutions. There is basic infrastructure in place such as the National School Health Policy of 2006 which states that school health services are to include provision of special health services for learners with special needs. These are very important systems and frameworks that enable the vision of asktoks.com; however, there is still a huge gap in the need for specialist care and the provision of quality services to these children. Every time I encounter a budding therapist, step into a new classroom, meet a new head teacher or proprietor of a school or learning establishment my hope is that our interaction results in the improvement of the quality of the services they are providing.

As with much in Nigeria, there are challenges every day. It can be difficult to find the right people to train; this isn't a prestigious job and the field is not well-advertised. There aren't many university courses focused around general psychology, developmental psychology, special education, or social care; so not many people step forward for the job. There are personal challenges too. I am coming into an established environment, and asking parents and the people working with their children to completely change the way they have been operating. I am asking people to trust me and let me lead the work. This has been a real learning process for me and in terms of my personal development, I have learnt to focus on what *my* instincts are telling me and on what I am good at.

Despite its challenges, I love this country because like a child, there is so much potential for growth. Working with neurodevelopmental disorders in Nigeria is like building a house. At a point, it was a little overwhelming. There were so many things that needed to be done and so many potential avenues I could focus on: counselling for parents, materials for teaching. Then there were all the information distribution streams I wanted to utilise for education and advocacy: TV, radio, SMS, newspapers, all the social media platforms. But I think you need to focus and run with what you know. For me that is the clinical stuff: singing *"If *you're happy and you know it"* to a three old and watching them copy you and clap their hands for the first time ever, or playing chase for the thirteenth time because "catch me" are the first words this child has ever used in the correct context with an adult. Now that's what I love!

I feel like asktoks.com has achieved more in Nigeria over 18 months than Toks Bakare ever achieved in England over 7 years. We have assessed 174 children, have provided ABA treatment services to 46 of the children assessed and even more have been impacted through our advocacy work. Part of my mission is to help create a tolerant and understanding perception of children with developmental disorders, and to break down stigma and attitudes that hinder our progress. We do this by educating the masses in a very real and tangible way. So, over the past 18 months I have conducted two community outreach projects in two different communities (one in the eastern region and one in the southern region of Nigeria). The first project involved a free two-day practical training session and a free one-day diagnostic clinic for all members of the public where parents could bring their children to be assessed and get free advice. The other involved collaborating with the Lagos State Ministry of Health to provide a free one-day training session for primary health care workers in a small urban community in Lagos. So far, there have been over 15 other training sessions and workshops in 11 different schools; I have made seven public appearances at conferences and talks and participated in three media campaigns for broadcast on TV. But I find meaning in more than just the numbers: because meaning is in giving the parents hope, restoring relationships and re-igniting their ability to believe in their child.

We launched the pilot of our skilled and experienced international experts programme this year. Our first international consultant arrived from the UK to gain experience in working with children on the continent and assisting in training of local therapists. We plan to continue to bring in four skilled professionals per year for the next five years to provide this unique experience for international consultants while meeting the growing demands of our own clinical practice here.

I've learnt a lot about my country and about us, as a Nigerian people. The different pressures we face every day, the way we respond to those pressures, and the way we express our anxieties and joys. For the future, I see many things but I'm unsure about the exact steps. I would like for us to convert our clinical practices into an institution that annually trains professionals who are qualified, capable and inspired to treat children across the country, maybe even across West Africa and beyond. I would also like to see my journey scaled – there are many more that can do what I have done; there are many more in the diaspora that can come home to blossom, to repair and nurture our communities.

Ms Toks Bakare is a Behaviour Analyst, Founder, asktoks.com and Principal Consultant, Bakare & Bakare Consultants. Ms Bakare is a UK trained Behaviour Analyst with over a decade of experience in developmental psychology with children across Europe and Africa. She is a Women for Africa's International Humanitarian of the Year Final Nominee (2015) and The Future for Africa Awards 2016 Prize for Advocacy Nominee (2016). As an independent specialist consultant, she provides ABA treatment and early intervention services for individuals with neurodevelopmental disorders; and collaborates with paediatricians to improve early identification. Much is yet to be done, however Ms Bakare strongly believes change *is* possible through education.

LueRachelle Brim-Atkins
Seattle Limbe Sewing Circle & Pads for Girls

As an African American, though separated from Africa for centuries through historical atrocities, I nonetheless feel a special bond to Africa. I am particularly interested in the success of girls and women on the continent. Guided by this connection and my commitment to the continent, I often reflect on the words of Kwame Nkrumah, former President of Ghana: *I am African, not because I was born in Africa but because Africa was born in me... The forces that unite us are intrinsic and greater than the superimposed influences that keep us apart...We face neither East nor West; We face forward...Action without thought is empty. Thought without action is blind.*

I have travelled to Africa 11 times, beginning in 1978 with a trip to Ghana and Togo followed by visits to Kenya, Egypt, Mali, Senegal, South Africa, The Gambia, Zanzibar, Nigeria and Togo. I have travelled 6 times to Kenya as a member of the 10-person Vision & Planning Team of Cultural Reconnection Missions (CRM). CRM is a delegation of women of African descent on a journey to become reacquainted and reconnected with their African ancestry; taking part in a 10-year participatory action research project begun by the leader of CRM, Marcia Tate Arunga.

After several visits to Kenya, I responded to two requests I heard from school children: books for leisure reading, and the need for feminine care products.

In response to the first request, working with other CRM sisters, I became the cultural custodian for the project that sent a shipping container filled with medical supplies and equipment for a rural clinic and 6,000 books to establish a regional library and supply 6 schools with library books.

On each visit to Kenya, school girls told us that they lacked feminine care products and that like many girls worldwide they suffered indignities, teasing, infection from using rags, leaves, mattress stuffing, newspaper, corn husks or anything else they could find when on their menstrual cycles. There was shame attached to a natural, normal function of the female body. Many girls spoke of being exploited by men (sometimes male teachers) simply because they need feminine care products to stay in school during their periods.

Upon returning to Seattle, I found a large body of global research linking menstruation with school absenteeism, engagement in transactional sex for money to buy sanitary pads, and lost workplace productivity for women. Without supplies, girls may miss a month or more of school and other opportunities every year, causing them to fall behind in school and eventually drop out. At this point in many cultures, girls are then considered to be women, even if they are only 11 or 12 years old. Lack of feminine care products exacts a tremendous human and financial toll on girls and women around the world.

Responding to the requests for products, on some of our trips to Kenya, we women of CRM took commercially produced feminine care products for the girls at the schools we were supporting. We realised, however, that once those products were used, the girls would find themselves back in their original state—struggling to stay in school because of lack of access to hygiene products.

I became determined to find a longer-term solution. I continued to read studies conducted in various parts of the world that reported the strong association between the challenges of managing menstruation and performance and attendance in school. The studies indicated that when menstrual supplies are provided along with education about female health and reproductive health and menstruation, school attendance increases significantly. Open and honest conversations about menstruation, reproductive health, and self-defence would increase the self-esteem, confidence, and classroom participation of girls. Though the topic is often uncomfortable and taboo in many cultures (including in the U.S.), I became a woman on a mission to address this issue with a more sustainable solution.

Many of my friends knew of my quest for answers to the issue of menstruation products for girls in Africa. In 2014 a friend called to say, "I believe I've found the answer you've been looking for!" She pointed me to an article in the *Seattle Times* about a non-profit organisation called *Days for Girls*—headquartered in Lynden, Washington that creates chapters world-wide to help girls gain access to quality <u>sustainable</u> (washable and reusable) feminine care products, reproductive health training, and income-generation opportunities. That day I made a phone call to *Days for Girls* and "the rest is history."

I had just become president of the *Seattle Limbe (Cameroon) Sister City Association*. Limbe is one of Seattle's 31 Sister Cities and one of its two African Sister Cities (Mombasa, Kenya being the other). The 31 *Seattle Sister City Associations* form a non-profit citizen diplomacy network whose mission is to create and strengthen partnerships between Seattle and its Sister Cities. The ultimate goal of Sister Cities is to increase global cooperation at the municipal level, promote cultural understanding and stimulate economic development. Representing the City of Seattle, each Association collaborates with private citizens, municipal officials and business leaders in their respective sister city to conduct long-term programmes of mutual benefit.

In the same year, I became co-chair of *Sarah Allen Sisterhood (SAS)* Women's Ministry at my church—First African Methodist Episcopal (FAME)—in Seattle, WA. I had been asked by our pastor to create a ministry that would help women of FAME and the Seattle community strengthen relationships between women and with God, demonstrate the relevance of the Bible to human relationships, and reach beyond the walls of the church to involve women throughout the Seattle area in creating cross-cultural community. I saw my dual roles at SLSCA and at FAME SAS as the perfect opportunity to encourage women from all walks of life to come together to benefit others without regard to artificial barriers of race, colour, religion, age, sexual orientation, beliefs, creed, etc. This was my opportunity to manifest things closest to my heart—creating cross-cultural community locally and acting globally to benefit girls in Africa.

As I recalled Kwame Nkrumah's words: *Thought without action is blind,* I unilaterally made the decision to act against conventional wisdom that "church & state" should not be combined. Thinking that it works better to ask *forgiveness* than *permission* when doing what you believe is right, I set about building community in the Seattle area to benefit girls in Cameroon. For me, it makes no sense to go all the way around the world to create community if we have not created community at home. Reaching beyond the walls of my church and increasing the membership of Seattle Limbe Sister City Association, I asked other organisations and churches to partner with SLSCA and Sarah Allen Sisterhood (SAS) to create a cross-cultural community and the *Days for Girls* feminine care products to take to school girls in Cameroon. Pacific NW African American Quilters (of which I am a member), Martin Luther King Baptist Church in Renton, WA, *Our Fabric Stash Fabric* consignment shop, and Delta Sigma Theta Sorority were the first to respond to our call. Thus, *Saturday Sewing Sisters (SSS)* was born.

Days for Girls sent an expert who trained a core group of us from my church to make the kits. We took the *Days for Girls* reproductive health training online. The first gathering of the *Saturday Sewing Sisters* was in June 2015. The group now meets from 8:30am-2pm on the 4th Saturday of each month, taking a break only in December and January. Men and children soon asked if they were welcome to join us and our answer was a resounding *Yes*. Later, a friend introduced me to a rabbi who is a member at Beth Shalom Congregation who was interested in what we were doing. She invited us to speak to her congregation about our work and invited women of the Amadiyyah Muslim Community to attend our presentation. Because members of Beth Shalom could not attend SSS on Saturday, we added a monthly session on a weekday evening at Beth Shalom where we are joined by some from our First AME gathering and women from Amaddiyah Muslim Community.

SSS quickly became a multi-cultural / multi-ethnic / multi-generational / multi-religious (or not) group of women, men, and children who were determined to help girls in Africa stay in school. People across the U.S.—from as far away as Michigan, Missouri, New Jersey, and California, heard about the work of SSS and sent financial contributions for supplies and shipping as well as donations of wash cloths, fabric, and Zip-Lock bags.

Our community has continued to expand as those who are active in SSS tell almost everyone they know: neighbours, family, seat mates on planes, and people they meet in stores. Few escape hearing our stories. Many who had given up on church attendance felt energised again, saying they "sew and worship at First AME". Because people in the Seattle area are excited to be a part of this work, membership in *Seattle Limbe Sister City Association* increased from 12 members to 101 and continues to grow. SLSCA now boasts the largest membership of all of Seattle's Sister City Associations. The SLSCA goal for 2017 is 250 members. There are now over 150 women, men, and children who come to First AME Church on Saturdays to create kits. We decided to change our name from *Saturday Sewing Sisters* to *Seattle Limbe Sewing Circle* to reflect the increasing diversity of participants.

There have been unexpected blessings as people respond to our work. Two Sewing Circle participants open their home on Mondays for others to join them in prepping components for the 4th Saturday gatherings. Several Sewing Sisters are known by first-name at local fabric stores where they go so often to purchase supplies. At least one participant works on creating shields on her vacations. One Sewing Circle Sister has raised money among her friends and colleagues to purchase 6,000 pairs of panties for the kits. People leave donations of fabric on my front porch and send fabric to me in the mail. One member of First AME Church is in a wheelchair and takes two public buses to come to help create kits. The youngest participant is 4 years old and the oldest are in their 80s.

In January 2016, I led a SLSCA/SAS delegation of 10 women to Cameroon; the youngest my 13-year old granddaughter and the oldest a 75-year old friend and church member. We delivered 1,200 feminine care kits and provided training on topics such as reproductive health, dental health, and hand washing to girls at six schools. Delta Airlines provided free shipping for 9 of our 37 duffle bags filled with kits. We trained YWCA staff and volunteers in Yaoundé, Cameroun to provide the health education to school girls. The YWCA used the training as a starter to establish YWCA Chapters at several schools in Cameroon (including Muslim girls' schools). The work of the Sewing Sisters continues to expand in Africa, creating community across artificial barriers of religion and ethnicity.

There is an adage—*No good deed goes unpunished*—which we have found to be true. When we travelled to Cameroon, we learned that several of the schools we visited do not have access to clean water for drinking, for the kits when they are used at school or for hand washing. This means that toilets do not flush and hands are not washed, leaving the school children vulnerable to disease. So now we are connecting with Rotary Clubs in Cameroon to write proposals to provide water at the schools.

On our January 2016 trip, we were invited by new friends in Cameroon to return for a funeral celebration in December 2016. We happily accepted the invitation so that we could participate in another cultural ritual. I led a second delegation of 12 on this second trip, including a different granddaughter who is 18 years old. We took with us supplies unavailable in country (P.U.L.—the moisture resistant fabric placed in the shields, gallon-size Ziploc brand baggies, flannel fabric, a die cutting machine, etc.) and trained 35 women to create *Days for Girls* kits at the YWCA in Yaoundé. On this trip, we carried 1,638 kits and, despite a teacher's strike in English speaking areas, we distributed over 900 kits to school girls in Yaoundé, Limbe, Tockem and Buea.

We use my friend and colleague Dr. Joye Hardiman's model established in our Cultural Reconnection work, where locals begin a project (their "1-2-3"), we contribute (our "4-5-6") and they continue the work (their "7-8-9"). Thus, remaining kits were left with our sisters at the YWCA in Yaoundé for later distribution as their cross-cultural community continues to create kits locally.

We have identified three potential sites at which we may conduct training in 2018 and met with a representative from the Rotary to initiate plans to collaborate on water projects where needed.

Meanwhile, back in Seattle, I have assembled a working board who will do strategic planning for SLSCA and guide the SLSCA/SAS commitment to: continue to strengthen citizen diplomacy, work with women to create businesses that can provide the feminine care kits in Cameroon to girls and women at minimal or no cost, fund/friend raise, and build water systems at schools so that children will have access to clean water.

The Municipality of Limbe includes a recently unearthed enslavement embarkation site at Bimbia, which the delegation visits on all trips. When we asked school children in Cameroon what they knew of who the African Americans were on the trip, they had a vague idea of the enslavement of their ancestors but had few details. As a result, SLSCA/SAS is collaborating with the Municipality of Limbe, the Pacific NW Chapter of the *Association for the Study of Classical African Civilizations*, and *Roots and Reconnection* to mount an exhibit in 2018 of the "American History Museum: The Unspoken Truths." It is a travelling museum of artefacts and storyboards compiled by Seattle Cultural Custodian & historian, Delbert Richardson. We hope the exhibit will serve to educate Cameroonians about slavery and Jim Crow so that they will be better informed about the atrocities visited upon Africans who were stolen from the continent. It is hoped that they will also understand the resilience of African peoples on the continent and in the diaspora and get a glimpse of why it is important for African Americans to "return" to Africa.

Having access to feminine care products is a major key to social change for girls and women all over the world. Who knows how far a girl can go in life when she has an education? In Kenya, we were told, "If you educate a man, you feed a family. If you educate a woman, you feed a nation."

I understand that we in SLSCA and FAME SAS might not change the world, but we believe we can change the feminine care situation for thousands of girls in Cameroon. Indeed, in two years we have already done so for almost 3,000 girls. I am grateful to *Days for Girls* for having developed a model that makes sustainable products possible. We continue to build community in Seattle and encourage cross-cultural communities in Cameroon. By training others in Africa how to make the kits, the numbers of girls impacted by our work will expand exponentially. We already see changes among the women, men and children in Seattle who, because of the *Sewing Circle*, are meeting, greeting, socialising, eating, and talking with people they may never have ventured out to meet otherwise. Racial attitudes change when people engage in open peer relationships.

We get challenged when people ask why we are working in Africa when there is so much need at home. My answer is that we are working both locally and in Africa and the continent IS our home as well. In turn I ask, "Tell me what you are doing here at home? Perhaps we can help you do your work." All too frequently the questioner is doing nothing here and has no answer.

In addition, we also get challenged when people ask how we know we are making a difference. Certainly, we know that we are making a difference in the lives of the girls because they thank us so profusely for helping them solve this problem and helping them understand that menstruation is a normal part of life and that there need be no shame attached. Many of the girls have never discussed this topic beyond receiving supplies from their mothers while others have had wonderful conversations not only with their mothers but with their fathers and brothers as well. Conversations with girls who received kits in January revealed that in addition to the kits being environmentally friendly, recyclable feminine care products are of economic benefit to their families who do not have to buy products each month and the kits help to empower the girls with more confidence to stay in school without fear that they will stain their clothes. Some shared that they divided their kit with a sister who did not receive one and others shared their kit with their mother. They report that they have not had to miss school because of their period.

Just as importantly, those of us who are building community here at home benefit as much if not more as we break down artificial barriers and establish new relationships.

As Kwame Nkrumah said, "*thought without action is blind. The forces that unite us are intrinsic and greater than the superimposed influences that keep us apart...We face neither East nor West; We face forward...*

Who will change Africa? We will when we make the decision to be the Sankofa bird who reaches back to get that which was forgotten/stolen/lost and do our share, however large or small. We will change Africa by changing ourselves. We will change Africa when we as descendants of the enslaved and the colonised lead others to join hands with descendants of enslavers and colonisers and descendants of those who stood by and watched it all happen. Then we will work for and demand change in public policy and private practice.

Some of the lyrics from the musical *Wicked* come to mind when I think of these changes for individuals both in the U.S. and on The Continent:

I'm limited…So now it's up to you …

I've heard it said
That people come into our lives for a reason
Bringing something we must learn
And we are led
To those who help us most to grow
If we let them
And we help them in return
Well, I don't know if I believe that's true
But I know I'm who I am today
Because I knew you:

Like a comet pulled from orbit
As it passes a sun
Like a stream that meets a boulder
Halfway through the wood
Who can say if I've been changed for the better?
But because I knew you
I have been changed for good.[39]

---

[39] https://www.allmusicals.com/lyrics/wicked/forgood.htm

Founder and Principal Consultant of Brim-Donahoe & Associates, LueRachelle Brim-Atkins has more than 30 years' experience working in organisation development and training in the public, private and non-profit sectors. Since 1988, she has designed customised, comprehensive training and education programmes that focus on leadership, management, cultural competence, diversity, and social change. She helps organisations become culturally responsive, actively reflect their stated values, and achieve their desired vision. She has spent time in 17 countries, thereby enhancing her ability to truly understand the struggle to become culturally responsive. To learn more and to contribute to the work of *Seattle Limbe Sewing Circle*, visit www.seattlelimbe.org or contact LueRachelle Brim-Atkins at BDA6@aol.com.

Pablo Imani
Yoga? African?

One day in 2006 I had a car crash. A head-on collision. I was in a small car and I hit a 7-seater car head-on. The police and the paramedics came and I got out of the car; my children were in the back seat and we were able to get them out. We were all unscathed. The car, however, was a wreck and the windshield was in the back seat. I was told I was supposed to be dead. "You're meant to be dead from this," they said, "we have seen people die from lesser accidents." Someone up there must love you. I was walking around for a couple of days afterwards a bit dazed.

I had an epiphany. My yoga practice was keeping me alive because the whole time of the ordeal I was able to stay relaxed. I had no broken bones. I put this down to two things. I had been kept alive for a particular reason. The reason was the yoga I was teaching was ancestral; it was African and not traditional. *I was teaching yoga from an African perspective. And for me, that isn't just about teaching something that's a fad. It is about raising the awareness of peoples of African descent.* It's about using my example about questioning things and finding out facts about Africa for myself to inspire others to also start questioning how Africa connects to the things in which they are interested. I think that if people of African descent start questioning like this, they will look into the areas that interest them and work on developing themselves. It will allow people to cultivate themselves physically, spiritually, and mentally.

I was born in the UK to Jamaican parents so I am of Jamaican heritage. However, I have a clear understanding that my genetic roots are in Africa. On my mother's side, my family line is from Mali and Morocco so my origin is Touareg. In terms of Africa itself, I was born in this body and in this skin and basically always had Africa in me. I have been travelling back and forth there since I was about 21 or 22 years old, first to Cameroon and now I have been to Ghana, Sierra Leone, Tanzania, Kenya, Uganda, Egypt and Morocco. I studied Africa growing up, black history and culture and African martial arts. I started martial arts when I was 12 and then I started dabbling with other forms of martial arts like Muay-Thai and then various forms until I was introduced to an African form of martial arts called Kazimba Ijakadi.

Then I heard about Egyptian yoga. It's an interesting story how I got into it. Sometime in 2000, Dr. Muata Ashby came to London and as I was working in radio at the time, I interviewed him. We talked about this idea of yoga coming out of Africa and I was fascinated and intrigued by the idea. He wanted me to go train with him in Florida but I couldn't take the 6 months training with him at the time. So he sent me information and I started self-studying.

I had been introduced to the classical forms of yoga before but it wasn't cool for me, a young black man in the UK, to say I was into yoga. I left yoga eventually to go back to martial arts but then I started seeing young men with all kinds of injuries. That got me into massage and kinesiology and somehow that took me back into yoga. When I got back into yoga, I turned to the yoga practice coming out of Africa. I started to understand that a lot of the forms of martial arts were African in origin. I found out that the oldest fighting system in the world is from Nubia. I learnt that Nuba wrestling was done in Africa before the Greeks. I learned that there are African fighter figures documented on ancient temple walls in Egypt. I became fascinated with the idea of these systems coming out of Africa. I wanted to get into the healing forms because of the injuries I had seen in people and because I myself had a bad back at the time as well. I had tried tai-chi and many different things but my back wasn't better. I wanted to find out how we can heal the body instead of destroying it through the martial arts.

So I tried Afrikan yoga posturing for one week and my bad back was gone. It was then I decided I will keep practicing. I studied it for a couple of years and started training myself, while keeping a journal of how it was working on my body. I documented my emotional, spiritual as well as physical changes. I documented the connections I saw happening in those areas of my life and also documented my dreams. I continued practicing and it wasn't until 2002/2003 that I started doing the work of teaching Afrikan Yoga. I serendipitously started teaching because I was invited by a group of women to teach. They had a sister circle and they wanted me to come and teach them Afrikan yoga. After the first month, they invited me the next month, and the next. Then they said - you have to teach - and I said I'm not a teacher.

Eventually though, I set up a class and started teaching once a week, while working a regular 9am - 5pm job and also working as a youth worker. I moved jobs at some point to become a community development officer where my job was to find young entrepreneurs and help them develop their ideas around business. I was going to schools and colleges and meeting up with youth organisations to source any of these young people who had a business idea. And that got me started working with the African Foundation for Development (AFFORD) based in London. They sent me to Sierra Leone and Ghana on a mission to help people develop their business in Africa. My role was to bring soft skills to business such as creative thinking and thinking more out of the box. We would meet up with micro-businesses to do work. For example, we'd meet with farmers to work with them and help them develop skills in their areas of work. I was doing all this 9am - 5pm while teaching yoga classes.

After the car crash, I realised that I had just been going along with whatever shows up. I KNEW that I'd been messing with my life, not really taking it seriously. I realised I have had near-death experiences since I was a child - probably every 3 years - and I noted it after that car crash because everything started coming back to me. I realised why then. It was so I would have a realisation that I had to seriously take whatever my gifts are and use them. It was so that I would take whatever I'm here to do to the next level, to really help people in an extraordinary way. I began to take my life seriously. The car crash happened in January and after that I was sent on a mission to Ghana. I sat in a hotel thinking about my life and yoga. And in that hotel in Ghana is when Afrikan Yoga was truly born. That's when I decided I had to do it full time.

So when I returned back to London, I stopped working. I began to launch myself back into yoga. I started writing a book about Afrikan Yoga and I also returned to Ghana teaching yoga. I linked with schools and started to support children by raising funds for school fees and sponsoring a few schools. I continued teaching and developing myself and breaking into the system. When I finished the book, I had lots of detractors and people questioning me.

People opposed to the idea of yoga coming out of Africa because the field is dominated by the idea that yoga came out of India. *I was told: "yoga? From Africa? Africans doing yoga? No!" I was also led to believe that many things that came out of Africa didn't come out of Africa, and when you begin to study and research you realise and you find out for yourself that there's a lot more to Africa.* Yoga is a multi-million-dollar industry and in North America probably hitting the billion-dollar mark. This idea that it is only Indians and Europeans that can do yoga is incredulous.

My work and what I am doing is to put back that balance and show that the planet is diverse and no one can make a singular claim to a practice that can really connect people to source. Every indigenous culture has some form of yogi practice and Africa being the continent where they say humans walked out of, the cradle of humanity, that to me says, come on, you have to give credit, where credit is due. That's primarily why I do the work I do. I'm constantly raising those questions and inviting people to rethink, to question what they've been taught; to raise awareness. In so doing we will bring more balance to the planet. That way the planet will not necessarily be better, but there will be less disruption and less chaos. People will take care of their own business and stuff and will do it fearlessly, will raise questions, not with carelessness, but with compassion and with love, and that can only be a good thing.

I also had many supporters. I had radio interviews and all kinds of publicity related to the controversy of Afrikan yoga. Then there were challenges, like I couldn't get insurance while teaching yoga from Africa. So, I had to train in the classical yoga systems to get my paperwork. Once I got the paperwork, I kept teaching Afrikan Yoga; now other people doing yoga outside of the country can get insurance, so I have been a pioneer in that way. Then I set up a virtual school and an actual school. I kept teaching and going back to Africa and by 2009 - 2010 the work just kept growing. I went back and forth between Uganda and Ghana in 2010, working and teaching and even did a retreat in Zanzibar in 2010. I started living and teaching in Uganda and working with street children as well.

There's a million street children in Kampala. That took me into training young men. I took a young man and trained him to be a yoga instructor and got him a job and his wages went toward his schooling for a private tutor. He's there now, training other street children. I set up a training programme and had to run a crowdfunding campaign for it to train Ugandans. One of the teachers is now teaching in Uganda and another country. Another teacher has now set up a women's fitness centre/gym for women and works with women in many circumstances; in addition, another is on NTV Uganda presenting Afrikan Yoga on the morning breakfast show.

So, from sister circle, to setting up classes, to going back and forth to Africa, my Afrikan Yoga business is growing. I am developing it as a business, but I am a social entrepreneur. For me, it is about developing yoga instructors so that they can develop and take care of themselves and then teach others. I've trained people in Africa to teach this style and system and this is impacting people's lives as they go on to teach others. In addition to being a youth worker/youth development officer, I come from creative industries with a background in the arts and photography. I was the first black artist of African descent to exhibit in the mayor's office in London. My work is cited in the national curriculum. I bring all of that together with my Afrikan Yoga practice to inspire others to develop themselves. I am encouraged to continue because I got very good feedback from the sister's circle when I started; 13 years on, I'm still getting great feedback. I have become an author and that has inspired others as well. I developed the first yoga app - for African based yoga. To summarise what I have done - I moved into the yoga world because of my zeal and desire to effect change. I felt I was told in my car crash experience, by the ancestors, that I was here to do more. I felt my life was not my own anymore and I had to live with a real purpose.

I also think that life is continuous change and I know I need to keep growing, changing, and learning as life continues to shift and move. It's dynamic in the sense of the changes I've undergone and experienced. I won't stop growing and learning and I have to stay open to that. I have learnt that life is never fixed and I can't expect it to be; it is continuous movement. I learnt to have compassion for people's circumstances. It is not really about saving people; it is about saving yourself. What you are doing isn't about other people, it's about you and a better you is a better environment. I want to go out there and help people but the reality is that if I am not good to myself, kind to myself, loving to myself, I can't engage others effectively. You have to have that compassion, love, and care for yourself. And I'm not just jumping on the self-love bandwagon so to speak. It is actually my experience. You have to start with and love yourself in order to bring that balance to the planet. If you are not grounded in yourself, you will create chaos in your environment.

I have also learnt that freedom comes at a certain price: you have to be completely honest with yourself and others. Some people may not like what you are doing and may not appreciate you doing your thing but you cannot be too concerned with them. You have to be true and honest with yourself. I've also learnt that things come around. Things always work out eventually, regardless of the challenges you face. Things work out - they are never too tragic. If you continue to live life and are open to learning, you understand that things work out in the end.

Moving forward, I am revising my book and continuing to train people. I'm training people in Jamaica in January 2017. I'm talking to people of African descent in Brazil who are undergoing an awakening and want to use Afrikan Yoga in Rio, Sao Paulo, and Fontazela. A young lady actually came all the way to London from Brazil just to meet and talk to me about it. There's also someone in South Africa who is setting up a studio dedicated to Afrikan Yoga that I may support with a series of workshops. *Moving forward my work seems to be continuing and I am passionate about continuing to build awareness about Africa through my work. African potential, African genius, African spirituality, and African healing have all been downplayed and this is criminal to me.* There are a lot of lies spread about African peoples and cultures and part of my work, in this particular field is partly to address that and to present the positive, present our genius, and help our healing.

I don't think I used to have huge ambitions. Now, I have people asking when I am coming back; I want to have 45 Afrikan Yoga studios around the continent helping to develop people. I want them to be living spaces where we house and train people to go back into their communities and train people. Most of the people I'm talking to or working with can't afford teacher training. In the UK, it's 2000 pounds or more and in the US $3000 or $4000. My idea is to train young people and help them develop a system of self-practice and healing for themselves, strengthen their bodies, and develop their minds. That's my vision now. I can't steer the whole ship of development on my own, but I trust that I can continue my work and make an impact. I'm creating a business and structure from a social entrepreneur perspective so that people can live and feed themselves by teaching Afrikan Yoga and earning from it. And so it goes.... on and on.

Pablo Menfesawe-Imani BA (Hons) MA, BSY, YRT, ITEC, is an Author, Yoga Teacher, Massage Therapist, Holistic Health and Wellbeing Consultant and Balanced Health practitioner trained in Kinesiology. He is the founder of Afrikan Yoga. Pablo's lineage comes from various masters in Health, African science, cosmology, and martial sciences. He is a member of the British School of Yoga, the International Association of Black Yoga Teachers, the Independent Yoga Network, the International Board of African Thinkers, Traditional Priest, Priestesses, Healers and Religion Inc. He is the Founder of Afrikan Yoga CIC. (Community Interest Company) He is also an artist and spent eighteen years exhibiting and teaching art to children with special needs and working in schools, youth groups and with mental health groups in crisis.

Robert Kalyesubula
Improving Health, Wealth and Knowledge of Rural Ugandans

I was born and raised in a small village in Nakaseke District, Uganda called Kalagi. I had quite a normal childhood until the age of six years when the war broke out in my homestead and surrounding villages. Unlike modern families, my father had nine wives and we were over 40 siblings living in different homesteads. I was the seventh child out of the ten children born to my mother. When the war broke out we would run from home and come back in the evening when the soldiers had left. With time this became impossible because the houses were taken over and we had to stay in the bushes and forests hiding away from the wrath of soldiers. Initially, we stuck together but whenever bullets were fired we would scatter and lose contact with each other. I was eventually separated from my mother in one such incident but was fortunate to be picked up by a village elder who took care of me for several months. By God's grace, we were able to reach Kampala after several weeks of harsh and dangerous trekking by foot.

In Kampala, I was reunited with my aunt who had nine other children between 3 and 12 years old to take care of in a single bedroom house. A few of my other brothers and sisters joined us after about two years but over 25 of them died in the war along with my father. I did not see my mother until she was rescued when I was 11 years old. During these troubled years, life became very difficult at my Aunt's place; the number of children living with her had increased and resources were scarce. We would eat only one meal a day. Two of my brothers and I dropped out of school due to lack of school fees. Fortunately, I was one of four children selected from our homestead to go and live in the orphanage. As I recall, this was one of the greatest days in my life! When I reached the orphanage (it was called Ambassadors of Hope; we called it "home") I was given new clothes, food, and for the first time in 2 years I had my own small bed to sleep in with bed sheets and a blanket. I was able to return to school and was later selected to join the 2nd African Children's Choir. We toured the United States, Canada and Europe singing and raising funds to help other orphans and vulnerable children. On my return to Uganda with the African Children's Choir, I furthered my education and became a doctor through the mentorship of Uncle Paul Matembe and Mummy Robinah Lubwama.

Once I became a doctor, I made the important decision to work in Nakaseke, the district where I was born. This was not an easy choice because access to the necessities and a good life is easier in the big towns. In fact, the Uganda Bureau of Statistics reports that 80% of Uganda's health professionals live in urban areas while 75% of the Ugandan population lives in rural areas. While on duty in Nakaseke hospital, I noticed a young woman who kept returning to the hospital with a variety of symptoms. I took special interest in this lady and found that she had migrated from Rwanda with her husband to escape the genocide. However, over the years her husband had fallen sick and died, leaving her with three children. By this time (2002) it was hard to diagnose HIV-AIDs but we ordered several tests and confirmed that she and two of her youngest children were infected with HIV. We counselled her and visited her regularly, taking care of her medical and social needs. My colleague, James Sewanyana and I bought her a piglet which she was able to rear and breed nine other piglets. We took this as a good example and decided to set up a clinic and an organisation for people living with HIV and AIDs in 2003.

The organisation we co-founded is the African Community Centre for Social Sustainability (ACCESS). We sought to provide a comprehensive model of health care services, education and economic empowerment in order to alleviate poverty and disease, help children obtain an education, and create sustainable development in the community. ACCESS cares for and supports people living with HIV-AIDS (PLWAs) as well as orphans and other vulnerable children (OVC). We formed a community board to help us reach out to the people we wanted to support, one patient and family at a time. With time, we realised that the needs of people with HIV-AIDs were beyond medical needs and would require a holistic approach. We therefore partnered with community volunteers whom we trained as community health workers. Since these individuals were local villagers, they were able to reach out to our supported families, monitor them on regular basis and give us monthly feedback about the status of each family. In 2006 we were awarded a $25,000USD grant from the Stephen Lewis Foundation, which enabled us to support 30 HIV-affected families.

My own leadership and development journey has been intertwined with my work with ACCESS. In 2004, I undertook a master's programme in internal medicine at Makerere University and in 2009 I was awarded a fellowship to study nephrology at Yale University in the United States, where I became a specialist in kidney disease management. This award came right after SAWA WORLD (a Canadian NGO) had just distinguished ACCESS as a superior grassroots organisation that was making a big difference in people's lives. As part of the award, I travelled to a Peace Summit in Vancouver, Canada. It was there that I met Janice Levine, who immediately recognised ACCESS's potential, and formed Partners for ACCESS, USA, to further help us realise our vision.

On returning to Uganda, I began practicing as a nephrologist and lecturer at Makerere University, and used some of the funds I made to support and grow ACCESS activities. We established a training school for low level health workers called Nursing assistants, and trained young girls who had either dropped out of school or were unable to continue with formal education. By 2011 we had trained over 280 nursing assistants who were working in over 20 districts of Uganda. Some are now even going beyond the borders of Uganda to Southern Sudan. But our early success met a roadblock, because our government soon phased out nursing assistant training programmes in favour of establishing professional nurse training schools. Rather than close our doors, we accepted the challenge to create an accredited nursing school, which was no easy task because of the overwhelming bureaucracy, expense, and intricacies involved. Over a period of 4 years we worked with community members and other partners to set up the required infrastructure. Finally, in July 2015 we were officially allowed to open the Nursing school under the name of ACCESS Health Training Institute (AHTI). We are currently in the second year of operation with 116 students attending the school.

AHTI is now our core, flagship programme. It is designed to be economically self-sustaining, and it holds an exponentially large potential to impact rural populations by returning trained nurses to provide health care in their many small villages. We continue our commitment to support PLWAs and the hundreds of orphans, elders, and vulnerable people we serve with our many other ongoing programmes. ACCESS provides primary medical care to the community through services at our clinic. We have an 8-bed facility that provides counselling for HIV/AIDS, primary care and minor surgery, as well as comprehensive pharmacy services. This programme not only generates revenue for the clinic, but ensures patients are able to access the full course of prescribed medication. Our programmes cover people of all ages. For example, we have an early childhood development programme as well as a Jaaja (meaning grandmother) project to support 80 elderly members of the community. There are virtually no social services for older people in Uganda and yet they are often the ones who take care of the orphans and other vulnerable children. Recently, a 16-year-old girl named Grace Herrick visited ACCESS and was so concerned that preschool aged children were receiving virtually no stimulating activities that she developed an early childhood education programme for ACCESS. Now, 30 children from 18 villages are able to receive medical care, meals, and learn reading, writing and number skills while engaging in stimulating play.

In addition, we have taken on women's health issues. Uganda has one of the highest fertility rates in the world (6.2 children per woman) and poor maternal mortality rates (438 per 100,000 live births - Uganda Demographic health survey, 2011). We therefore have developed a large family planning programme that focuses on providing education and clinical services to pregnant women and their families. Working with One World Children's Fund and Erik E and Edith H. Bergstrom's foundation, we have trained 25 community health workers who provide family planning to over 250 beneficiaries every month.

We now have a global health programme at ACCESS that welcomes students and faculty from around the world. Our hope is to collaborate with our global partners in combating poverty, improving health, and finding lasting solutions for rural community problems.

Through this journey, I have come to learn that once one decides to make a difference they should pursue their passion and endeavour to recruit like-minded people who will increase the opportunities to realise this dream.

Another lesson I have learned is that many of the problems of rural societies can be improved by engaging community health workers. These are lay people who live within the community and are more likely to be trusted by the community members. Once they are empowered with new knowledge and skills, it is much easier for them to have an impact.

Everyone who wishes to grow and minimise mistakes, both at an organisational and personal level, should work with mentors to not only help steer them in the right direction, but also to provide a shoulder when things do not go as expected. Most of the people and organisations I now work with were introduced to me by my mentor(s) in one way or another. Creating and nurturing this network of friends and partners can help both small and big organisations access the resources they need to help make a difference in the communities they serve.

Good leaders must be willing to invest in themselves in order to develop the necessary skill set to help make a difference. Becoming one of four Nephrologists in Uganda gave me an opportunity to spearhead the developments in the field of nephrology. As a result of finishing the nephrology training, I was able to work with numerous international partners to organise the first International Kidney meeting in Uganda. This was a ground-breaking meeting for the field of nephrology. After this conference, we established the Uganda Kidney Foundation to which I was elected the first president in 2012. Through concerted efforts we have been able to increase the number of dialysis units from three (with 12 dialysis machines) in the whole country to eight dialysis units with over 58 dialysis machines. We have negotiated for reduction in cost of dialysis from $100 to $20 per session at Mulago National Referral Hospital which has seen the number of patients accessing life-saving dialysis rise from 30 to 260 per year.

In addition, in my role as lecturer at Makerere University I feel proud to have established a chief residency programme, as well as a post-graduate directorate and a revised curriculum that captures the changing dynamics of patient needs. In addition, we have set up a research database at Mulago National Referral Hospital (the largest hospital in the country) to track 5-year trends in morbidity and mortality rates, all with an eye to improving patient care. We have partnered with several institutions to study hypertension, kidney disease and HIV and I have co-authored over 30 publications to inform the public about inroads in the field. PACT (Partnership for Cohort Research and Training) is a collaboration between Nigeria, Uganda, South Africa and Tanzania looking at non-communicable diseases (NCDs) in collaboration with Harvard School of Public Health. Through this collaboration, we have been able to establish the drivers of NCDs in African communities. As a member of the European Group on Hypertension and National NCD committee for the Uganda Ministry of Health, I have been able to advocate for development of guidelines for the prevention of hypertension and kidney diseases. I am the principal investigator for a 1.26 million pound highly competitive GlaxoSmithKline NCD Open Lab grant we recently won in collaboration with the Medical Research Council, the London School of Hygiene and Tropical Medicine, and Malawi Epidemiological Research Unit. This research is going to help characterise chronic kidney diseases in Uganda and Malawi and will set stage for understanding the drivers, peculiarities and treatments for kidney diseases in sub-Saharan Africa.

ACCESS has grown tremendously over the last 4 years, thanks to our partners in the USA and our Board of Directors in Uganda who worked to ensure that we get the necessary resources. In the coming years, we plan to upgrade the training programme to a diploma level for the nurses and midwives. We also plan to begin other institutes of allied health that will include clinical officers, laboratory technicians, pharmacy assistants and health administrators who are few in the country. The scarcity of professional health workers is most acute in rural areas like Nakaseke - a trend we are working very hard to overturn by ensuring that our trainees have a deep grasp of the health needs of rural communities. We have also set up a scholarship programme that we hope to expand so that girls from very poor families can access this training and be able to return to serve their communities.

To date we have created strategic partnerships with Yale University, University of Erlangen, University of British Columbia, and University of Vermont, alongside our local partnerships with Nakaseke Hospital and Makerere University. With these and many more partnerships in the pipeline we hope to establish a research centre of excellence that can explore how community health worker models can be used to strengthen health care and social service delivery in Africa and beyond.

Dr. Robert Kalyesubula graduated from Makerere University College of Health Sciences (MUCHS) in medicine. He completed his master of Medicine from MUCHS and a nephrology fellowship and research training from Yale University (USA). He has Health Management training from Manchester University, UK. He is a consultant nephrologist at Mulago Hospital, the founding president of the Uganda Kidney Foundation, a lecturer and a member of ethics review board at MUCHS. He is Adjunct assistant clinical professor for McMaster University, Canada and the executive director of ACCESS Uganda, a community based organisation aimed at improving health, wealth and knowledge of rural communities.

V.   Media & Communications

Mimi Kalinda
Moving from Changing the African Narrative to Owning it

Growing up in a family that travelled constantly and having to adapt from a very young age to different cultures at a moment's notice is the kind of story that is often met with mixed reviews. "Sounds so glamorous and adventurous!" "I would have loved to travel so much as a kid!" "What a shame; you must have been so lonely!" "Must have been difficult to make any real friends!" Everyone has an opinion - do children benefit from changing their environments often or does it impede their growth process?

I loved travelling as a child. I loved meeting new people, trying new things and the challenge of adapting to new environments. My family lived in the Democratic Republic of Congo (DRC), Belgium, and Portugal, amongst other countries. I was a fast learner, especially when it came to languages. I absorbed my surroundings and I was in turn easily absorbed by them. When we moved to South Africa in the early 90s, a new challenge awaited me – learning to speak English. French was my first language and I learned to speak Portuguese in Lisbon when I was eleven years old. I had been obsessed with the English language for years, mainly from watching badly lip-synched movies and wondering what the characters sounded like in real life. As soon as we arrived in Johannesburg, my mother took me out of the French school system and threw me into a South African school to sink or swim. The first few months of school were terrible and it took me what seemed like an eternity to make friends. But I had a secret. I was addicted to soap operas and would rush through my homework after school so that I could catch an episode of "*Days of Our Lives*. I was so desperate to follow the storyline that I would watch the show for hours. Before I knew it, my determination paid off. I went from understanding a full episode to having a vocabulary that was developed enough to hold a conversation. Everything else flowed from there. I could finally fit in.

It feels strange to admit this now but my love for all things communications started with *Days of Our Lives*. It dawned on me very early on that media had the power to change people's lives and that stories can, quite literally, shape the world in which we live. I started my career in communications more than twenty years ago. At the time, I could not have guessed where I would end up. From Channel O to MTV, I carved my niche as a multilingual presenter in Africa and Europe. Soon, my curiosity led me to explore content production in New York. Coming back to the continent, I was lured into the world of public relations and now, I own and manage my own pan-African public relations firm, the Africommunications Group (ACG). All roads, however, led to my mission: to enable the ownership of the African narrative by Africans.

I believe that stories shape perceptions and perceptions shape behaviour. In our efforts to transform Africa into the continent we all dream of, it is pointless to focus on shaping or changing the behaviour of Africans without taking into consideration their perceptions of the world – and these perceptions are catalysed by the stories we are told. We must start with storytelling if we hope to incentivise a shift in behaviour. Stories are important and powerful. I am convinced that there can be no sustainable transformation in Africa until we can truthfully share our stories with each other and the world in a way that works for us and doesn't reinforce the hegemonic relationship we have cultivated with the West – a relationship that we have unfortunately grown accustomed to. As long as we are not documenting and sharing our stories, the narrative about Africa will remain out of our control. When the world says Africa is the "lost continent," we will believe and manifest that reality; and when it says Africa is "rising," we will buy into that narrative too, without applying any critical thinking to the concept. When are we going to start defining Africa's rise or lack thereof for ourselves? When are we going to break the cycle of dependency altogether and reclaim our truth, starting with our own stories?

Having travelled the length and breadth of our beautiful continent, I am convinced that the time to "change" the African narrative is long gone. It is time for Africans to fully, consciously and deliberately start *owning* the narrative of the continent.

My business partner, Addis Alemayehou, and I started ACG because we believed there was an opportunity for us to contribute to Africa's reputation as a continent full of opportunities for growth while leveraging our skills and experience in communications. The clients we attract at ACG are fellow believers in the power of narrative and storytelling. Whether they are private equity funds or innovation leaders, they share our conviction that shaping Africa and transitioning from a continent that is "rising," to one that moves beyond potential has to start with the stories we tell ourselves, about ourselves and others. What I bring to my work is a deep desire to tell the stories of Africa's promise, capabilities, and realities. We see enough of the stereotypical images of Africa, and volumes have been written on the subject, so I am not concerned with the condemnation of the Western media or other narrative-drivers who participate in the denigration of Africa's image.

I unapologetically declare my main concerns to be: first, to tell Africa's positive stories of transformation, triumph and success; and second, to campaign for the ownership of storytelling platforms by Africans for Africa's stories. The latter is a logical extension of the first – we cannot hope to tell our stories without bias if we don't own the platforms on which they are told. Take books, for example. Access to statistics on how many Africans write books are almost impossible to find. Hans M. Zell, in his paper entitled "How many books are published in Africa?"[40], points out that "the need for more reliable statistical information about African book publishing output, and aspects such as book imports and exports for each country, has always been chronically difficult to obtain, and the picture has become progressively worse in recent years." Yet, access to statistics of authors from Europe, America and Asia are much easier to find and chances are, they are higher than those of African authors. Africans must start creating their own platforms for storytelling, publishing, and distribution so that we don't continue to be imprisoned by the status quo.

I am passionate about ACG and the work we do because it gives me an opportunity to position our clients' African stories of impact with a wider audience. Our pan-African experience helps. In my recently published book, *Talking to Africa: Considering Culture in Communications for a Complex Continent*, I review how understanding the cultural dynamics of four major African markets (Nigeria, Kenya, Ethiopia and South Africa) can lead to the

---

[40] How Many Books are Published in Africa? The Need for More Reliable Statistics." *The African Book Publishing Record* 39, no. 4 (2013): 397-406.
Pre-print online version (freely accessible)
http://www.academia.edu/4549278/How_many_books_are_published_in_Africa_The_need_for_more_reliable_statistics

development and more successful implementation of communications strategies that are results-driven.

Research and insights drive our thinking; our own African experience guides our instincts. And in all we do, we are committed to weaving in a narrative that uplifts and empowers Africans while re-positioning the continent's narrative. We hope that, through our work, we can bring more positive stories about Africa to the fore. We are storytellers first and foremost. This is a conscious choice in our quest to shift perceptions of the continent, internally and externally. We believe this shift will lead to behaviour change by Africans and our global counterparts that will benefit the continent in the long term.

In 2014, I worked on a campaign, commissioned to a South Africa-based PR firm by African Union Commission chairperson Dr Nkosazana Dhlamini Zuma, to raise money to send health workers to Liberia, Guinea, and Sierra Leone during the Ebola crisis. The campaign helped raise $55 million dollars for the health initiative and also reshaped the narrative of Africa from latecomers to the table to proactive champions of authentic home-grown solutions.

Back to South Africa. More than 20 years since I learned English from a popular soap opera, the importance of storytelling on perceptions and behaviour resurfaced during the recent xenophobic attacks that notoriously put the country under the global spotlight. I will not dive into the murky waters of the socioeconomic and political factors that brought about the attacks, but on a personal level, I was saddened to see that, as in so many cases where behaviour is dealt with in isolation, storytelling was not part of the discussion. Yet, I remember clear discriminatory behaviour against foreigners in the South African school I attended all those years ago. Songs were made, children were taunted, and insults were thrown around with little consequence. The narrative of separation and difference was allowed to infiltrate the fabric of South African black society for years. And we all know that the resulting behaviour was devastating to victims of the attacks on all sides. Watching the news during those dark days, I wondered if things would have been different if all parties involved had confronted the "African foreigners in South Africa" narrative back when I was a student.

What if, instead of watching *Days of Our Lives*, children my age were offered television shows that portrayed tolerance and acceptance of people who come from different countries, stories of similarities between Africans, or films that confirmed that they are a part of a wider African family with intertwined roots that date back to our forefathers? I bet their perceptions of Africa, themselves and "the other" would not have led to devastating conflict twenty years later, but to constructive dialogue.

We have a long way to go in documenting, retelling and reimagining our African stories. However, there is no better time than the present. Much work has already been done and many have paved the way. Through my work, I am playing my part. The ultimate goal is to own our stories so that we can own our future. As the African proverb goes, "until the story of the hunt is told by the lion, the tale of the hunt will always glorify the hunter." Until we insist on owning our stories, our rise or fall will be recounted to fit agendas that are not our own.

Mimi Kalinda is the Managing Director of Africommunications Group (ACG), an African-owned pan-African public relations and communications agency headquartered in Johannesburg, South Africa. She is the author of *Talking to Africa: Considering Culture in Communications for a Complex Continent*. Mimi is a New York University graduate, sits on the Africa Brand Counsel, and is the Rebranding Africa Champion for Africa 2.0. She was nominated for the Women4Africa Awards 2016 as a finalist in the International African Woman of the Year category. From 2003 to 2006, Kalinda worked in New York City as a content producer and filmmaker with Director Spike Lee, and she was the first African woman to host a show on MTV in 2000, based in London.

Nereya Otieno
The Role of the Diaspora

My father left Kenya when he was a young adult. He landed in his new home of the United States — the southern state of Tennessee — in the early seventies. Picture that: a boy from the farmlands of Kisumu, Kenya in Tennessee without even a decade having passed since Civil Rights. "I never knew I was black until I moved to the States. Then everyone kept telling me," he tells me, a weighted smile always playing on his lips.

That line has troubled me ever since he first said it. How does that happen? To *know* you're black? To be told your black? Surely my father knew he was black before he arrived in the land of McDonald's fries and apple pies. He had met white people, he had met Indian people and — given that he is not blind— there cannot really be anything about his colour that became a sudden lesson in the US. As I matured, I came to realise he was not speaking literally about his colour. What he had meant is that he had not been aware that blackness meant something, that the concept of black carried a certain weight to it.

This was my father's introduction to blackness as a lived and shared concept. Many of us have this realisation that we are black in the sense that my father meant it. Sometimes it happens when we are young, sometimes we are older — but many of us do, in fact, have it. As a concept, it is peculiar, this blackness that so many of us share. The French created a word for it: *negritude.* But the invention of this word does not help us form what its essence is. Blackness is an entity unto itself that is deeply understood but nearly impossible to explain. Even the most talented wordsmiths lack the vocabulary to define it. Blackness is a bit like love in that sense.

But it is exactly this force, this shape-shifting, all-encompassing black force that makes up the diaspora. It is from the shared burden, celebration, and understanding of blackness that the diaspora itself is born — how we all form the basis of interacting with one another. It is a unique kinship in that it is generated from one simple yet frustratingly complex factor. This blackness belongs to you regardless of your particular skin shade, hair type or vernacular. Being black is not something you are told you are or categorised as - being black is you. It is not a box to be checked nor an asterisk or footnote next to your name, but a holistic and grounding fiber in your essence. This blackness belongs to you because you know and live what blackness is —which is to say it belongs to you because it is you.

For much of my life, I struggled with this context of blackness as it related to me. While I carried it, I lacked ownership of it. I was struck by how I could represent something so strongly and be uncertain if I was 'doing it right' (before I realised there was no right way to do it and, frankly, we all do it just fine). Eventually, I decided I needed to go back to the source and interact with the spearhead of blackness and the heroine of this anthology. I decided to go back to Africa.

When I went to Africa, I felt easy, comfortable and welcomed when interacting face-to-face with others who did not share my mother tongue but shared this great blackness. If you understand this blackness, this *negritude,* you have a responsibility to it. For whatever reason — and this is a question many minority factions carry but it seems particularly prevalent for blacks — any individual black person is constantly representative of all black people to non-black people. Whether you are from Kingston or Atlanta, if you have a kink in your hair many non-people of colour will take your actions to be 'black customs' or your thoughts to be 'black thoughts.' I do not think this is fair, but it certainly is fact. It is here that our consciousness of *negritude* must be alert because while I — an American black — does not often represent African people when I act, I do always represent black people.

What am I getting at with this? I am getting at the responsibility of the diaspora and how those of us outside the continent can impact and influence the things that are emerging from the continent. I am talking about the duty that rests within our shared identity of blackness. I am saying we, too, can lead from afar because an African future is a diasporic future. For this reason, I proffer these basic guide lines as to how those of us in the outer spheres of the continent can contribute consciously to Africa and her future.

A critical point in the role of the diaspora — and I believe I am speaking mostly to those of us in North America and Europe — is to be supportive and not directive of the practices and innovations being put forth by those on the continent. *Much of the woes and inner turmoil of Africa is caused by the overexcited, zealous flare of outside influences. It is crucial for us, as partners with one another, to take a step back and observe how it is that Africa wants to lead herself.*

As Africa increasingly earns and demands respect from a world that has trod on her so long, it is imperative for those of us who reflect the ancestry that so violently drives us to be forthcoming about our beliefs. And that belief is that Africa simply will, whether you 'let' her or not. It is by empowering and standing behind Africa that we support her. A significant shift cannot be made from the outside in and — though you may be as black as night — change must come primarily from those who have lived the majority of their lives breathing the air. The voices coming out of the continent have not propagated for centuries; the diaspora should set the example of opening our ears first and acting only after listening. Take heed of the military action to 'fall in,' which is to take one's place in a designated position. Key word: designated.

I arrived in South Africa after having lived for some years in Copenhagen, Denmark. That place is not known for its diversity. Now people of all variances of melanin have their trials and issues in Denmark. There has been an influx of immigration that has led to discussions that typically fall between uncomfortable and outright racist. For me, when leaving a place where I was a stark minority, it was a beautiful and blissful relief to be surrounded by people who would 'get it.' However, while we may be on an even par when it comes to being judged by others for the colour of our skin and the kink in our hair, my experience in Europe and the United States is not at all like that of an African. I could not and should not act as I do in the other places I have called home. I am a guest in Africa; I am a guest in these communities and I will wait to operate in the ways in which the people who live there (and know the land and culture in ways I never could) will educate me. I will fall in. Because you cannot make any decisions when the choice is not actually yours to make.

Within our 'falling in,' we shall be diligent in demanding greatness. This call for support is not to be blindly shepherded but to ensure that we are supporting that which can further and improve the state of our *negritude*. Do your research and find the minds and businesses that you truly believe are doing work in a productive way, an innovative way. Being black is most often not reason enough; we must demand excellence from one another and then put that excellence forward. If we choose good leaders, our following will in turn be good.

In travelling through South Africa, I met a young man named Dillion. He and his wife, Lunga, had created an innovative creative platform called Creative Nestlings to mentor and help young, black creative professionals. They were, from an initial glance, another hub offering wi-fi and a place for ideas to convene. But a closer look (or even simply five minutes speaking with them) revealed that they were different. Dillion and Lunga had more than a desire to create things, they had a desire to help people. They had a desire to make people seen. They had a desire to demand attention, to be bold and to – most importantly – make sure young black kids with ideas knew that that was okay to do.

I chose to hang around Dillion and Lunga. I chose to interact with them and the artists they were pushing along because I felt that the talent they were surrounding themselves with was not only black and proud, but also pushing forward a new agenda. Their own agenda. An uncompromising agenda full of art, documentaries, photography, writing, apps, inventions, and music that was comfortable the further it was from the requirements of the white, western culture that has shrouded the global concept of 'good' for so long.

I chose them. Because they were doing more and I knew by supporting them and spreading their gospel, their work would increase exponentially. It would reach the artists they were assisting; it would reach the black production houses and investors looking for that sort of talent; and it would, eventually, come back to me in the type of creative fodder made available to me for purchase and consumption. So don't settle for anything simply because it is black and comes from the continent – follow what you see promise in.

The average person has an arsenal of ways to bolster that which they believe in. You have multiple choices as to how you will spend any and all forms of your currencies. I'm not only talking about monetary currencies — though that is essential to the success of African ideas. Please know that your buying power and financial support is a critical tool in cementing the future success of Africa. But engage your myriad other currencies as well.

Your social currency: if you have a loyal following on social networks let them know and don't neglect the power of simple word of mouth. Tell your circles and your outer network, regardless of what their associations and identifications may be. Any improvement on culture or practice is a global benefit — not specific to a particular demographic. Black people aren't the only folks who benefit from black excellence.

Use your currency in time, by this I mean quite simply giving yourself to a space and taking the time to either physically or mentally assist in the production of what you believe in. To give time is also to give attention, and there is a great deal to be said in the simple act of willingly giving an entity attention. But I also mean to use this specific time in a greater historical context — the world, for all the inventions we have made, is smaller. Distances are less significant. Obstacles can shrink. Use this to your advantage and operate in the moment we occupy now to ensure better footing for tomorrow.

Currently, I spend some of my time writing for OkayAfrica, an online platform that has taken great strides in making African voices and news heard both on and outside the continent. It has its issues, but it is a vanguard force in modern information about Africa and the diaspora. When I first began pitching and drafting stories for them, I found that I quickly shifted from editorials and descriptive pieces to interviews. I don't want my writing to colour their voice. I don't want their stories to be told through my words but instead to proffer a dialogue. I find it much more honest and interesting to learn what the subjects of my pieces do and think in their own words.

That was my time currency: time to listen and engage. Spending my time feels much less like an expense and much more like an investment. When the pieces are published, I use my social currency and connections at a respected international platform as my elbow in the door to a good portion of the spectators of the world wide web. This results in exponential exposure of African voices and opinions. I hope so, at least. So, think of what you have to give and how.

In the last year, I have visited Johannesburg, Cape Town, Upington, Kimberly, Grahamstown, Paarl, and Springbok among other cities in South Africa. I talked to some folks at the top of a hill in Lesotho. I observed a lot and I learned a great deal. It was extremely evident that my voice in that space was not to be the lead but to be the choir. Or else, I could compromise the whole play.

In the context of bettering Africa and leading it the way it wants to be led, the role of the diaspora is paramount. We have a responsibility. In leading Africa, we lead black people. We lead a very large multi-hued, multi-faith, multi-haired demographic. In leading Africa, we must choose the right leaders and then we must stand by them. This act of the diaspora is one that not only breeds and deepens solidarity, but it invites dialogue. It invites action. It causes those of us interested in and borne of *negritude* to be agents in the future ideas, perceptions and productions that will inevitably surround us.

I have come back to the continent. I am certain I will again go back into the diaspora. But being here, on this soil, has taught me one very crucial aspect of my blackness: accountability. I am not dictating who you should support nor with whom you should invest your currencies — but I am saying you — you there! — you are accountable for the state of blackness. Whether you lay your head in Port-au-Prince, Kingston, Berlin, San Francisco, Maputo, Harare or Cairo — you are accountable. Because you are accountable to you. As the diaspora, we must be vigilant in choosing strong, bold, creative and relevant leaders of Africa. Then we must earnestly lead by following. And we must follow them with the strength of our collective hearts.

Nereya Otieno never truly grew up, but she got bigger in San Francisco, California, USA. Her father is Kenyan. Her mother is Swedish, Danish, and Jamaican with a dash of Chinese wrapped in an American blanket. She loves everything about a world that makes that last sentence possible. Nereya is a writer based globally. Read her work at www.nereyaotieno.com.

Adeline Sede Kamga

Connecting the dots: *FabAfriq Magazine*, Corporate Awards & Bloggers Hangout

I started my first business at age nine. This was a not-for-profit business aimed at inspiring and educating others. Growing up in a disadvantaged society, I had always wanted to support my community to grow through knowledge acquisition. I was not a very intelligent kid, but my dad was a teacher and this gave me an upper hand amongst most of the kids in my neighbourhood. Being a Catholic teacher, my dad taught us many values amongst which is the value of sharing the little things we had. He could have been nicknamed "Charity" in our modern days because of his overly generous personality.

At the time, my first venture, a school, had one classroom of about 9 to 15 children, depending on how many of them were not out on the streets helping their parents to hawk instead of attending class. The pupils were from the poorest homes around my area where many children were not schooling at all. Of course I did not know what I was actually teaching them, but I remember teaching whatever I was taught at school. Was it accurate? Well, who cared at that time?! Running my school lasted for two terms only, simply because my second term results were disastrous and my dad decided to dissolve it. The school was based in our abandoned poultry at the back of our home, giving him an easy access to everything I had carefully put together.

Despite this setback, from then onwards, I have been engaged in different activities that involved passing on my knowledge, paid or unpaid. I studied a Bachelor's degree in Corporate Communication, which landed me my first official job at a local radio station in Douala, Cameroon. I spent a few months running voice overs for big companies like Telecom giant Orange Cameroon, Signal Toothpaste, Colgate brands, and many local products. Unfortunately, this was not the future my family had planned for me. They organised for me to travel to Europe for greener pastures as believed back in those days.

It is usual for people to work when they travel abroad to settle, and I too had to work very hard to survive. The first few years were devoted to work to earn some money and help those at home. With enough work experience, I gained admission to study an MA in Human Resource Management in the United Kingdom. This is when I had to switch back to the old question: How do you want to help your community?

My educational experience was a mixture of studies and community work (as an outreach career advisor), arming me with the ability to work across diverse groups of people and projects. I am naturally very passionate about community engagements, one of the reasons why I partnered with some friends to set up one of the first ever African community networks in the West Midlands of England. Our aim was to help newcomers from other African countries to have a smooth settlement in the United Kingdom. We advised on everything from health to family and educational options. Looking back at this, I am pleased our services had an impact on more than 280 beneficiaries from over 16 African Countries and that we have helped shape some of the stories they now share.

Everything I do leads to the quest to do more, so this was not enough. I was on the lookout for other ways to contribute. Life is not always about wearing the most comfortable pair of shoes; however, once the shoes start pinching, your first instinct is to take it off. As a leader, I have come to understand that sometimes you might need to wear those shoes a bit longer and trek along the tedious route to another accomplishment. This is that point when people will ask you to get out of your comfort zone and try other things. My case was a simple one. After working in the corporate environment for more than 10 years, I decided to do something different, something to change lives, inspire others, empower many, and portray my continent in a positive light.

I learned a long time ago, that no one else has the right to tell my story, so I must tell it first, act fast and share it as it truly is. My story is that of my continuous efforts to put Africa on the map, to share our African story, our beautiful culture, our wonderful fashion, our delicious cuisine, our musical rhythms, our tourist attractions, some of them already named part of the Seven Wonders of the World. To achieve this, I ventured into an entrepreneurial journey in 2010 by creating *FabAfriq Magazine*, an African lifestyle magazine aimed at narrating our stories as Africans. Six years later, *FabAfriq Magazine* has accomplished its primary objective by sharing more than a thousand stories, by being recognised on different platforms, by winning two awards as the best African lifestyle magazine and other recognition awards across the globe.

During this journey, we've recruited more than 15 full-time staff and mentored more than 35 millennials looking for career progression and growth. The role I play in impacting lives is by organising structured mentorship programmes for our younger generation. As a returnee from the United Kingdom to Cameroon, I am leaving my mark as I forge deeper in both the corporate and community environments. The challenges have been difficult to overcome but my resilience has helped me to play smart and to be focused on the goal. Although I still face some challenges, especially with regards to working with trustworthy people – hence impacting delivery timeframe, credibility and to some extent the quality of my final products - I have since learnt to quickly re-strategise when obstacles appear and strike while the iron is hot.

My focus has been (and always will be) the promotion and uplifting of African culture and helping to improve standards. *FabAfriq* is currently distributed in most Africa cities, the United Kingdom and some of Europe's cities. The magazine and its associated website (www.fabafriq.com) serve as platforms through which inspiring Africans are showcased and celebrated; it is also a stage on which the privileged and underprivileged can be heard. *FabAfriq Magazine* is as informative as it is inspirational and provides a wealth of information on everything from lifestyle issues, fashion, culture and features, to tourism, parenting, and healthcare. Through publishing articles on people providing a positive impact on change in Africa, which inspire change and innovation, we have touched the lives of many Africans living at home and abroad with a minimum print readership of 60,000 readers a year, and website and social media platforms circa 400,000 readers a year.

Although we have shared many stories that have impacted the community, we were impressed when Cambridge University Press decided to re-publish our cover story on Oreoluwa Somolo Lesi, Founder of W.TEC-Women's Technology Empowerment Centre.

This was re-published in an Academic English book called *English 4eme Student's Book* and all credit for the interview, images and creation was given to the *FabAfriq Magazine* editorial team. This is a typical example to showcase that as Africans, we must incorporate giving back to our community, and create initiatives that will help both economic and community growth just like our covergirl, Oreoluwa.

As a continuation of my work with *FabAfriq*, I found another avenue for spotting and sharing African stories through my day job in my business. When my family and I moved to Douala, Cameroon in 2013, I used the first few months to understand how I could add value to the corporate environment. I realised something was lacking between employer-employee relationships in most corporate organisations. Many companies were spending billions of dollars on marketing and advertising, but the staff were either disgruntled about working practices, standards or management style. This observation made me put on my HR hat.

Human resource is one of the most important areas of business development, which is also the centre and custodian of the most valuable resource – *people*. But it has suffered several attention deficits and has been relegated to the background. The words of Frederick Herzberg resonate with me: 'true motivation comes from achievement, personal development, job satisfaction and recognition.'[41] I believe the time has come to cash in on the wealth of successful organisations by recognising best practices and setting enduring human resource standards and practices. I started a campaign to help build internal change in companies. This has been very challenging so far, but has also led me to be part of creation of the first ever Corporate Awards of its kind in Cameroon and, possibly, Africa. I have currently found a purpose in running a Corporate Public Relations (PR) and a HR policy consulting firm in Africa.

I work mostly with companies in petroleum, oil and gas, financial institutions, and aviation. My mission is simple: to implant international ways of managing corporate communication and help to create a benchmark on HR policies and Procedures in companies.

---

[41] http://www.azquotes.com/quote/660702

The PR firm runs alongside the magazine, giving me a strong platform to help share corporate successes and stories. I am passionate about charitable causes; therefore, I also use the opportunities to help raise funds for charities.

In 2016, we partnered with very reputable organisations to create awards that recognise excellence in people management. The objective of the award is simply to recognise and reward enterprises who place a great and unrivalled premium on different aspects of commitment to staff and customers. It intends to recognise organisations that are high-achievers and game-changers, who exude positive change and innovation, who create role models and provide a platform for people to excel. By celebrating these organisations and raising the bar of performance, we create healthy competition that sets them on the same pedestals as other international organisations around the world. Our hope is to enlist the free participation of organisations across different industries, which are ready to work in partnership with this initiative aimed at driving change. The categories that have been considered for the maiden edition of this award cuts across community spirit, corporate social responsibility, and employee engagement and empowerment. Subsequent editions will be expanded to embrace more categories that will add value to the performance of the organisations and the people that work within them.

Thanks to my high level of networking skills, it is easy for me to get access to company directors. Sadly, this is not the case for some of the younger generation with whom I work. As part of my job as a corporate PR executive, I have to design innovative ways of getting my clients' products online. I realised many youths are unemployed and could actually make money writing online. I started a movement called Camer Bloggers Hangout. Its core activity is to hang out with corporate Directors and catch up on new products developments or services. I organise events between them and get the blogger community to generate quality content. I am constantly encouraging many graduates to start their own blogs and to act as the voice for companies looking for online presence. Through these hangouts, they could make some money while developing future skills. Fast forward two years, and they have hung out with more than 15 corporate directors, earned enough money to buy a domain name, built a strong online following, and gained self-confidence. Although I have not made money directly from this activity, I am pleased there has been a culture shift as a result of it. The most obvious one is the creative of the Bloggers Forum, spearheaded by some of the bloggers we have worked with, a conference that is now hosting its second edition. Moreover, thanks to this initiative, one of the bloggers recently won a round trip to any African country of their choice awarded by Ethiopian Airlines, as a reward for being the most consistent Blogger on the Camer Blogger Hangout.

As the global secretary of the Global Visionary Women Network, I have met and shared my story with thousands of women. This international women's network, for women from all nations and all walks of life, is a platform which I used to touch the lives of women in different professions, women seeking motivation and inspiration, and women looking for change. It is a platform for women taking charge of their lives and women willing to help other women grow. We have successfully organised women in leadership conferences, symposiums, leadership meetings and summits in different parts of the world such as the United Kingdom, Cameroon and Poland with approximately 2300 women in total since its inception in 2013.

Although I feel satisfied with the level of changes that I have spearheaded or been part of, I still believe we have a long way to go. While working on any project, I always try to connect dots, which I believe is especially important in our context in Africa. This is the spirit I got from my dad, the spirit I got from my mom, the spirit I get from my family, and the spirit I get each day from my most supportive fan, my husband Nelson Nkwenkam. Connecting the dots in your life is very important because it is part of self-actualisation and boosts your esteem. Sometimes, you might feel you have been involved in a useless educational journey as you are not working or practicing in the area you studied. My advice will be to look at any form of education as a bank credit, which you will use for a later date in your future. Keep on educating yourself in the areas of interest and remember only you can create or seize opportunities for yourself.

This experience is a learning curve; although I am still learning, I am glad I took on this journey. It has taught me to believe in myself and to have confidence. I have also learnt about collaborating to gain a greater outcome. The best part of this has been the mentoring. I love the smile on the faces of each mentee, the "oh-oh" on their lips and the successful results that they have achieved so far. I look forward to creating a stronger network, which will act as a platform for continuous learning.

From fulltime paid jobs, to project management to having my own personal projects - *FabAfriq Magazine* and The Corporate Awards - I have sought to inspire and develop the next generation so they can follow their own dreams, much as I have followed mine. My favourite quote of all time is by Albert Camus: "Don't walk behind me; I may not lead. Don't walk in front of me; I may not follow. Just walk beside me and be my friend."[42] This has been true in my journey to share stories about Africa because I give people an equal opportunity to work with me as a peer and I offer everyone a platform to share their success story. Any contribution from members of my staff to that of my clients is taken into consideration for the project we work on. Leading people simply means leading by example and supporting those who truly need your support.

The future is bright; the future has room for more leaders, for inventors, for innovators, and for people willing to support the growth of our continent. While connecting my dots, I implore the Lord to guide us in every step that we make and to one day lead me to the missing dot, which I am sure will form my beautiful necklace.

---

[42] https://www.brainyquote.com/quotes/quotes/a/albertcamu100779.html

Adeline Sede Kamga is the CEO and Founder of *FabAfriq Magazine*, a Pan-African glossy magazine published and distributed in the UK and some African countries. She also runs a PR firm and specialised in Corporate PR and Communications and a HR Consulting firm. Her mercurial nature has found plenty of creative outlets in the business world and as an expert at the things she does, she has used her skills to make a positive change by influencing policy making and instigating change where possible to make people's lives better. Most importantly in everything she does, Adeline aims to empower men and women to achieve their dreams.

Julian Spezzati
A Human of Mozambique

I believe.

Two weeks ago, my mother organised a lunch at home in Mozambique with a few of my good friends with whom I trained martial arts for many years. Some of us had grown up without or having never met our fathers and as a group we wanted to thank our Master for the role he played in our lives. What he did was train us not only to kick and punch, but also to develop a warrior mentality that we've all applied in our lives ever since. He taught us to act like champions, and now, I can truly say that each of us is excelling and doing the best we can in the individual paths that we've chosen. We're all operating at the top of our level, and it is in a huge way due to do his role in shaping us. People ask me whether I still train and, no, I don't throw kicks and punches any more. But every single day I apply the mind-set that I developed in training, and that mind-set is so rich with potential and so powerful. The winner isn't necessarily the fittest or the most skilled, but it's the one who thinks he can win; who knows he can win. I think that what he taught us, and what we all now know, is that we are champions – we don't doubt ourselves. You can't enter something with doubt. When we were training, "I can't do this" or "it's impossible" wasn't allowed – that would get you some push-ups. You quickly learned to wipe those words from your vocabulary, and just get on with it; even if you fail the first few times, eventually you get it right and realise you can do anything. I think people often underestimate their capabilities, particularly in the long term. Most people overestimate what they can do in a year and underestimate what they can do in ten.

I believe it's useful to set goals, to have something to aim at. But keeping in mind that reaching it isn't always the most important thing; progress is what matters. I have many ambitions, and they serve as a guide and an inspiration, allowing me to keep working even if it's two steps forward and one step back. As a leader, I think this mentality is more than important; I think it's essential.

I am.

I'm a *third culture kid*. Technically I'm 50% Swedish, 25% Belgian, 25% Italian yet I feel 100% Mozambican. Although my parents are a mix from abroad, I feel more Mozambican than anything else. I've spent over half my life in Africa, including my formative years, building relationships and interests, especially in Mozambique. I started going out here and have most of my closest friends here, the ones that I consider family, that I hang out with and will continue to hang out with until my last days. You could say I'm *assimilated*... I'm used to life here and it would be a culture shock for me to return to Europe.

However, I've lived in and been exposed to Europe too. And being exposed to these two extremes has given me a broader perspective and many lenses through which I can view the world. And as a leader I believe that's important, because before you try to be revolutionary and reinvent the wheel, you need to understand the broader context you're in and what you can replicate. *There are many things that I learned while I was studying in Europe and that I would like to implement here in Mozambique. And I think people from across the globe have a lot to learn from Mozambique. Mozambique is more than the poverty and famine you see on the news – we have a lot of great things to offer.* And showcasing what we have in Mozambique, in terms of amazing people and experiences, is what I've taken on as a personal challenge and responsibility.

I share.

I've been spurred on by the fact that lots of *people* I know from abroad have never come to visit me here because they have this stereotypical misconception of Mozambique, and Africa in general, as a backwards place with little to offer. When I went to university I realised how ignorant people were. I had people asking me, "why are you going back to Africa?" as if it was inconceivable to do so. I remember sharing a news story about protests due to the price of bread rising and someone being completely shocked that there were people that couldn't afford bread. And people are equally ignorant about the good things: this is a prosperous continent, with lots to do and see and lots of interesting people to meet. Of course, there are lots of challenges, but I have always felt that we need to show a more balanced view of Africa to the world.

That's how the *Humans of Mozambique* project came about, based on the *Humans of New York* photographic storytelling project. We present photo portraits of ordinary people alongside summaries of their extraordinary stories. We tell their inspirational stories – both the good and the bad – and give them a time in the spotlight of our followers (we are currently at over 10,000 and growing). This country is so young, and has gone through so much that everything in society is much more diverse; whereas I feel that in Europe everything is more homogenous. A few 100 kilometres apart in a different province people have a completely different life. Even across generations, people from the last generation have had a completely different life than those in this generation. There are so many stories to capture, and Humans of Mozambique seeks to capture and show this historical richness and variety in a simple and appealing way. We've collected stories of all kinds of characters from Maputo province, host to the country's capital. We're now expanding our collection to the rest of the 10 Mozambican provinces to really get a complete picture of the country and its people.

My second project is about putting the spotlight on *experiences*. One of my favourite things to do is scuba dive, and I've reached a point where yes, it's recreational but it's more than that because I'm now looking to explore places where few people, if any, have ever been before. There's so much that is unexplored, so much more to discover. Many people know what's living on land, but few know what it's like underwater. And in Mozambique the oceans are filled with life. You have over 2,000km of coastline with whale sharks, mantas, dolphins, whales, turtles and a bunch of other exotic looking fish. I remember the first time I saw an Oriental Sweetlip and thinking how it looked like a mix between a zebra and a cheetah, but it was a fish! And it's not just the ocean experience, but it's the car ride through the elephant reserve or the beach you have completely to yourself or camping in the wild with a few billion stars above your head.

I decided to launch a blog to showcase the adventures and natural beauty you can have here that you couldn't have elsewhere. Experiences with animals, nature, and adventure sports in places many people have never heard about. They're places that are completely extraordinary and really accessible, yet people just aren't aware. Sharing my adventures has made some friends want to visit, and I want more people to be pleasantly surprised and say, "I didn't know you could experience that there" and give them a new view of what Mozambique is about.

I create.

I have always been interested in business. Since middle school I turned many of my ideas into businesses, from running a cinema at school to opening a shop and managing it from school, after school and on weekends. I then went abroad to complete a Masters in Strategic Management and I think my exposure to variety across a spectrum between the *developed* and *developing* world, has created an entrepreneurial drive in me. I take ideas and solutions from one place and replicate it in another; I look for gaps and challenges and ways to address them. I like to solve problems and see my solutions materialise.

When I came back from university I joined a newly formed investment and advisory firm – ThirdWay Africa Partner – I was one of their first employees. The firm focused on Mozambique and Impact Investing: social and environmental returns alongside the traditional financial returns. I've been here for a few years now and I've come to realise that Impact Investing isn't only good for society and the environment, but also good for business. The economics make sense and sometimes are even more attractive than more traditional methods of investing. Creating a sustainable business with a long-term horizon is valuable and can deliver catalytic impact, especially in the developing world, where it's most needed. I've now also adopted this long-term perspective in looking at private-sector led investments as a means of sustainable development and I'm keen to one day measure the fruits of my labour not only by how much money was made but also by how many jobs were created, how many people were provided education, healthcare and so on.

I aspire

My work has really helped me better understand the challenges that we have and are facing as a country. I'm learning to create solutions in this context. I think that my multi-faceted, multi-cultural experience and upbringing has taught me to take a broad perspective. I'm learning to analyse and see things from new perspectives. And now I've got the chance to address problems far greater than those I ever encountered in my school days. I feel that I can be an effective enabler of growth in this environment. I think my background and skillset are a perfect match and I'm confident about the future of Africa and Mozambique in particular. In fact, I know I am made to be here.

Julian Spezzati grew up as the son of a diplomat, giving him the opportunity to travel the world and see its extremes. He was born in Belgium, moved to Guinea-Conakry before his first birthday, leaving 4 years later to spend 6 years in New York and then 8 in Mozambique before moving to the Netherlands to complete his university studies. He holds a Master's Degree in Strategic Management and a Bachelor's Degree in International Business Administration from the Rotterdam School of Management. Julian is now back in Mozambique working as an Associate for ThirdWay Africa Partners – an Investment and Advisory firm focused on Impact Investing in Indian Ocean Africa.

VI.   Science, Technology & Engineering & Math

Chuma Asuzu
Electronics are made of Silicon

Getting into an engineering programme in a Nigerian university is a big deal. You would have scored relatively high in JAMB (the pre-university examination in Nigeria) and passed your School Leaving Examinations usually at one sitting. Your parents would be so proud of you; after all, you are going to study a professional course. A professional course with a high chance of getting a good job when you finish school: 'good job' being the parlance for a job with an oil and gas multinational or at least with a leading FMCG (fast-moving consumer goods) company.

This was my story on entering the University of Ibadan. With my parents in academia, there was increased pressure to attain a strong graduating grade. Not from them, but from their colleagues who taught you or saw you around the university.

'Are you Asuzu's boy?' They often asked.
'Yes, sir.' The only standard reply.
'Ah, na first class we dey expect o.' [Ah, we expect a First-Class Honours!].

In the University of Ibadan, as an engineering student, you get to undergo three internships in the course of your degree. My first stint was in a mechanic shop near the university, fixing minor car problems for the two months of the holiday. My second was with an airline at the Lagos airport. My third was with Schlumberger – the oil services company. At that time, interning with the company was a big deal; it meant they had a file with my name and would give me a call on graduation. My classmates and I had to write a test to apply; only six of us got accepted.

I moved to Port Harcourt for six months: one semester of my fourth year and the holiday period. Schlumberger had assigned me to the Drilling Tools and Remedial segment of the company's operations. I was to work in the shop fixing tools brought back from the oil rigs and preparing them for shipping to the rigs. In the first month, we had set up hydraulic jars, kitted boring rims, and prepared an

218

anchor for directional drilling; I was excited. Then we went on to do the same thing for five more months. Midway into the fourth, I was bored.

I saw no engineering here. Yes, I handled tools and performed maintenance operations on different drilling tools, but those are not engineering jobs. Engineers here went on rigs and operated the tools we prepared, but to me that is not engineering. Engineering is building the tool. Engineering is selecting the materials and manufacturing processes to make the tool.

I left Port Harcourt and returned to Ibadan to finish my degree with the conviction that I would look extensively for a product engineering job on graduation. With my classmate, Kunle Adeleke, I engaged in product design competitions on GrabCAD.com. We won one – organised by Lomography to design an accessory for their Konstructor camera – and got interviewed on their website. It was a good day; finally, we had a little validation of our decision to design.

Our winning design – a hand-holder grip for the Konstructor camera

Just after my final examinations, General Electric brought their Garages event to Lagos. As Lagos is two hours from Ibadan where I lived, I could only attend one day of the month-long event. The event had fabrication machinery installed in a floor of the GE building in Lagos, everything was there: 3D printers, a mini injection mold, a laser cutter, a vinyl cutter, and a CNC mill. The organisers had gotten TechShop (the US workshop) to run the tools for the duration of the programme. It was the first time I was in a digital fabrication lab and I loved it, the idea of rapidly prototyping designs from a computer to a physical product in minutes made me ecstatic.

During NYSC (the National Youth Service Corps, a compulsory one year programme for Nigerian graduates), I worked for an engineering consultancy. Here, we did design work for building services: plumbing, air-conditioning and fire-fighting. It was exciting at first, but it wore off once we could design using heuristics. But this experience taught me discipline and the structure that comes with established business.

As I had planned while in school, I looked for product engineering jobs during this service year. There simply were none. I then looked for internships. Two companies replied to my e-mails: BRCK (in Kenya) and Vayu (in the US). After forwarding my CV and cover letters, and in Vayu's case two recommendations from former lecturers, the internships did not materialise. BRCK only took interns from Nairobi, and Vayu stopped replying my e-mails. In hindsight, companies exist here that require design engineering (and are building hardware) but exist in their silos with almost no interaction with each other. No network to connect the entrepreneurs and graduates interested in the space. Interestingly, most entrepreneurs in the space complain of a dearth of talent.

But working helped me. I learnt to do a full day's work then catch up on my own reading and design. With the salary, I got an Arduino Kit and started learning to prototype electronic circuits. After a year of work, I saved up and bought my first 3D printer: a PrintrBot Simple Metal.

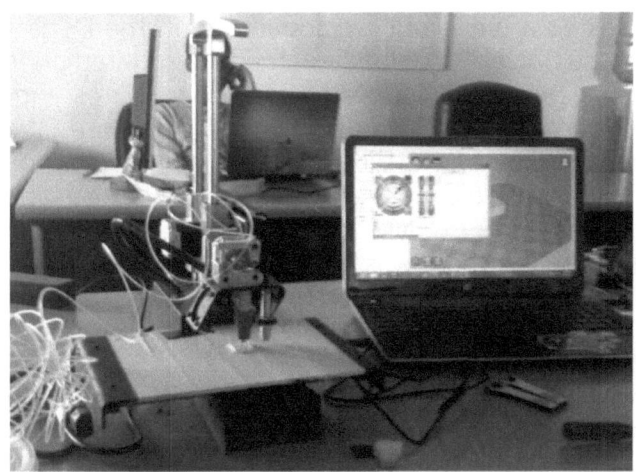

My 3D printer

With this printer, I set up Involute as a 3D printing and design lab. A former roommate of mine from university had spoken to his dad, who allowed me use some part of his office space for my work. I quit the engineering consultancy and moved there. Having only used a 3D printer once, it took me two days to get mine up and running. After this, I designed a website with my email and phone number and waited for clients.

It was difficult to get clients; a lot of people did not know what 3D printing was. Another group of people knew what it was but only wanted to see it in action. As a result of this, I started a newsletter on the website. Week by week, new subscribers joined the fray. I gave a talk at my old university and did a showcase with my printer – it was nice to meet students in whose shoes I had been just over a year before. They ate it up and took turns to get a closer look at the 'printing' process. To get more clients, I wrote emails to architectural firms and got invited to give presentations at some.

About this time, some former colleagues of mine got together and decided to build a drone. They asked me to join the team and lead the mechanical engineering, I acquiesced. We wrote a blog that documented the whole process: design, procurement, and building. It was the first time I built a full prototype since graduation, and the process kept dragging on. Initially, we thought we could build the drone in 6 weeks, this became 9 months very fast. When attempting to build a frame out of wood, we could not use a carpenter as it had to be accurate. We had to find a machine saw; it took us a while but we found one in the Department of Physics of the University of Ibadan. Having 3D printed plates for the design, we needed M3 screws to join them (plates and wooden frame). We could not find M3 screws anywhere. We looked everywhere: online and offline. Visiting markets and local screw shops, they simply did not sell M3 screws because not enough people requested it. In my mind, I was sure that someone would have M3 screws but there was no way to reach whoever that person was. In the long run, we had to redesign the plates for bigger screws. This setback is one that I would revisit later.

When this was done, a friend and I founded a company to solve a problem that is dear to us: the metering of petroleum products. Building a prototype was easier this time, but we had to source electronic components from online stores. Some of these stores did not ship to Nigeria. Others had area distributors. Most of the distributors (for Nigeria) were based in South Africa. It's a little indication of where our reception of hardware development is. By a stroke of luck, we found a distributor for Sparkfun in Nigeria and he has helped tremendously since then. Aliexpress (the China store) ships regularly to Nigeria but it takes about three weeks to arrive here by post; three weeks being the earliest time. Waiting for a single component for three weeks can be frustrating. In this time, you wonder why we have to wait three weeks for a single component. Why can't we make the components ourselves, after all electronics are made of Silicon? If you are on earth right now, the sand you walk on is made of silica – a combination of Silicon and Oxygen. To build real technology, we need industries that produce electronics, maybe not robots or self-driving cars yet, but surely some capacitors. It will take a bit of time to get there, but we need to start working towards it.

However, we live in the now and building hardware in Nigeria is still difficult. People are surmounting the challenges and making progress; students like me, with a passion for design, graduate from university every year. How do we make sure that the people building hardware face less structural challenges, students have mentors or places to seek an internship? By coming together and forming a strong, open network.

In April 2016, I planned a meetup for hardware enthusiasts and 'makers.' We had fifteen people in attendance and we talked about hardware we could build to make lives better. In two hours, we had discussed everything from internet connectivity to engineering education and energy generation. In the group were mainly students, a few recent graduates and a couple of entrepreneurs. One of them told us about how his company had started out intending to build mobile phones but had to pivot to digital content as they did not have prototyping equipment. We decided to meet quarterly and named the group Hackaday Hardware Lagos.

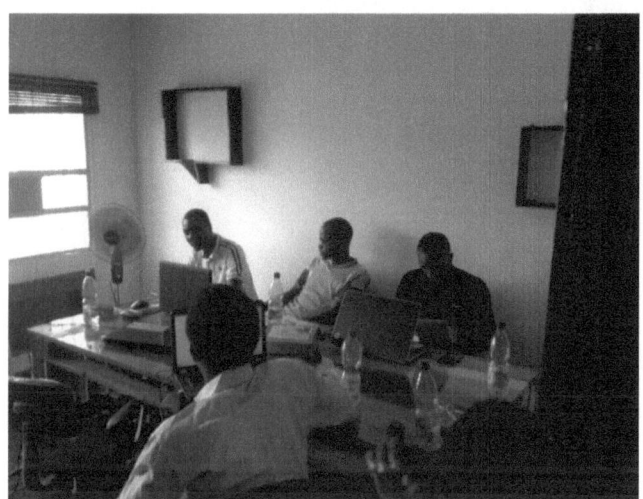

The first meetup (other attendees behind the camera)

At the next meetup, three months later, we had a bigger group – a good mix of entrepreneurs and students. This time we had sessions on designing a Printed Circuit Board (PCB), business models for hardware, and prototyping. The sessions were given by entrepreneurs developing hardware in Nigeria and had a lot of input from others in attendance, as much as it was about learning there was also a lot of networking.

Next, we started two initiatives. The first, an accessible online resource of hardware service providers in Nigeria; the list containing 3D printing outfits, sheet metal fabrication workshops, electronic components resellers, and a lot more. Just like I thought, there were a number of people who offer these services but no one person knows everyone. A group like this makes it possible to know everyone. The second, a pool of privately-owned 3D printers. A number of people own 3D printers they purchased for personal use which do not get used very often; in a population where such machinery is scarce, other people could get to use these machines for cheaper than they would at a 3D printing shop. This way, the printers also get used a lot more.

The meetups will continue; my goal is that it keeps being accommodating for students and entrepreneurs; a place where everyone can learn something and meet people. For two hours a month, a place where people can dream about the future of Africa – An Africa that builds hardware.

Chuma Asuzu is an engineer with keen interests in product development, digital fabrication, and interaction design. He leads Involute, a hardware product development outfit, and organises Hardware Lagos – a quarterly meetup of makers and entrepreneurs in the hardware space. He writes three blogs and can be found in Ibadan, Lagos or on the expressway between both cities.

A Closing Conversation

Why we will lead?

Yabome (Y): For me, I think it was 2014, I remember there was a day sometime before Christmas that year; I remember being in one of those times where you just wake up on the wrong side of the bed and think: *What am I doing with my life?* ... I don't know why I was in that space. It had been a few years since graduation and I had all these visions of what I'd be doing after the Doctorate and I felt like I wasn't *doing* stuff. Which also wasn't true. But long and short, to get myself through that I grabbed a notebook and started writing and journaling. My brain felt flooded that morning. So I started writing and journaling to get rid of the ball of stuff around what I was doing and what I was not doing.

After that, I remember having this odd memory of myself at eight, and I'm thinking, *why am I thinking about that right now?* I hadn't

thought about it for years, but it was a memory of me giving a speech at the foundation laying of a secondary school my father was building in Northern Sierra Leone. There were lots of dignitaries, diplomatic corps people and so on in the audience. I was giving this speech, and I don't really remember it, I was only eight years old, but the speech basically became, in my family and in that area (from what I'm told!) a legend. People came running to see who this little eight year old girl was; in this Northern Sierra Leonean town where girls generally didn't go to school, talking in perfect English; and apparently I was even pausing when people were applauding, waiting to continue. I even have the picture - I'll share it with you all later on - giving that speech and I'm perfectly poised. My siblings would repeat the speech and mimic the way that I was delivering it. And for the town, I represented this possibility or this vision of what they hadn't seen before. And I just remember thinking: *There it is.*

The idea of resonance stories was something I had been using with people. Resonance stories are stories from your past that signify your purpose now. So I had this moment where I was like: *ok, here's mine.* So what is it about this story? And I remember thinking that if I could stand, at eight, with that amount of confidence - not stressed about what my purpose was and what I was leading or why I was leading - then why can't I do it now?

And in the flood that came right after that, in the things that I wrote, We Will Lead Africa is *actually* on that list. I have the page in my notebook. We Will Lead is there. And so for me, We Will Lead Africa represents the possibility of change, and that if I could stand for that when I was eight years old, what's stopping me from doing the things that I wanted to do with African leadership now without being worried about it?

Sarah (S): Just on that last thing you said about the "possibility for change," that really resonates for me. My friend, who knows me really well, said that to me the other day. He was like, "Sarah, change is your constant." It's just how I've always been; I'm just really comfortable in change. And so I think there's something about being with you all (and there are other groups of people that I connect in with, but the three of us especially), there's something really inspiring to me around our willingness to imagine and then step into a different future, right? That's always really energising to me about being part of this.

But, more specifically - stories... two stories came to mind. One is from work. I was leading this big piece of work and I genuinely don't think anyone in the business really knew what it entailed. It was my first big job, on internal culture change, the first work that I did in OD [Organisation Development] - and it literally just broke me. It was just a huge, huge, huge piece of work to carry and no one really knew how to do it, and I was trying to work it out and I started to lose my voice. I had to have time off work, and I physically lost my voice. And it was one of the first times where I had to go and reflect on, *what does it mean for me to speak my truth, and keep my voice?* ... and to speak without fear, especially in a space where there is a lot of fear because it was quite a toxic environment. And also, it was the point at which I realised that for things to change, whether it's in an organisation, a family, or a team, you have to start with conversations and you have to start by really listening out for people's stories and trying to hear what they want to say and want to share. And so that was part of my experience. And it was also at that time that I met Judith and so it feels like a really critical moment, where I began to connect in with storytelling and how stories can move you to change and build relationships and connect you with others in a way that is much more meaningful than the way we quite often try to communicate with others.

And then later on, when I left that job and went travelling. One of the main objectives was to go and collect my father's story - because I never really knew him as an adult - and it turns out he was an amazing story teller. And there are parts of his character, which it wasn't till I went and collected his story (I spoke to my family in Ghana, and the family he left behind in Botswana), that I realised how similar we are. I always in my head imagined that I'm more like my mother, but there are just some things, some parts of him that live really strongly in me. And really over the last three years since I've moved back to Mozambique I kind of feel that side of myself coming out much stronger. And if there's one thing to learn from him, then it's that you can tell your story and be joyful and it can move others to change.

Judith (J): So for me... the WHY... I think I've always been fascinated with stories. I'm a super active dreamer and day-dreamer. I've always imagined worlds and futures and realities both what exists and what doesn't. And I've always been intrigued by the history and the culture of what's around me. I think that came into play in even greater ways every time I was in Nigeria. For example, as a child growing up there would be that curiosity but there wasn't much information available. My education was still centred around a very British-based curriculum. And certainly as I got older, education followed a certain format. What that meant was that definitions of leadership also followed a certain format. I would encounter lots of stories and have discussions - I mean I can't count the number of times I sat with people. I remember one particular time in Europe I sat with a guy from one of those big tobacco companies and he was telling me that they had operations in Senegal, and had attempted Nigeria, but it was too difficult. The stories were all the same - it was about leadership... this thing that didn't seem to exist on the African continent for them. Hearing that would always rub me the wrong way. I would try to compare those stories with what I saw when I was back here. From what I know about working and living in places like Nigeria. And I just could not connect it. I thought, *what is the problem we are having here? why is there no appreciation of leadership beyond a certain view or perspective?* And I think part of that was for me, *why aren't our leadership stories out there - why don't they even exist? Why aren't there things we can look for?* And playing with that in my head and going back into the *curious child* or the *wandering child* who would look for the parables or the stories from her heritage, I kept thinking that perhaps the way to go is to dig into culture and find ways to link it to leadership. For many years I thought about how I could play in that space and what that might look like. Could we have leadership development that was crafted based on culture? Those sorts of thoughts. I used to think about it often. And it's quite fascinating because then later I would look at other African cultures apart from my local Nigerian ones and start to explore them for what *they* might bring.

So, that was the background context of leadership and African culture in my head. Then a number of things happened. I met Sarah, and after working together, one day in the fall of 2013, Sarah said to me, "I've got this thing; I'm going to Ethiopia to the African Union to do something on leadership, will you come with me?" That was a real turning point, because I had been studying, asking the question: what is African leadership, but I had done that from Europe. And here was the opportunity to take all of those thoughts and all of those ideas and walk it and put it into practice. That trip then, is one of the reasons I'm in Lagos now - it's one of the reasons I'm back here. It certainly changed the game; it opened up new possibilities. It allowed me to believe that coming back, this was the time for it. And also that the work, the stories around leadership are now more important than ever and this is the time. So doing the work at the African Union and after that, working together at ODN [Organisation Development Network] and getting to meet you too, Yabome - it all came together really beautifully. That's my why...

Why this team?

Y: Just picking up right there Judith, at ODN. I really feel like ODN was... it's almost one of those moments that... it was by design in some ways. Because as I hear you express all the things that had gone before, for me it sort of was like that too. There was what I described about that morning in 2014. And then there were a couple of things after that, like writing and speaking at the Kwame Nkrumah Biannual Conference. I submitted an abstract, in protest actually. Someone sent me the call for abstracts and my reaction was an African hiss *kissing teeth*. These topics were all the same that you always hear on African leadership: colonial, post-colonial, conflict, pan-Africanism...the usual. And so I submitted an abstract that said: "this is what I think about African leadership now and for the future; I know you didn't ask for this in your list of topics but I can offer this." And it was accepted. And so I wrote that paper, and that got me even more into the literature and validated that the literature was mostly negative on "African leadership". Having done that and having played with that, I then went off to South Africa in 2015 - and we met in 2015 - I went off to the Appreciative Inquiry conference, and someone who knows someone saw my information (and is now actually a contributor to our volume) and was introduced to me. She saw my bio and the abstract for that same paper and said, "hey, we are trying to transform the leadership conversation for the public service in South Africa, love what you're up to, would you come do a workshop for us?" I said yes. And doing that just spiralled my mind further into this work. So, it was so present for me when I met you all at ODN 2015 - I was in that place of saying yes to anything that moves me further into the African leadership conversation. When I saw your bios on the programme, I got super excited. I knew I couldn't make your session because I had another meeting planned, but went to meet you anyway. And literally, walking into the room, and the minimal interaction we had, the way you had set up the opening of the workshop, and me just walking over and saying, "hey, this is who I am, love what I saw of the workshop and who you are, I want to talk more." And both of you, were instantly like "absolutely, let's get in touch afterwards." That was pretty much all I needed for why this team.

The kind of reception I got from both of you was validated afterwards, because as you know that was the only time we met. I wasn't even in the session more than half an hour. I left and didn't see you at the conference again. I emailed you and you both emailed back. Followed up to set up a skype and you both said yes. Got on a skype, and literally all I remember - I remember having separate skypes because we couldn't make the joint one. Talking to you Judith, I got really excited about who you are and what you were up to - same with you Sarah. It was just a 'who are you and what are you up to' call. Then I remember the first call that we all three were on after that. I don't remember the details, but remember Sarah saying, "That sounds awesome, let's do it!" And later that week we had google docs, and we were exchanging information and setting stuff up. And I'm walking around in this haze of: *how did that just happen?!* So, why this team? Because you said yes to an idea that was percolating for me and that I knew I would get into, but you were there and ready, and it was the best way to do it in my mind, so I had no hesitation in jumping in.

S: For me, that question is really simple. It's just like, it just couldn't have been any other way. It's both completely unplanned and completely perfect. You know? I don't really have more words for it than that. It just couldn't have been any other way. It was just completely effortless saying yes. Completely... I didn't even think it through, what it entailed. I didn't think anything except: *Well obviously, we have to connect in this way!* I don't know, maybe that's just how I live but it's just been really easy. And last year, I don't think was a particularly easy year for me. The amount of support, just personally, knowing that I have this group to come to, the laughs that we have and everything that sits around us actually getting the work done (because I'm kind of baffled at the fact that we've managed to pull that off) ... but just the personal interaction that we've had as well, it just came at a really important time for me as well, to know that I have you two. So I think that's another reason why: it's not just for the book, but I think we needed each other in some way.

J: Yeah, I think I'm kind of in the same space as you Sarah, as in, "Yes, of course!" It makes sense, it's the way things were supposed to be.

S: Right? It's like how could it *not* be.

J: Exactly. That we would meet. That we would do this thing. That we would be able to do this thing. How amazing is that? My God, how amazing is that!? I keep thinking about the fact that we were just in a room, we saw each other once - just once - such a brief moment, and then two years later we're putting a book out. I don't know about you guys, but that's pretty incredible.

Anyway, so I think there's something about... not so much that we chose it, but that it chose us. That this thing we all believe in, that this is the time for it, and that we are the ones. We are the ones.

S: I also just think, there's something really beautiful about the three of us, about how different we are. We're clearly connected by something and that's why we all said yes to jump into this thing. And Yabome, that was your call - it resonated with us deep in our bellies. So obviously we came together for something that's common. But we're so different! It's hilarious when we come together, and I just love that kind of kaleidoscope of personalities that happens every time we're on a call. I learn so much from you as well, *because* we are so different.

Y: Absolutely.

J: I like that, that we are really, really different, and despite that - it's like it shows what diversity really is - because despite that we still flow, we support and catch each other...

Y: We call each other out...

J: Exactly. It's incredible, everything from "What the hell was that idea?!" to "Oh my god, you're so amazing!"

Y: You know what's interesting for me? I completely 100% agree, we are very different, even in how we think and process and all of that. And when we met, there was something about your bios - there's something about the way they were written that had me going, "I think I'm going to like these women." And then when I walked in, there was something about both of you - Sarah, I remember you looking at me with a complete twinkle, chuckle in your eye, thinking, *who is this crazy lady?* But at the same time totally with me in whatever I was babbling on about. And Judith, the same for you - you were like, "that's amazing, [who ever you are], yes, that's amazing what you are saying." There was a level of connection. And I've said this before, there was a way in which... you guys know me well enough now, I'm not really afraid of a lot, but there's a funny way in which I'm cautious about who I work with. Let's just be honest, there's a way in which I hide behind my personality when I really don't want to go deep with people and for some reason there was none of that with the two of you, which hardly ever happens...I would easily spend time laughing with you, but getting to know you, that doesn't happen until I actually think I can go deep with you, otherwise it just won't happen. You'll just know me as that girl that laughs a lot and is happy to do whatever. But I won't really go there. And for me, talking about this work and stepping into it was pretty important to me at the time that we met, because I was really there with it and wanting to do more and more with it. So it wasn't a simple thing that I just blurted out to the two of you, but there was a lot of comfort there when I did it. It wasn't with recklessness either. Just from the energy of meeting you I knew it wasn't a risky thing. But that is pretty unusual for me.

Why now?

Y: The why now for me is the simplest piece. I mean we've all said why this work called us and all of that, but what a time in the world to be engaging in this conversation and to be putting it out there in the way that we are. What a time on the continent, at this bubble where, 50-something years post the whole independence movements, and the bubble of people in this next generation that are saying, "forget about those traditional ways of being and knowing and talking about leadership on the continent. Let's just think about it differently, and think and be our *own* way." I think there's a whole mass of people that are doing things. And as the volume has shown us, they are thinking in these ways and wanting to just lead and turn things on their head. Like, the growing youth population on the continent, conditions are changing faster than we're talking. What a time. I don't know where this is going, but it just feels like the right time.

S: Yeah, and so I would use those exact same words: *what a time.* I will put a more spiritual spin on it. Like for me it's - I don't know, maybe every generation feels this way - for me it feels like there is genuinely, on a global, maybe universal scale, a shift of consciousness happening. A paradigm shift. The cracks are all there, and the light is shining through. And as humanity, I think we are faced with the realisation that we know we can't continue this way and we really just want to reconnect with our humanity. And so, I think in all the work that I do, I want to be part of that thing that's next. What would radical transformation look like? And We Will Lead is just one of the ways I think, where we can create a space for people to imagine into that new way of being. So I think it's all around us, I think it's in the planets, in the earth. Now is the right time for imagining new ways of being.

J: What a time, I'll echo that as well. I would like to go back to last year. Sarah and I did an Acumen plus course that was centred on Martin Luther King Jr's Letter from a Birmingham Jail. It talks about a lot of things: and was focused on leadership including your moral responsibilities. One thing that it really drove home was the fact that we can't afford to be bystanders. We can't afford to just do the nice, to do the politically correct, to do the respectable. If we want things to change, and things must change - never mind whether we want them to - then we have to do something about it. And I think that, in ways, maybe that we won't even realise any time soon, being a part of this, telling these stories, putting this out there, will really make a difference. And this is the time it must happen. I mean, Yabome when you were talking about the demographics, the growing population and what that may or may not mean on the continent, everyday we are faced with stories about whether Africa is rising or falling or if there's a yo-yo thing going on. The one thing I reckon we know for sure, at the end of the day, is that our destiny will be in our own hands. The sooner we're equipped to rise to that responsibility the better, and any way in which we can - for ourselves, for those who came before us, and for those that will come after us - any way in which we can contribute towards being ready, we must. So, this is the time.

What's next?

Y: Uhm...I don't know! *laughing* I spend a lot of time dreaming about different things, they just pop up in my head and I bring you gals along with a lot of those dreams! *loud laughing* With We Will Lead, the platform, I don't know what's next but I have a lot of hope and desire that this will snowball beyond our wildest imaginations. Not because of us, but because of the need to be in this conversation. And for me, that it will be more than a conversation; that it will really move, touch and inspire people to be in action.

More than anything, *collective* action and movement is what is needed.

I was just having a conversation today about how there are always those outliers, no matter the extreme, dire conditions people are in. There's always gonna be that person who rises above, that individual excellence, dreamer, story of someone that goes from rags to riches. There's always going to be those stories about human nature, positive deviance, whatever you want to call it. No matter what the adversity, people will rise. But I think what is needed is beyond that, this is not about individuals rising. This is about collective action, and networking and working together, and supporting each other and really defying the odds of everything out there about what's possible. And I think the way we get there is through that collective action. So for me, my hope, my dream, is that this work will be part of creating movement towards the collective action that's needed to raise people on the continent to live the lives they want to live, of dignity and prosperity and hope. Raising people enough to live well, and to enjoy their lives with dignity. I think for me that's my hope and dream, more than what is next. Because any which way - it could look like more of these volumes whether they are written by us or not, it could look like hosting conversations (we've talked about that), it could look like having some platform for sharing - it doesn't matter. For me, I just want to be part of that movement of collective action.

S: Hmmmm....I also don't know... everything you're saying really resonates but I guess maybe a way to answer the question would be, what would success look like for me? And, I think that that's simple. I would just love this to live beyond us. Like for others to pick up the mantle and recreate it and remix it and make it their own. That's it.

J: Echoing you all, I'm not sure what's next... Like you said Sarah, I very much hope, believe that this will live beyond us for sure. You know, I'm kind of excited. I feel really good that we did this at this time, in this moment, because it must live beyond us in some way. Because we used the different avenues and channels that we have, because it's a much more connected world, in some way it *will* grow. I hope it does that with purpose though. I know that this is something that is very dear to me, so in some way I see connection happening beyond but I don't know what that means or what that looks like. I also think there will be surprises. That the connectedness that exists right now, out of that will come something that we haven't even imagined, and I'm looking forward to that.

S: I'm getting a little emotional now... actually, what's next for the three of us right? What happens when we've launched, when we no longer need to be on these weekly calls?

Y: ...We create a new reason. Because this can't be it.

J: No, I'm sure this is not it. I'm sure it isn't. In some way, I think there is beauty in an ending. I'm one of those people that can't stand TV series that go on forever, it really annoys me. Have a purpose, have an end, and I like that. There will be something else. Or it's evolution, maybe that's what I should call it. Rather than an ending, it's a transformation into something else.

Y: Sarah, say more about what you are thinking or feeling?

S: I think, endings are kind of sad - so I guess the feeling is a kind of sadness. But I really like what you just said Judith about, it's just the cycles, it's an ebb and flow. It's nice that there will be a kind of close, and then a transform and a rebirth and we start again. That's a really uplifting thought for me.

Because.

Africa, my Africa, no not Diop's, mine!
An open expanse for my
learning,
love, and
life.
Yet some say, this,
my Africa,
calabash for my soul,
is only a place of strife.
And yet,
here my heart,
always free,
finds time.

Africa, our Africa,
both brash and subtle,
both bold and humble.
Carrying a legacy of story,
drumming to its heartbeat alone
Loving and loud,
too patient, proud?
Performing,
Providing,
and waiting for us to shape futures untold

Africa, your Africa,
but wait
...will you be hers?
The mother, the bride, the nurturer, life giver.
With dedication, and action, into a future of our own making.
We choose...
no longer a-waiting,
because this Africa...
She is mine, yours, ours.

By Judith, Sarah and Yabome.
An improv poem created by passing each new sentence on to the next
person, blind.

About the Editors

Yabome Gilpin-Jackson was born in Germany, grew up in Sierra Leone, West Africa, and completed her undergraduate & graduate studies in Canada and the United States. Yabome is a social scientist, consultant, academic, and writer and curator of African identity & leadership stories. She has presented on and taught about African Leadership: Now and for the Future. Yabome has most recently spoken on the issue of global African Identities, which led to her writing and publishing a short story collection titled *Identities*.

Sarah Owusu is an Organisation Development specialist focused on culture, employee engagement and change navigation. A planetary citizen she is Danish / Ghanaian, born in Botswana and is currently based in Maputo, Mozambique. She has worked with Africa 2.0 (and is their Champion for Capacity Building), Peace One Day and British Airways leading transformational change programmes and in 2014 she won the Women4Africa award for Inspirational Woman of the Year. She has a Masters in Philosophy, is an Integral Coach and a Reiki practitioner.

Judith Okonkwo was born in London and grew up in Austria, Sierra Leone, Nigeria, Indonesia & Japan. She is a Business Psychologist, Organisation Development Consultant & Technology Evangelist. Her passion for inclusive leadership models was a key driver for Judith's move to Lagos in 2014. She sits on the Board of the European Organisation Design Forum; is a guest lecturer at the Lagos Business School & University of Westminster; & is the creator of the Oriki Coaching ModelTM. Judith is a Fellow of the Royal Society of Arts and an Associate Fellow of the British Psychological Society. In 2016 she set up Imisi 3D, a virtual reality creation lab, in Lagos.

www.ingramcontent.com/pod-product-compliance
Lightning Source LLC
Chambersburg PA
CBHW050439290526
45786CB00006B/2083